The Book of a Thousand Poems

THE · BOOK · OF · A
·THOUSAND·
·POEMS·

A Family Treasury

P E T E R
BEDRICK
BOOKS
NEW YORK

This edition published by
Peter Bedrick Books
2112 Broadway
New York, NY 10023

Library of Congress Catalog in Publication Data

The Book of a Thousand Poems
  Includes Indexes.
  Summary: A collection of poems by writers ranging from William
Blake and Henry W. Longfellow to Emily Dickinson and Robert L.
Stevenson, arranged by topics such as "The Seasons," "Nursery
Rhymes," and "Lullabies and Cradle Songs."

  1. Children's poetry, English. 2. Children's poetry, American.
1. English poetry—Collections. 2. American poetry—Collections.
PR1175.3.B66 1986 821'.008'092082 86-7862
ISBN 0-87226-084-4
ISBN 0-87226-218-9 (pbk.)

Manufactured in the United States of America
First American edition September, 1986
10 9 8 7 6 5 4

Contents

The Anthology

It is hoped that this anthology of verse for young children will be found to be full of interest to the child of today. In addition to favourites chosen from well-known poets, much original verse, on subjects within the child's own experience and environment, has been included from the pages of *Child Education*. To suggest ways in which the anthology may be used may seem superfluous or even unnecessary, but in these unquiet days it is good sometimes to recall—even for ourselves—something of our pre-war ideals and aims (still present with us) when language training, clear speech, understanding of humour and fun, revelation of beauty in thought and appreciation of high values, were—and are—matters worthy of our preoccupation. It will be remembered that the use of poetic ideas in learning to speak and read, trains children in literary appreciation. We may watch idly the sunshine and the rain, but it takes a poet to tell of 'the uncertain glory of an April day'. Poetic study gives a fuller, richer meaning to the reading of word or phrase, the effect of which, if introduced in early years, will continue through life.

Almost parallel with this is the thought that a child need not always comprehend fully all that a poem may mean, but in later years of understanding, to recall such a poem, once learnt, may bring him the greatest happiness. Again—for who can fathom the workings of the human spirit?—a poem seemingly beyond a child's years or comprehension may communicate to him—like the highest teaching—something far beyond mere speech. It may be only a gossamer thread of delicate sparkle, but it can weave and bind; or it may open a window through which he can see to far horizons—'magic casements opening on the foam of perilous seas in faery lands forlorn'. Wonder, in a child, is the beginning of worship. It is we (the upgrown) who often miss 'the many-splendoured thing'.

Some Examples for the Older Children

Again, we know that all children need adventure: it is almost as necessary to them as their sense of security. If it is not abundantly provided in their own lives they get a kind of delicious, fearful joy when they experience it in poem or story. For the older children, therefore, such poems as *The Pedlar's Caravan, The Wraggle Taggle Gipsies, Meg Merrilees, The Jovial Beggar, The Toy Band*, provide this experience, while the longing of *The Old Woman of the Road* touches something of its antithesis—the need of rest and home. *Robin's Song* gives a feeling of thinking backward in time, 'before the Legions came', and so suggests the passing show exemplified in history.

The Wood of Flowers is an example of sheer happiness, while wonder lingers in *The Darkening Garden* and *Who Has Seen the Wind?* A domestic baby ballad is *Little Dame Crump*, whose adventures can be joyously shared round, verse by verse. *The Clothes Line*, with the Flip, Flap, Flop of its fluttering creatures, reveals a hitherto unsuspected source of poetic expression. Lastly, the eternal loveliness of the Christmas story sings its musical way in:

> Winds through the olive trees softly did blow
> Round little Bethlehem, long, long ago.
>
> *A Christmas Song*

Suggestions for Practical Use
The following further suggestions are offered for the practical use of the anthology:

1 *Rhyme and Rhythm* Images, jingle, pattern, music, repetition—all satisfy an early rhythmic need of the child, and hark back to primitive language days. Two examples which will give delight to the little ones are: *A Cat Came Fiddling out of a Barn*, and (with four little stresses in each line):

> Hów many dáys has my Báby to pláy?
> Sáturday, Súnday, Móndáy,
> Tuésday, Wédnesday, Thúrsday, Fríday,
> Sáturday, Súnday, Móndáy

Incidentally the days of the week are playfully remembered.

Inner rhymes and cross rhythms will later bring delight and interest to the older children.

2 *Speech Purposes* Training in speech, clear articulation and correct pronunciation are obvious aims in the presentation or speaking of verse, as well as modulation of the voice to indicate meaning—surprise, fear, expectation, longing, delight, or mere narration, as in a story poem or ballad.

3 *Natural Punctuation* Much practice can be achieved in natural phrasing before knowledge of comma or full stop. Observation of rhyme-phrases—where each is a complete unit of thought—is

helpful later in 'reading for content', and has its parallel in music where the phrase gives meaning, also in sentence methods of teaching reading.

4 *Verse Speaking* Opportunities here abound in variety for ensemble work, solo and refrain, dialogue, or other antiphonal ways as in question and answer.

5 *Individual Work* A poem may be spoken individually or shared, verse by verse, as in a narrative. This latter allocation to different voices brings out dramatic qualities and varying tone-colour. Moreover, alertness is achieved, and joy in sharing.

6 *Own Choice* In an extensive anthology much individual choice is provided so that the child can, after hearing the verses spoken by the teacher, choose those he wishes to memorise. It is significant that he learns and interprets best where his preference lies.

7 *Memory and Imagination* A poem, like a beautiful piece of music, is mostly a record of an experience—an emotional experience 'recollected in tranquillity'—or sometimes is mere narration of an incident or story. If the experience is a familiar one, memory is drawn upon; if unfamiliar, imagination bodies forth or is nourished by description of the unknown.

8 *Addition to Vocabulary* Poetry or verse is one of the chief channels through which the vocabularly is enriched. New words and phrases should be explained separately, then in their context. Poetic licence, too, might also be anticipated.

9 *Training in Observation* This training will have ample and particular scope in the many nature verses, also animal poems, throughout the anthology, and the children will take delight in verifying facts in their gardening activities and walks farther afield. Here beauty and truth are faithfully sought, and it may be that:

> Truth embodied in a tale
> Shall enter in at lowly doors

1942

J. MURRAY MACBAIN

Nursery Rhymes
and Traditional Verse

Round about in a fair ring-a
Thus we dance and thus we sing-a

Bell horses, bell horses,
   What time of day?
One o'clock, two o'clock,
   Three and away.

Round about in a fair ring-a,
Thus we dance and thus we sing-a;
   Trip and go, to and fro,
      Over this green-a;
   All about, in and out,
      Over this green-a.

Here we come a-piping,
In Springtime and in May;
Green fruit a-ripening,
And Winter fled away.
The Queen she sits upon the strand,
Fair as a lily, white as wand;
Seven billows on the sea,
Horses riding fast and free,
And bells beyond the sand.

   Here we go up, up, up,
And here we go down, down, downy,
And here we go backwards and forwards,
And here we go round, round, roundy.

On Mayday we dance,
On Mayday we sing,
For this is the day
We welcome the Spring.

2

Full early in the morning
  Awakes the summer sun,
The month of June arriving,
  The cold and night are done;
The cuckoo is a fine bird,
  She whistles as she flies,
And as she whistles "cuckoo,"
  The bluer grow the skies.

As I went up the garden
I found a little farthing;
I gave it to my mother,
To buy a little brother;
My brother was a sailor,
He sailed across the sea,
And all the fish that he could catch
Were one, two, three.

Bless you, bless you, bonnie bee:
Say, when will your wedding be?
If it be to-morrow day,
Take your wings and fly away.

How many miles to Barley Bridge?
  Fourscore miles and ten!
Shall we be there by candlelight?
  Yes, and back again:
If your heels are nimble and light,
You may get there by candlelight.
Open the doors as wide as wide,
And let King George go thro' with his bride!
A curtsy to you, and curtsy to you,
If you please, will you let the king's horses go through?

Monday's child is fair of face,
Tuesday's child is full of grace,
Wednesday's child is full of woe,
Thursday's child has far to go,
Friday's child is loving and giving,
Saturday's child works hard for a living,
But the child that is born on the Sabbath day
Is bonny, and blithe, and good, and gay.

A cat came fiddling out of a barn,
With a pair of bagpipes under her arm,
She could sing nothing but "Fiddle-de-de.
The mouse has married the bumble bee."
Pipe, cat—dance, mouse—
We'll have a wedding at our good house.

Cock Robin got up early
  At the break of day,
And went to Jenny's window
  To sing a roundelay,
He sang Cock Robin's love
  To the little Jenny Wren,
And when he got unto the end,
  Then he began again.

The lion and the unicorn
  Were fighting for the crown;
The lion beat the unicorn
  All round the town.
Some gave them white bread,
  And some gave them brown;
Some gave them plum cake,
  And sent them out of town.

Dame, get up and bake your pies,
    Bake your pies,
    Bake your pies,
Dame, get up and bake your pies,
On Christmas Day in the morning.

Dame Trot and her cat
Sat down for to chat;
The Dame sat on this side,
And Puss sat on that.

"Puss," says the Dame,
"Can you catch a rat,
Or a mouse in the dark?"
"Purr," says the cat.

On the wind of January
    Down flits the snow,
Travelling from the frozen north
    As cold as it can blow.

If all the seas were one sea,
What a great sea that would be!
If all the trees were one tree,
What a great tree that would be!
And if all the axes were one axe,
What a great axe that would be!
And if all the men were one man,
What a great man that would be!
And if the great man took the great axe
And cut down the great tree,
And let it fall into the great sea,
What a splish-splash that would be!

5

"Little girl, little girl,
    Where have you been?"
"Gathering roses
    To give to the Queen."
"Little girl, little girl,
    What gave she you?"
"She gave me a diamond
    As big as my shoe."

Diddle, diddle, dumpling,
My son John
Went to bed
With his stockings on:
One shoe off,
And the other shoe on:
Diddle, diddle, dumpling,
My son John.

Draw a pail of water
For my lady's daughter;
My father's a king, and my mother's a queen,
My two little sisters are dressed in green,
Stamping grass and parsley,
Marigold leaves and daisies.
One rush, two rush,
Prithee, fine lady, come under my bush.

In the month of February,
When green leaves begin to spring,
Little lambs do skip like fairies,
Birds do couple, build, and sing.

Girls and boys come out to play,
The moon doth shine as bright as day;
Leave your supper and leave your sleep,
And come with your playfellows in the street,
Come with a whoop and come with a call,
Come with a goodwill or not at all.
Up the ladder and down the wall,
A halfpenny roll will serve us all.
You find milk and I'll find flour,
And we'll make a pudding in half an hour.

Where are you going,
My little kittens?

We are going to town
To get us some mittens.

What! mittens for kittens!
Do kittens wear mittens?
Who ever saw little kittens with mittens?

Once I saw a little bird going hop, hop, hop,
So I cried, "Little bird, will you stop, stop, stop?"
And was going to the window to say "How do you do?"
When he shook his little tail and away he flew.

One misty moisty morning
    When cloudy was the weather,
There I met an old man
    Clothèd all in leather;

Clothèd all in leather,
    With cap under his chin,—
How do you do. and how do you do,
    And how do you do again?

The first of April, some do say,
Is set apart for All Fools' Day,
But why the people call it so
Nor I nor they themselves do know.

Go to bed early wake up with joy;
Go to bed late—cross girl or boy.
Go to bed early—ready for play;
Go to bed late—moping all day.
Go to bed early—no pains or ills;
Go to bed late—doctors and pills.
Go to bed early—grow very tall;
Go to bed late—stay very small.

The grand old Duke of York,
    He had ten thousand men;
He marched them up to the top of the hill
    And he marched them down again!
And when they were up, they were up,
    And when they were down, they were down,
And when they were neither down nor up,
    They were neither up nor down.

Willie boy, Willie boy, where are you going?
    I will go with you, if I may.
I'm going to the meadows to see them mowing,
    I'm going to see them make the hay.

Hey diddle, dinkety, poppety pet,
The merchants of London they wear scarlet;
Silk in the collar and gold in the hem,
So merrily march with the merchantmen.

The dove says Coo,
What shall I do?
I can hardly maintain my two.
Pooh, says the wren,
Why, I've got ten
And keep them all like gentlemen!

Hickety, pickety,
My black hen,
She lays eggs
For gentlemen;
Sometimes nine,
And sometimes ten.
Hickety, pickety,
My black hen!

Hot-cross buns! Hot-cross buns!
One a penny, two a penny,
Hot-cross buns!
If you have no daughters,
Give them to your sons,
One a penny, two a penny,
Hot-cross buns!
But if you have none of these little elves,
Then you may eat them all yourselves.

I had a little hobby-horse,
And it was dapple grey;
Its head was made of peastraw,
Its tail was made of hay.

I sold it to an old woman
For a copper groat;
And I'll not sing my song again
Without a new coat.

I had a little pony,
    His name was Dapple-gray,
I lent him to a lady,
    To ride a mile away;
She whipped him, she slashed him,
    She rode him through the mire;
I would not lend my pony now
    For all the lady's hire.

Pitty Patty Polt!
Shoe the wild colt,
    Here a nail,
    There a nail,
Pitty Patty Polt!

Here's to the poor widow from Babylon
With six poor children all alone:
One can bake and one can brew,
One can shape and one can sew,
One can sit at the fire and spin,
One can bake a cake for the king.
Come choose you east, come choose you west,
Come choose you the one that you love the best.

I had a little nut-tree, nothing would it bear
But a silver nutmeg and a golden pear;
The King of Spain's daughter came to visit me,
And all was because of my little nut-tree.
I skipped over water, I dancèd over sea,
And all the birds in the air couldn't catch me.

Little Boy Blue, come, blow up your horn,
The sheep's in the meadow, the cow's in the corn;
But where is the boy that looks after the sheep?
He is under the haystack, fast asleep.
Will you wake him? No, not I;
For if I do, he'll be sure to cry.

Juniper, Juniper,
  Green in the snow;
Sweetly you smell
  And prickly you grow.

Juniper, Juniper,
  Blue in the fall:
Give me some berries,
  Prickles and all.

Said a frog on a log,
  "Listen, little Bunny.
Will you ride by my side?
  Wouldn't that be funny!"

Jeanie, come tie my,
  Jeanie, come tie my,
Jeanie, come tie my bonny cravat;
  I've tied it behind,
  I've tied it before,
And I've tied it so often, I'll tie it no more.

I had a little hen, the prettiest ever seen,
She washed me the dishes and kept the house clean.

She went to the mill to fetch me some flour,
She brought it home in less than an hour.

She baked me my bread, she brewed me my ale,
She sat by the fire and told many a fine tale.

Peter and Michael were two little menikin,
  They kept a cock and a fat little henikin;
  Instead of an egg, it laid a gold penikin,
  Oh, how they wish it would do it againikin!

I had a little husband,
    No bigger than my thumb;
I put him in a pint pot,
    And there bade him drum.

I bought a little horse
    That galloped up and down;
I bridled him, and saddled him,
    And sent him out of town.

Little Robin Redbreast
Sat upon a tree,
He sang merrily,
As merrily as could be.
He nodded with his head,
And his tail waggled he,
As little Robin Redbreast
Sat upon a tree.

Welcome, little Robin,
    With your scarlet breast,
In this winter weather
    Cold must be your nest.
Hopping on the carpet,
    Picking up the crumbs,
Robin knows the children
    Love him when he comes.

A little cock sparrow sat on a tree,
Looking as happy as happy could be,
Till a boy came by with his bow and arrow,
Says he, "I will shoot the little cock sparrow.

"His body will make me a nice little stew,
And his giblets will make me a little pie too."
Says the little cock sparrow, "I'll be shot if I stay,'
So he clapped his wings and flew away.

Where are you going,
My little cat?

I am going to town,
To get me a hat.

What! a hat for a cat!
A cat get a hat!
Who ever saw a cat with a hat?

A man went a-hunting at Reigate;
He wished to jump over a high gate.
Said the owner, "Go round,
With your gun and your hound,
For you never shall jump over my gate."

Rock-a-bye, baby, thy cradle is green;
Father's a nobleman, mother's a queen;
And Betty's a lady, and wears a gold ring;
And Johnny's a drummer, and drums for the king.

"Who's that ringing at the front door bell?"
Miau! Miau! Miau!
"I'm a little Pussy Cat and I'm not very well!"
Miau! Miau! Miau!
"Then rub your nose in a bit of mutton fat."
Miau! Miau! Miau!
"For that's the way to cure a little Pussy Cat."
Miau! Miau! Miau!

Pussy Cat, Pussy Cat. where have you been?
I've been to London to look at the Queen.

Pussy Cat, Pussy Cat, what did you there?
I frightened a little mouse under the chair.

13

From house to house he goes,
   A messenger small and slight;
And whether it rains or snows,
   He sleeps outside in the night.

                              Answer: A Lane.

Robin sang sweetly
   In the Autumn days,
"There are fruits for every one.
   Let all give praise!"

Poor old Robinson Crusoe!
Poor old Robinson Crusoe!
   They made him a coat
   From an old nanny goat,
I wonder how they could do so!
   With a ring-a-ting tang,
   And a ring-a-ting tang,
Poor old Robinson Crusoe!

Ride a-cock horse to Banbury Cross,
   To see a fine lady upon a white horse;
Rings on her fingers and bells on her toes,
   She shall have music wherever she goes.

"Which is the way to London Town,
To see the King in his golden crown?"

"One foot up and one foot down,
That's the way to London Town."
"Which is the way to London Town,
To see the Queen in her silken gown?"
"Left! Right! Left! Right! up and down,
Soon you'll be in London Town!"

Lilies are white,
    Rosemary's green;
When you are king,
    I will be queen.

Roses are red,
    Lavender's blue;
If you will have me,
    I will have you.

To market, to market, to buy a fat pig;
Home again, home again, jiggety jig.
To market, to market, to buy a fine hog;
Home again, home again, joggety jog.

Six little mice sat down to spin,
Pussy passed by, and she peeped in.
"What are you at, my little men?"
"Making coats for gentlemen."
"Shall I come in and bite off your threads?"
"No, no, Miss Pussy, you'll snip off our heads."
"Oh, no, I'll not, I'll help you to spin."
"That may be so, but you don't come in!"

There was a crooked man, and he went a crooked mile,
He found a crooked sixpence against a crooked stile:
He bought a crooked cat, which caught a crooked mouse,
And they all lived together in a little crooked house.

The doggies went to the mill,
This way and that way;
They took a lick out of this one's sack,
They took a lick out of that one's sack,
And a leap in the stream, and a dip in the dam,
And went walloping, walloping, walloping home!

15

High in the pine-tree
　　The little Turtle-dove
Made a little nursery,
　　To please her little love.
"Coo," said the Turtle-dove,
　　"Coo," said she;
In the long shady branches
　　Of the dark pine-tree.

Cock a doodle doo!
My dame has lost her shoe;
My master's lost his fiddling stick,
And don't know what to do.

Cock a doodle doo!
What is my dame to do?
Till master finds his fiddling stick,
She'll dance without her shoe.

Cock a doodle doo!
My dame has found her shoe,
And master's found his fiddling stick,
Sing doodle doodle doo!

Cock a doodle doo!
My dame will dance with you,
While master fiddles his fiddling stick,
For dame and doodle doo.

There was a little dog, and he had a little tail,
　　And he used to wag, wag, wag it.
But whenever he was sad because he had been bad,
　　On the ground he would drag, drag, drag it.

He had a little nose, as of course you would suppose,
　　And on it was a muz-muz-muzzle,
And to get it off he'd try till a tear stood in his eye,
　　But he found it a puz-puz-puzzle.

Robin and Richard
 Were two little men,
They did not awake
 Till the clock struck ten:

Then up starts Robin,
 And looks at the sky:
"Oh! Brother Richard,
 The sun's very high!"

They both were ashamed
 On such a fine day,
When they were wanted
 To make new hay.

Do you go before,
 With bottle and bag,
I will come after
 On little jack nag.

When I was a little boy
 I lived by myself,
And all the bread and cheese I got
 I put upon the shelf.

The rats and the mice,
 They led me such a life,
I was forced to go to London
 To get myself a wife.

The roads were so bad,
 And the lanes were so narrow,
I could not get my wife home
 In a wheelbarrow.

The wheelbarrow broke,
 And my wife had a fall;
Down came the wheelbarrow,
 Wife and all.

Robin Hood, Robin Hood,
In the mickle wood!
Little John, Little John,
He to the town has gone.

Robin Hood, Robin Hood,
Is telling his beads
All in the green wood,
Among the green weeds.

Little John, Little John,
If he comes no more,
Robin Hood, Robin Hood,
He will fret full sore!

This is the Key of the Kingdom:
In that Kingdom is a city;
In that city is a town;
In that town is a street;
In that street there winds a lane;
In that lane there is a yard;
In that yard there is a house;
In that house there waits a room
In that room an empty bed;
And on that bed a basket—
A Basket of Sweet Flowers:
   Of Flowers, of Flowers;
   A basket of Sweet Flowers.

Flowers in a Basket;
Basket on the bed;
Bed in the chamber;
Chamber in the house;
House in the weedy yard;
Yard in the winding lane;
Lane in the broad street;
Street in the high town;
Town in the city;
City in the Kingdom—
   This is the Key of the Kingdom.
   Of the Kingdom this is the Key.

A knight and a lady
    Went riding one day
Far into the forest,
    Away, away.

"Fair knight," said the lady,
    "I pray, have a care.
This forest is evil;
    Beware, beware."

A fiery red dragon
    They spied on the grass;
The lady wept sorely,
    Alas! Alas!

The knight slew the dragon,
    The lady was gay,
They rode on together,
    Away, away.

Little Jenny Wren,
    Fell sick upon a time;
In came Robin Redbreast,
    And brought her bread and wine.

"Eat of my cake, Jenny,
    And drink of my wine";
"Thank you, Robin, kindly,
    You shall be mine."

Jenny she got well,
    And stood upon her feet,
And told Robin plainly,
    "I love you not a bit."

Robin he was angry,
    And hopped upon a twig,
"Out upon you, fie upon you,
    Bold-faced jig!"

A dis, a dis, a green grass
   A dis, a dis, a dis;
Come, all you pretty fair maids
   And dance along with us.

For we are going roving,
   A roving in this land;
We take this pretty fair maid,
   We take her by the hand.

She shall get a duke, my dear,
   As duck do get a drake;
And she shall have a young prince,
   For her own fair sake.

And if this young prince chance to die,
   She shall get another;
The bells will ring, and the birds will sing,
   And we clap hands together.

A farmer went trotting on his grey mare,
   Bumpety, bumpety, bump!
With his daughter behind him so rosy and fair,
   Lumpety, lumpety, lump!

A raven cried "Crook" and they all tumbled down,
   Bumpety, bumpety, bump!
The mare broke her knees, and the farmer his crown,
   Lumpety, lumpety, lump!

The mischievous raven flew laughing away,
   Bumpety, bumpety, bump!
And said he would serve them the same the next day,
   Lumpety, lumpety, lump!

Down by the meadows, chasing butterflies,
Two little folk were taken by surprise,
When a tiny gallant came, with a bow and a smile,
And begged them to be seated, in his mushroom house awhile

Spring is coming, spring is coming,
　Birdies, build your nest;
Weave together straw and feather,
　Doing each your best.

Spring is coming, spring is coming,
　Flowers are coming too;
Pansies, lilies, daffodillies,
　Now are coming through.

Spring is coming, spring is coming,
　All around is fair;
Shimmer and quiver on the river,
　Joy is everywhere.
We wish you a happy May.

Which is the way to London Town?
Over the hills, across the down:
Over the ridges and over the bridges,
That is the way to London Town.

And what shall I see in London Town?
Many a building old and brown,
Many a real, old-fashioned street
You'll be sure to see in London Town.

What else shall I see in London Town?
Many a maiden in silken gown;
Pretty pink faces, tied up in laces,
You'll certainly see in London Town.

Then onward I hurried to London Town,
Over the hills and across the down,
Over the ridges and over the bridges,
Until I found me in London Town.

Whether the weather be fine, or whether the weather be not,
Whether the weather be cold, or whether the weather be hot,
We'll weather the weather, whatever the weather,
　Whether we like it or not.

Three Riddles

The man in the wilderness asked of me
How many strawberries grew in the sea.
I answered him, as I thought good,
As many red herrings as grew in the wood.

In Spring I look gay
Deck'd in comely array,
In Summer more clothing I wear;
When colder it grows
I fling off my clothes,
And in Winter quite naked appear.

Answer: A Tree

I have a little sister, they call her Peep, Peep,
She wades the water so deep, deep, deep;
She climbs the mountains, high, high, high;
Poor little creature, she has but one eye.

Answer: A Star

One, two,
    Buckle my shoe;
Three four,
    Knock at the door;
Five, six,
    Pick up sticks;
Seven, eight,
    Lay them straight;
Nine, ten,
    A good fat hen.
Eleven, twelve,
    Dig and delve;
Thirteen, fourteen,
    Maids a-courting;
Fifteen, sixteen,
    Maids in the kitchen;
Seventeen, eighteen,
    Maids a-waiting;
Nineteen, twenty,
    My plate's empty.

Once there lived a little man
Where a little river ran,
And he had a little farm and a little dairy O!
  And he had a little plough,
  And a little dappled cow,
Which he often called his pretty little fairy O!

  And his dog he called Fidèle,
  For he loved his master well,
And he had a little pony for his pleasure O!
  In a sty, not very big,
  He'd a frisky little pig
Which he often called his little piggy treasure O!

Simple Simon

Simple Simon met a pieman
  Going to the fair;
Says Simple Simon to the pieman,
  "Let me taste your ware."

Says the pieman unto Simon,
  "Show me first your penny";
Says Simple Simon to the pieman,
  "Indeed I have not any."

Simple Simon went a-fishing
  For to catch a whale;
All the water he had got
  Was in his mother's pail.

Simple Simon went to look
  If plums grew on a thistle;
He pricked his fingers very much
  Which made poor Simon whistle.

When the wind is in the east,
'Tis good for neither man nor beast;
When the wind is in the north,
The skilful fisher goes not forth;
When the wind is in the south,
It blows the bait in the fishes' mouth
When the wind is in the west,
Then 'tis at the very best.

My mother said that I never should
Play with the gipsies in the wood;
The wood was dark, the grass was green,
In came Sally with a tambourine.

I went to the sea—no ships to get across,
I paid ten shillings for a blind white horse.
I jumped on his back, and was off in a crack;
Sally, tell your mother I shall never come back.

There was a little Rabbit sprig,
Which being little was not big;
He always walked upon his feet,
And never fasted when he eat.
When from a place he did run away,
He never at that place did stay;
And when he ran, as I am told,
He ne'er stood still for young or old
Tho' ne'er instructed by a cat,
He knew a mouse was not a rat;
One day, as I am certified,
He took a whim and fairly died:
And, as I'm told, by men of sense,
He never has been walking since.

Little Dame Crump

Little Dame Crump, with her little hair broom,
One morning was sweeping her little bedroom,
When, casting her little grey eyes on the ground,
In a sly little corner a penny she found.

"Ods bobs!" cried the Dame, while she stared with surprise.
"How lucky I am! bless my heart, what a prize!
To market I'll go, and a pig I will buy,
And little John Gubbins shall make him a stye."

So she washed her face clean, and put on her gown,
And locked up the house, and set off for the town;
When to market she went, and a purchase she made
Of a little white pig, and a penny she paid.

When she'd purchased the pig, she was puzzled to know
How they both should get home, if the pig would not go;
So fearing lest piggie should play her a trick,
She drove him along with a little crab stick.

Piggie ran till they came to the foot of a hill,
Where a little bridge stood o'er the stream of a mill;
Piggie grunted and squeaked, but no farther would go;
Oh, fie! Piggie, fie! to serve little Dame so.

She went to the mill, and she borrowed a sack
To put the pig in, and took him on her back;
Piggie squeaked to get out, but the little Dame said,
"If you won't go by fair means, why, you must be made."

At last to the end of her journey she came,
And was mightily glad when she got the pig hame;
She carried him straight to his nice little stye,
And gave him some hay and clean straw nice and dry.

With a handful of peas then Piggie she fed,
And put on her night-cap and got into bed;
Having first said her prayers, she extinguished the light
And being quite tired, we'll wish her good night.

An Old Rhyme

I went to market and bought me a Cat.
Cat had four legs, I had but two.
'Tis almost midnight, what shall I do?

I went a little further and found me a Dog.
Dog wouldn't carry the cat; Cat wouldn't goo.
'Tis almost midnight; what shall I do?

I went a little further and found me a Boy.
Boy wouldn't carry the dog;
Dog wouldn't carry the cat; Cat wouldn't goo.
'Tis almost midnight; what shall I do?

I went a little further and found me a Stick.
Stick wouldn't beat the boy;
Boy wouldn't carry the dog;
Dog wouldn't carry the cat; Cat wouldn't goo.
'Tis almost midnight; what shall I do?

I went a little further and found me a Fire.
Fire wouldn't burn the stick;
Stick wouldn't beat the boy;
Boy wouldn't carry the dog;
                    Repeat as before

I went a little further and found me some Water.
Water wouldn't quench the fire;
Fire wouldn't burn the stick;
                    Repeat as before

I went a little further and found me an Ox.
Ox wouldn't drink the water;
Water wouldn't quench the fire;
                    Repeat as before

I went a little further and found me a Butcher.
Butcher wouldn't kill the ox;
Ox wouldn't drink the water;
                    Repeat as before

I went a little further and found me a Rope.
Rope wouldn't hang the butcher;
Repeat as before

I went a little further and found me some Grease.
Grease wouldn't grease the rope;
Repeat as before

I went a little further and found me a Rat.
Rat began to eat the grease; Grease began to grease the rope,
Rope began to hang the butcher; Butcher began to kill the ox;
Ox began to drink the water; Water began to quench the fire;
Fire began to burn the stick; Stick began to beat the boy;
Boy began to carry the dog; Dog began to carry the cat;
Cat began to goo,
So now it's all over and I am happy.

Thoughts for a Cold Day

A little bit of blowing,
A little bit of snow,
A little bit of growing,
And crocuses will show;
On every twig that's lonely
A new green leaf will spring;
On every patient tree-top
A thrush will stop and sing.

Scaring Crows

O all you little blackey tops,
Pray, don't you eat my father's crops,
While I lie down to take a nap.
Shua-O! Shua-O!

If father he perchance should come,
With his cocked hat and his long gun,
Then you must fly and I must run.
Shua-O! Shua-O!

27

When good King Arthur ruled this land,
  He was a goodly king;
He stole three pecks of barley meal,
  To make a bag-pudding.

A bag-pudding the queen did make,
  And stuffed it well with plums:
And in it put great lumps of fat,
  As big as my two thumbs.

The king and queen did eat thereof,
  And noblemen beside;
And what they could not eat that night,
  The queen next morning fried.

The Mouse, The Frog and The Little Red Hen

Once a Mouse, a Frog, and a Little Red Hen,
  Together kept a house;
The Frog was the laziest of frogs,
  And lazier still was the Mouse.

The work all fell on the Little Red Hen,
  Who had to get the wood,
And build the fires, and scrub, and cook,
  And sometimes hunt the food.

One day, as she went scratching round,
  She found a bag of rye;
Said she, "Now who will make some bread?"
  Said the lazy Mouse, "Not I."

"Nor I," croaked the Frog as he drowsed in the shade,
  Red Hen made no reply,
But flew around with bowl and spoon,
  And mixed and stirred the rye.

"Who'll make the fire to bake the bread?"
   Said the Mouse again, "Not I,"
And, scarcely op'ning his sleepy eyes,
   Frog made the same reply.

The Little Red Hen said never a word,
   But a roaring fire she made;
And while the bread was baking brown,
   "Who'll set the table?" she said.

"Not I," said the sleepy Frog with a yawn;
   "Nor I," said the Mouse again.
So the table she set and the bread put on,
   "Who'll eat this bread?" said the Hen.

"I will!" cried the Frog. "And I!" squeaked the Mouse,
   As they near the table drew:
"Oh, no, you won't!" said the Little Red Hen,
   And away with the loaf she flew.

Old Mother Hubbard

Old Mother Hubbard
Went to the cupboard
To get her poor dog a bone;
   But when she got there,
   The cupboard was bare,
And so the poor dog got none.

She went to the baker's
   To buy him some bread;
But when she got back
   The poor dog was dead.

She went to the joiner's
   To buy him a coffin;
But when she got back
   The doggie was laughing.

She took a clean dish
 To get him some tripe;
But when she came back
 He was smoking his pipe.

She went to the fishmonger's
 To buy him some fish;
And when she came back.
 He was licking the dish.

She went to the tavern
 For white wine and red;
But when she came back
 The dog stood on his head.

She went to the hatter's
 To buy him a hat;
But when she came back
 He was feeding the cat.

She went to the cobbler's
 To buy him some shoes;
But when she came back
 He was reading the news.

The Dame made a curtsey,
 The dog made a bow;
The Dame said, "Your servant,"
 The dog said, "Bow-wow."

This wonderful dog
 Was Dame Hubbard's delight;
He could sing, he could dance,
 He could read, he could write.

She gave him rich dainties
 Whenever he fed,
And erected a monument
 When he was dead.

A Party Song

Merry have we met
And merry have we been;
Merry let us part,
And merry meet again.

With a merry sing-song,
Happy, gay and free,
With a merry ding-dong
Again we'll happy be.

The Squirrel

The winds they did blow,
    The leaves they did wag;
Along came a beggar boy
    And put me in his bag.
He took me to London;
    A lady did me buy,
And put me in a silver cage,
    And hung me up on high;
With apples by the fire,
    And hazel nuts to crack,
Besides a little feather bed
    To rest my tiny back.

The Cuckoo

In April
Come he will,
In flow'ry May
He sings all day,
In leafy June
He changes his tune,
In bright July
He's ready to fly,
In August
Go he must.

The House that Jack Built

This is the house that Jack built.

This is the malt
That lay in the house that Jack built.

This is the rat
That ate the malt
That lay in the house that Jack built.

This is the cat
That killed the rat
That ate the malt
That lay in the house that Jack built.

This is the dog
That worried the cat
That killed the rat
That ate the malt
That lay in the house that Jack built.

This is the cow with the crumpled horn
That tossed the dog
That worried the cat
That killed the rat
That ate the malt
That lay in the house that Jack built.

This is the maiden all forlorn
That milked the cow with the crumpled horn
That tossed the dog
That worried the cat
That killed the rat
That ate the malt
That lay in the house that Jack built.

That is the man all tattered and torn
That kissed the maiden all forlorn
That milked the cow with the crumpled horn
That tossed the dog
That worried the cat

That killed the rat
That ate the malt
That lay in the house that Jack built.

This is the priest all shaven and shorn
That married the man all tattered and torn
That kissed the maiden all forlorn
That milked the cow with the crumpled horn
That tossed the dog
That worried the cat
That killed the rat
That ate the malt
That lay in the house that Jack built.

This is the cock that crowed in the morn
That waked the priest all shaven and shorn
That married the man all tattered and torn
That kissed the maiden all forlorn
That milked the cow with the crumpled horn
That tossed the dog
That worried the cat
That killed the rat
That ate the malt
That lay in the house that Jack built.

Sing Ivy

My father left me three acres of land,
Sing ivy, sing ivy;
My father left me three acres of land,
Sing holly, go whistle, and ivy!

I ploughed it with a ram's horn,
Sing ivy, sing ivy;
And sowed it all over with one peppercorn,
Sing holly, go whistle, and ivy!

I harrowed it with a bramble bush,
Sing ivy, sing ivy;
And reaped it with my little penknife,
Sing holly, go whistle, and ivy.

Poems for the Very Young

Now rocking horse, rocking horse, where shall we go?
The world's such a very wide place, you must know

Merry Birds

Merrily, merrily,
All the spring,
Merrily, merrily
Small birds sing.
All through April,
All through May,
Small birds merrily
Carol all day.

Rodney Bennett

Seven Little Pigs

Seven little pigs went to market,
One of them fell down;
One of them, he ran away,
And five got to town.

Shower and Sunshine

Shower and sunshine,
Sunshine and shower,
Green are the tree tops
And blooming the flower,
Nesting are wild birds,
Air full of song;
Hark! now the cuckoo—
He does not stay long.

Maud Morin

A Rhyme for Washing Hands

Wash, hands, wash,
Daddy's gone to plough.
Splash, hands, splash,
They're all washed now.

Writing Letters

Every time I write a letter,
 If I do not write too fast,
It is sure to be a better,
 Neater letter than the last.

Rodney Bennett

The Queen Bee

When I was in the garden,
 I saw a great Queen Bee;
She was the very largest one
 That I did ever see.
She wore a shiny helmet
 And a lovely velvet gown,
But I was rather sad, because
 She didn't wear a crown.

Mary K. Robinson

Action Rhyme

The policeman walks with heavy tread,
 Left, right, left, right,
Swings his arms, holds up his head.
 Left, right, left, right.

E. H. Adams

A E I O U

We are very little creatures,
All of different voice and features;
One of us in glass is set,
One of us you'll find in jet.
T'other you may see in tin,
And the fourth a box within.
If the fifth you should pursue,
It can never fly from you.

Jonathan Swift

37

The Rain

Rain on the green grass,
And rain on the tree,
And rain on the house-top.
But not upon me!

Little Clotilda

Little Clotilda,
Well and hearty,
Thought she'd like
To give a party.

But as her friends
Were shy and wary,
Nobody came
But her own canary.

The Pancake

Mix a pancake,
Stir a pancake,
Pop it in the pan.

Fry the pancake,
Toss the pancake,
Catch it if you can.

Christina Rossetti

Daffodils

We make both mead and garden gay,
We spend the sweet spring hours in play,
And dance like sunbeams gone astray.

P. A. Ropes

Out of Doors

Birds and bees and butterflies,
  Bobbing all about!
What a jolly world it is,
  Sing and laugh and shout!

E. North

A Baby Verse

Tit-tat-toe,
My first go,
Three jolly butcher boys
All in a row;
Stick one up,
Stick one down,
Stick one in the old man's crown.

White Sheep

White sheep, white sheep
  On a blue hill,
When the wind stops
  You all stand still.
You all run away
  When the winds blow;
White sheep, white sheep,
  Where do you go?

W. H. Davies

Two Little Blackbirds

Two little blackbirds singing in the sun,
One flew away and then there was one;
One little blackbird, very black and tall,
He flew away and then there was the wall.
One little brick wall lonely in the rain,
Waiting for the blackbirds to come and sing again.

39

A Chill

What can lambkins do
All the keen night through?
Nestle by their woolly mother,
The careful ewe.

What can nestlings do
In the nightly dew?
Sleep beneath their mother's wing
Till day breaks anew.

If in field or tree
There might only be
Such a warm, soft sleeping-place
Found for me.

Christina Rossetti

Buttercups

Buttercups golden and gay,
Sway in the wind all day.
They tickle the nose of the cow as she goes,
And they call to the bees, "Come away."

"Banbury Fair"

"Where have you been,
    Miss Marjorie Keen?"
"To Banbury Fair,
    In a carriage and pair."
"And what could there be
    That was funny to see?"
'A dame in a wig
    A-dancing a jig."
'And what did you get
    For six pennies, my pet?"
"A pink sugar mouse
    And a gingerbread house."

Edith G. Millard

The Donkey

My donkey has a bridle
Hung with silver bells,
He feeds upon the thistles
Growing on the fells.

The bells keep chiming, chiming
A little silver song;
If ever I should lose him
It would not be for long.

Rose Fyleman

Boots and Shoes

My Wellington boots go
Thump-thump, thump-thump,
My leather shoes go
Pit-pat, pit-pat,
But my rubber sandals
Make no noise at all.

1. *Children beat loudly on the floor with their feet.*
2. *They beat softly with their feet.*
3. *They beat with their feet making no noise at all.*

Lilian McCrea

Rain

Pitter-patter, hear it raining?
Slow at first, then faster, faster.
Put on your raincoat,
Hold up your umbrella,
Pull on your Wellingtons
And splash in the puddles.

1. *Children clap hands slowly and lightly, gradually getting faster and louder.*
2. *They pretend to button up raincoats, open umbrellas and pull on Wellington boots.*
3. *They stamp their feet on the ground.*

Lilian McCrea

Who has seen the Wind?

Who has seen the wind?
Neither I nor you:
But when the leaves hang trembling
The wind is passing through.

Who has seen the wind?
Neither you nor I:
But when the trees bow down their heads
The wind is passing by.

Christina Rossetti

What the Weather Does

The rooks are alive
On the tops of the trees;
They look like a hive
Of jolly black bees;
They all squawk together,
And loud is their squawking—
It must be the weather
That sets them a-talking.

What Does the Bee Do?

What does the bee do?
Bring home honey.
What does father do?
Bring home money.
And what does mother do?
Lay out the money.
And what does baby do?
Eat up the honey.

Christina Rossetti

Summer Breeze

Summer breeze, so softly blowing,
In my garden pinks are growing,
If you'll go and send the showers,
You may come and smell my flowers.

A Tug-of-War

Three little chickens
And one little worm,
Oh what a tug-of-war!
And each little chick
Thinks he knows very well
What fat little worms are for.

M. M. Hutchinson

The Dandelion Puff

The dandelion puff
Is a very queer clock,
It doesn't say tick,
And it doesn't say tock,
It hasn't a cuckoo,
It hasn't a chime,
And I really don't think
It can tell me the time!

Mary K. Robinson

Finger Folk

Putting on gloves

Finger Folk, Finger Folk,
Four Fairy Finger Folk;
Wearing suits of leather,
All of them together—
    Funny Finger Folk!

Finger Folk and Thumb-man,
Short, sturdy Thumb-man:
Just as quaintly dressed
In a leather vest—
    Funny Thumb-man!

H. M. Tharp

Daisies and Grasses

Daisies so bright,
Grasses so green,
Tell me, I pray,
How you keep clean?

Summertime showers,
Summertime rain,
Wash dusty flowers
All clean again.

"Good Night," Says the Owl

"Tu-whitt, Tu-whitt, Tu-whoo, Tu-whoo,
Good night to me, good night to you."
'Tis the old white owl in the ivy tree,
But I can't see him, and he can't see me!
Lady Erskine Crum

Three Plum Buns

Three plum buns
To eat here at the stile
In the clover meadow,
For we have walked a mile.

One for you, and one for me,
And one left over:
Give it to the boy who shouts
To scare sheep from the clover.
Christina Rossetti

Bachelors' Buttons

Bill the Bachelor lived by himself,
He'd little of comfort in cupboard or shelf,
But skill with his needle he ever did show
With Bachelors' Buttons sewed on in a row.
Maud Morin

I Spy

One, round the candytuft,
Two, round the tree,
Three, round the hollyhock,
Then find me.

Candytuft! Hollyhock!
Where can you be?
I've looked in front, I'll look behind,
One—two—THREE!

N. E. Hussey

Finger Play

Each finger is touched in turn

This little bunny said, "Let's play,"
This little bunny said, "In the hay."
This one saw a man with his gun.
This one said, "This isn't fun."
This one said, "I'm off for a run."
　　"Bang" went the gun,
　　　They ran away
And didn't come back for a year and a day.

Kind Deeds

Little drops of water,
　Little grains of sand,
Make the mighty ocean,
　And the pleasant land.

This the little minutes,
　Humble though they be,
Make the mighty ages
　Of eternity.

Little deeds of kindness,
　Little words of love,
Make this earth an Eden
　Like the heaven above.

Isaac Watts

The Disappointed Shrimper

My net
Is heavy with weed.
My net
Is heavy indeed
With wet,
Wet weed.

For an hour I tried,
For two, for three,
I fished,
I kept looking inside
My net to see
Some shrimps for tea.
I wished
For shrimps for tea.

And the day is done,
And I haven't one
Shrimp
        for
           tea.

P. A. Ropes

Getting Up

When I get up in the morning
I'll tell you what I do,
I wash my hands and I wash my face,
Splishity-splash, splishity-splash.
I clean my teeth till they're shining white,
Scrubbity-scrub, scrubbity-scrub,
Then I put on my clothes and brush my hair,
And runnity-run, I run downstairs.

Children dramatise all the actions as they say the story. For the last line they raise both arms and lower them quickly, making running movements with their fingers.

Lilian McCrea

46

Conversation

Mousie, mousie,
Where is your little wee housie?
Here is the door,
Under the floor,
Said mousie, mousie.

Mousie, mousie,
May I come into your housie?
You can't get in,
You have to be thin,
Said mousie, mousie.

Mousie, mousie,
Won't you come out of your housie?
I'm sorry to say
I'm busy all day,
Said mousie, mousie.

Rose Fyleman

Robin Hood

I've got a bow and arrow,
And I take them to the wood,
And don't the rabbits scuttle
For they think I'm Robin Hood!

Rachel MacAndrew

Billy Boy

Billy Boy, Billy Boy, what will you bring for me?
Riding Old Dobbin to Banbury Fair.
Billy Boy, Billy Boy, shall you be long away?
Just twice as long as it takes to get there.

Billy Boy, Billy Boy, what will you bring for me?
One golden fiddle to play a fine tune,
Two magic wishes and three fairy fishes,
And four rainbow ropes to climb up to the moon.

Dorothy King

47

A Frisky Lamb

A frisky lamb
And a frisky child
Playing their pranks
In a cowslip meadow:
The sky all blue
And the air all mild
And the fields all sun
And the lanes half shadow.

Christina Rossetti

Four Scarlet Berries

Four scarlet berries
Left upon the tree,
"Thanks," cried the blackbird,
"These will do for me."
He ate numbers one and two,
Then ate number three,
When he'd eaten number four,
There was none to see!

Mary Vivian

Eggs For Breakfast

Get up at once, now, Margaret May!
There are eggs in the kitchen for breakfast to-day;
We have porridge on Mondays,
On Wednesdays and Sundays,
But we've brown eggs for breakfast to-day.

Get up at once, now, Margaret May!
Our white porridge bowls are all put away;
We have them on Mondays,
On Wednesdays and Sundays,
But we've little blue egg-cups to-day.

Irene F. Pawsey

48

Bed-Time

Robin Friend has gone to bed,
Little wing to hide his head.
Mother's bird must slumber, too—
Just as baby robins do.
When the stars begin to rise
Birds and Babies close their eyes.

L. Alma Tadema

The Blackbird

1st Child:
Out in the garden,
Up in a tree,
There is a blackbird
Singing to me.

2nd Child:
What is he singing
Up in the tree?
What is he piping
So merrily?

1st Child:
Come out in the garden,
Come out and hear!
Stand still and listen
(But not too near).

Blackbird:
I love the wind, and the stars, and the moon.
I love the sun when it shines at noon;
I love the trees, but I love best
My little brown wife in our cosy nest!

1st Child:
That is the song
He's singing to me,
That's what he's piping
So merrily!

Phyllis Drayson

Baby-Land

"Which is the way to Baby-land?"
"Anyone can tell;
    Up one flight,
    To your right;
Please ring the bell."

"What can you see in Baby-land?"
"Little folks in white—
    Downy heads,
    Cradle-beds,
Faces pure and bright!"

"What do they do in Baby-land?"
"Dream and wake and play,
    Laugh and crow,
    Shout and grow;
Jolly times have they!"

"What do they say in Baby-land?"
"Why, the oddest things;
    Might as well
    Try to tell
What a birdie sings!"

"Who is the Queen of Baby-land?"
"Mother kind and sweet;
    And her love,
    Born above,
Guides the little feet."

George Cooper

My Toys

My red engine goes chuff-chuff-choo! chuff-chuff-choo!
My shiny drum goes rum-tum-tum, rum-tum-tum.
My teddy bear goes grr . . . grrr . . . grrr . . .
And my wooden bricks go clitter-clatter, clitter-clatter,
    rattle-bang—BUMP!

Lilian McCrea

When We Are Men

Jim says a sailor man
　　He means to be;
He'll sail a splendid ship
　　Out on the sea.

Dick wants to buy a farm
　　When he's a man
He'll get some cows and sheep
　　Soon as he can.

Tom says he'll keep a shop;
　　Nice things to eat,
Two windows full of cakes,
　　Down in the street.

I'd hate a stuffy shop—
　　When I'm a man
I'll buy a trotting horse
　　And caravan.

E. Stella Mead

My Doggie

I have a dog,
　　His name is Jack,
His coat is white
　　With spots of black.

I take him out,
　　Most every day,
Such fun we have,
　　We run and play.

Such clever tricks
　　My dog can do,
I love my Jack,
　　He loves me too.

C. Nurton

51

A Giant's Cake

Each year I have a birthday,
When people buy me toys,
And mother gives a party
To lots of girls and boys.

I have a cake with candles,
And icing, pink and white,
With rosy candles lighted,
It makes a lovely sight.

Each year the cake grows larger,
Another light to take,
So if I grow much older
I'll need a giant's cake.

Evelina San Garde

The Bells of London

Gay go up and gay go down,
To ring the bells of London town.
Halfpence and farthings,
Say the bells of St. Martin's.
Oranges and lemons,
Say the bells of St. Clement's.
Pancakes and fritters,
Say the bells of St. Peter's.
Two sticks and an apple,
Say the bells of Whitechapel.

Kettles and pans,
Say the bells of St. Ann's.
You owe me ten shillings,
Say the bells of St. Helen's.
When will you pay me?
Say the bells of Old Bailey.
When I grow rich,
Say the bells of Shoreditch.
Pray when will that be?
Say the bells of Stepney.
I am sure I don't know,
Says the great bell of Bow.

Here We Come A-haying

Here we come a-haying,
  A-haying, a-haying,
Here we come a-haying,
  Among the leaves so green.

Up and down the mower goes
  All the long field over,
Cutting down the long green grass,
  And the purple clover.

Toss the hay and turn it,
  Laid in rows so neatly,
Summer sun a-shining down,
  Makes it smell so sweetly.

Rake it into tidy piles
  Now the farmer's ready,
Load it on the old hay cart,
  Drawn by faithful Neddy.

Down the lane the last load goes,
  Hear the swallows calling.
Now at last our work is done,
  Night is softly falling.

Eunice Close

Hide and Seek

Baby loves to play with me,
Peek-a-boo! Peek-a-boo!
She goes and hides behind a tree,
I see you! I see you!

Baby is so very wee,
Hiding's easy as can be!

Phyllis Drayson

The Balloon Man

This is a little "action poem" for the littlest ones, in which five children may take part. It includes some useful "colour training".

Characters:	Properties:
Balloon man	Coloured balloons
Mother	
Three children	

Balloon Man:
> I stand here every afternoon,
> Waiting for someone to buy a balloon.
> Look at the colours bright and gay.
> Just one penny is all you pay.
> Plenty for all who come, have I,
> Come and buy! Come and buy!

First Child:
> I have a penny, Mother said,
> So I think I'd like one of red.

Second Child:
> I would like that one of green.
> It is the prettiest that I've seen.

Third Child:
> Lucky am I, please give me two,
> One of yellow, and one of blue.

Balloon Man:
> Now with your balloons just run and play,
> I like to see you happy and gay.
> *(Children play with balloons.)*

Mother:
> Children! Children! Come home to tea!

First Child:
> That is my Mother calling me.

All Together:
    Balloon man, don't go away,
    We'll come and see you another day.
    (Children run out saying "Good-bye!")
                                        E. Herbert

To Let

    Two little beaks went tap! tap! tap!
    Two little shells went crack! crack! crack!
    Two fluffy chicks peeped out, and oh,
    They liked the look of the big world so,
    That they left their houses without a fret
    And two little shells are not to LET.

                                D. Newey-Johnson

Little Blue Apron

    "Little Blue Apron,
        How do you do?
    Never a stocking
    And never a shoe!"

    Little Blue Apron
        She answered me,
    "You don't wear stockings
    And shoes by the sea."

    "Little Blue Apron—
        Never a hat?
    How do you manage
    To go out like that?"

    "Why, what is the use
        Of a hat?" said she,
    "You never wear hats
    When you're by the sea."

"Why, little Blue Apron, it seems to me
Very delightful to live by the sea;
But what would hatters and shoemakers do
If everyone lived by the sea like you?"

                            From an Old Story Book

The Furry Home

If I were a mouse
And wanted a house,
I think I would choose
My new red shoes.
Furry edges,
Fur inside,
What a lovely
Place to hide!
I'd not travel,
I'd not roam—
Just sit in
My furry home.

J. M. Westrup

The Mouse

There's such a tiny little mouse
Living safely in my house.

Out at night he'll softly creep,
When everyone is fast asleep.

But always in the light of day
He softly, softly creeps away.

Thirza Wakley

Five Sisters

Five little sisters walking in a row;
Now, isn't that the best way for little girls to go?
Each had a round hat, each had a muff,
And each had a new pelisse of soft green stuff.

Five little marigolds standing in a row;
Now, isn't that the best way for marigolds to grow?
Each with a green stalk, and all five had got
A bright yellow flower, and a new red pot.

Kate Greenaway

High June

Fiddle-de-dee!
Grasshoppers three,
Rollicking over the meadow;
Scarcely the grass,
Bends as they pass,
So fairy-light is their tread, O!

Said Grasshopper One,
"The summer's begun,
This sunshine is driving me crazy!"
Said Grasshopper Two,
"I feel just like you!"
And leapt to the top of a daisy.

"Please wait for me!"
Cried Grasshopper Three,
"My legs are ready for hopping!"
So grasshoppers three,
Fiddle-de-dee,
Raced all the day without stopping.

C. A. Morin

My New Umbrella

I have a new umbrella,
A bright red new umbrella,
A new red silk umbrella,
I wish that it would rain,

And then I could go walking,
Just like a lady walking,
A grown-up lady walking
Away 'way down the lane.

I could not step in puddles,
The shiny tempting puddles,
No lady walks in puddles,
Then turn, and home again.

M. M. Hutchinson

57

The Holiday Train

Tall children or boys are arranged in double file to form train. Other children as passengers enter train after first verse. Train proceeds to rhythm of voices.

Here is the train!
Here is the train!
Let us get in!
Let us get in!

Where shall we sit?
Where shall we sit?
When will it go?
When will it go?

What does it say?
What does it say?
"Let us get on!"
"Let us get on!"

Look at the trees!
Look at the trees!
See all the cows!
See all the cows!

Isn't it fun?
Isn't it fun?
Going along!
Going along!

Hurrying on!
Hurrying on!
Nearly there!
Nearly there!

Look at the sea!
Look at the sea!
See all the ships!
See all the ships!

Here we are!
Here we are!
Out we get!
Out we get!

Irene Thompson

Jack Tar

Jack Tar, Sailor Man,
   Can you tell me
How much water
   Is in the sea?

Yes, Miss, Yes, Miss,
   Certainly!
There's just as much
   As there ought to be.

Emile Jacot

The Pony

I've got a pony
All of my own;
So has Tony,
But his is roan
Mine is a black one,
With such a long mane;
"Let's have a gallop
Right down the lane!"

Rachel MacAndrew

Honey Bear

There was a big bear
Who lived in a cave;
His greatest love
Was honey.
He had twopence a week
Which he never could save,
So he never had
Any money.
I bought him a money box
Red and round,
In which to put
His money.
He saved and saved
Till he got a pound,
Then spent it all
On honey.

Elizabeth Lang

59

The Robin

When father takes his spade to dig,
  Then Robin comes along;
He sits upon a little twig
  And sings a little song.

Or, if the trees are rather far,
  He does not stay alone,
But comes up close to where we are
  And bobs upon a stone.

L. Alma Tadema

The Bus

There is a painted bus
With twenty painted seats.
It carries painted people
Along the painted streets.
They pull the painted bell,
The painted driver stops,
And they all get out together
At the little painted shops.

"Peter"

The Ferryman

"Ferry me across the water,
  Do, boatman, do."
"If you've a penny in your purse
  I'll ferry you."

"I have a penny in my purse,
  And my eyes are blue;
So ferry me across the water,
  Do, boatman, do."

"Step into my ferry-boat,
  Be they black or blue,
And for the penny in your purse
  I'll ferry you."

Christina Rossetti

60

Yesterday

Where have you gone to, Yesterday,
    And why did you have to go?
I've been wondering all the day,
    And nobody seems to know.

Say, is it true that you've journeyed far,
    Over the hills to Spain,
And no one to see which road you took
    Nor call you back again?

Hugh Chesterman

The Woodpecker

Last night I heard him in the woods,
    When everything was still,
Tappity-tap on the dreaming trees
    Under the fairy hill.

I wonder if he lost his way,
    As I did long before.
So had to tap and tap until
    He found the fairies' door.

Joyce Sambrook

Fish and Bird

How happy to be a fish,
To dive and skim,
To dart and float and swim
And play.

How happy to be a bird,
To fly and sing,
To glide on feathered wing
All day.

Rosemary Brinckman

61

The Snowman

Come in the garden
And play in the snow,
A snowman we'll make,
See how quickly he'll grow!
Give him hat, stick, and pipe,
And make him look gay,
Such a fine game
For a cold winter day!

E. M. Adams

The Wind

What can be the matter
  With Mr. Wind to-day?
He calls for me so loudly,
  Through the key-hole, "Come and play."

I'll put my warm red jacket on
  And pull my hat on tight,
He'll never get it off, although
  He tries with all his might.

I'll stand so firm upon my legs,
  I'm strong, what do I care?
Now, Mr. Wind, just come along
  And blow me if you dare.

Dorothy Gradon

The Frog

A little green frog once lived in a pool,
The sun was hot but the water was cool;
He sat in the pool the whole day long,
And sang a queer little, dear little song.

"Quaggery do, quaggery dee,
No one was ever so happy as me."
He sang this song to his little green brother,
And if you don't like it then make me another.

Rose Fyleman

Doves

High on the dove-cot
  In the sunny weather,
The doves nod and bow,
  Crooning together:

"Oh, how do you do?
  How do you do?"
Nodding and crooning
  "How do you do?"

E. J. Falconer

The Dustman

Every Thursday morning
Before we're quite awake,
Without the slightest warning
The house begins to shake
  With a Biff! Bang!
  Biff! Bang! Biff!
It's the Dustman, who begins
  (BANG! CRASH!)
To empty all the bins
Of their rubbish and their ash
  With a Biff! Bang!
  Biff! Bang! Bash!

Clive Sansom

The Dragon

What do you think? Last night I saw
A fiery dragon pass!
He blazed with light from head to tail,
As though his sides were glass.

But when my Mummie came to look
Out through the window-pane,
She laughed, and said: "You silly boy—
It's an electric train!"

Mary Mullineaux

63

Calendar Rhyme

January falls the snow,
February cold winds blow,
In March peep out the early flowers,
And April comes with sunny showers.
In May the roses bloom so gay,
In June the farmer mows his hay,
In July brightly shines the sun,
In August harvest is begun.
September turns the green leaves brown,
October winds then shake them down,
November fills with bleak and smear,
December comes and ends the year.

Flora Willis Watson

Sing-Song Rhyme

One! two! three!
Outside the school,
Three small ducks splash in a pool.

Quack! quack! quack!
That door is wide.
Say the ducks: "Let's peep inside."

Flip! flap! flip!
A waddling row,
Right into the school they go.

Oh! oh! oh!
'Tis fun to see
These new scholars—one! two! three!

Look! look! look!
The children shout:
'Teacher, shall we drive them out?"
(Teacher) "Yes"—sh! sh! sh!

Feet

Big feet,
Black feet,
Going up and down the street;
Dull and shiny
Father's feet,
Walk by me!

Nice feet,
Brown feet,
Going up and down the street;
Pretty, dainty,
Ladies' feet,
Trip by me!

Small feet,
Light feet,
Going up and down the street;
Little children's
Happy feet,
Run by me!

Suggestions for rhythmic action:
Children are arranged in three groups:
(1) Tall children or boys, slow walking step;
(2) Girls, quick walking or tripping;
(3) Smallest children, running.
Each Group interprets movements of verses as indicated by words. The verses are spoken by one child or in Choric Speech by several children.   *Irene Thompson*

An Egg for Easter

I want an egg for Easter,
A browny egg for Easter;
I want an egg for Easter,
So I'll tell my browny hen.
   I'll take her corn and water,
   And show her what I've brought her,
   And she'll lay my egg for Easter,
   Inside her little pen.

Irene F. Pawsey

65

Wash-Day

This is the way we wash our clothes,
Rub-a-dub-dub, rub-a-dub-dub!
Watch them getting clean and white,
Rub-a-dub-dub, rub-a-dub-dub!

This is the way we mangle them,
Rumble-de-dee, rumble-de-dee!
Round and round the handle goes,
Rumble-de-dee, rumble-de-dee!

This is the way we hang them out,
Flippity-flap, flippity-flap!
See them blowing in the wind,
Flippity-flap, flippity-flap!

This is the way we iron them
Smooth as smooth can be!
Soon our wash-day will be done,
Then we'll all have tea.

Lilian McCrea

Wishes

Said the first little chicken,
    With a queer little squirm,
"I wish I could find
    A fat little worm."

Said the next little chicken,
    With a sharp little squeal,
"I wish I could find
    Some nice yellow meal."

Said the third little chicken,
    With a small sigh of grief,
"I wish I could find
    A little green leaf."

"See here," said the mother,
    From the green garden patch,
"If you want any breakfast,
    Just come here and scratch."

66

Best Of All

I've got a lovely home,
With every single thing—
A mother and a father,
And a front-door bell to ring.
A dining-room and kitchen,
Some bedrooms and a hall,
But the baby in the cradle
Is the nicest thing of all.

J. M. Westrup

Lucy Lavender

Little Lucy Lavender,
　Aged just three,
Dances over the water,
　Dances over the sea,
Dances by the streamlet,
　Dances on the hill—
Little Lucy Lavender
　She can't stand still!

Little Lucy Lavender,
　Aged just three,
Sang as she clambered
　Up the apple tree;
Sang in her bath-tub,
　Sang in her bed,
For—"I can't stay quiet,"
　Little Lucy said.

Ivy O. Eastwick

To The Bat

Little bat, little bat,
Pray, when you speak,
Speak a bit louder,
You've such a high squeak,
That only those people
With quite a good ear,
Who know all about you,
Can possibly hear.

Edith King

Wishes

I wish I were an Emperor,
　　With subjects of my own,
And sat in royal robes upon
　　A splendid golden throne.

I wish I were a Muffin Man,
　　And rang a muffin bell,
And every day for tea I'd have
　　The ones I didn't sell.

I wish I were a Pirate Chief,
　　And sailed the stormy sea,
With lace and earrings and a sword
　　As fine as I could be.

I wish I were a Railway Guard,
　　With bright green flag to wave,
Watching the people catch their train
　　By such a narrow shave!

I wish I were a Drummer Boy,
　　And beat upon a drum,
And heard the crowd all shouting out:
　　"Look, here the soldiers come!"

I wish I were Aladdin, or
　　I knew some magic way
To make my wishes all come true
　　And not be only play.

F. Rogers

Dancing on the Shore

Ten in circle. Queen in centre.
　　Ten little children
　　Dancing on the shore;
　　The queen waved a royal wand
　　And out went four.

Four step outside circle.
> Six little children
> Dancing merrily;
> The queen waved a royal wand
> And out went three.

*Three step out and join hands with four, making an outside circle
around the smaller one.*
> Three little children
> Danced as children do;
> The queen waved a royal wand
> And out went two.

Two join larger circle.
> One little maiden,
> Dancing just for fun;
> The queen waved a royal wand
> And out went one.

M. M. Hutchinson

Three Mice

Three little mice walked into town,
Their coats were grey, and their eyes were brown.

Three little mice went down the street,
With woolwork slippers upon their feet.

Three little mice sat down to dine
On curranty bread and gooseberry wine.

Three little mice ate on and on,
Till every crumb of the bread was gone.

Three little mice, when the feast was done,
Crept home quietly one by one.

Three little mice went straight to bed,
And dreamt of crumbly, curranty bread.

Charlotte Druitt Cole

Things I Like

I like blowing bubbles, and swinging on a swing;
I love to take a country walk and hear the birdies sing.

I like little kittens, and I love puppies too;
And calves and little squealing pigs and baby ducks, don't
    you?

I like picking daisies, I love my Teddy bear;
I like to look at picture books in Daddy's big armchair.

Marjorie H. Greenfield

Twinkle, Twinkle, Little Star

Twinkle, twinkle little star,
How I wonder what you are!
Up above the world so high
Like a diamond in the sky.

When the blazing sun is gone,
When he nothing shines upon,
Then you show your little light,
Twinkle, twinkle, all the night.

Then the traveller in the dark
Thanks you for your tiny spark!
He could not see which way to go,
If you did not twinkle so.

In the dark blue sky you keep,
And often through my curtains peep,
For you never shut your eye
Till the sun is in the sky.

As your bright and tiny spark
Lights the traveller in the dark,
Though I know not what you are,
Twinkle, twinkle, little star.

Jane Taylor

Primrose Hill

On Primrose Hill in the early spring
The soft winds blow and sweet birds sing
And the little brown thrush is king—is king.

On Primrose Hill in the sunny weather
The children dance on the grass together
And the larch's bough has a bright green feather.

Rose Fyleman

My New Rabbit

We brought him home, I was so pleased,
    We made a rabbit-hutch,
I give him oats, I talk to him,
    I love him very much.

Now when I talk to Rover dog,
    He answers me "Bow-wow!"
And when I speak to Pussy-cat,
    She purrs and says "Mee-ow!"

But Bunny never says a word,
    Just twinkles with his nose,
And what that rabbit thinks about,
    Why! no one ever knows.

My Mother says the fairies must
    Have put on him a spell,
They told him all their secrets, then
    They whispered, "Pray don't tell."

So Bunny sits there looking wise,
    And twinkling with his nose,
And never, never, never tells
    A single thing he knows.

Elizabeth Gould

71

Topsy-Turvy Land

Will you come to Turvy Land,
To Tipsy-Topsy-Turvy Land,
And see the fishes growing, like the apples on the tree?
The houses are of silk there,
And the sea is made of milk there,
And the rain comes down in strawberries for Mother and
for me.

Phyllis M. Stone

Jenny and Johnny

Jenny gay and Johnny grim,
In your house so green, so trim,
Tell me truly, tell me, pray,
What's the weather for to-day?
Jenny's standing at her door,
So dull days are surely o'er . . .
Ah, but John's popped out again
Just to say, "It's going to rain."

Dorothy King

Jeremy Hobbler

Sing a song of cobbler!
Jeremiah Hobbler
Mended boots and shoes
By ones and by twos.
His room had a floor and a ceiling
And he did soling and heeling.
But oh, he was so funny!
He always expected his money;
And—oh, would anybody believe it?
He generally used to receive it
When the boots and shoes were mended.
And now the song is ended—
The song of Jeremy Hobbler
Who followed the trade of cobbler.

Whisky Frisky

Whisky Frisky,
Hipperty hop,
Up he goes
To the tree top!

Whirly, twirly,
Round and round,
Down he scampers
To the ground.

Furly, curly,
What a tail,
Tall as a feather,
Broad as a sail.

Where's his supper?
In the shell.
Snappy, cracky,
Out it fell.

A Watering Rhyme

Early in the morning,
   Or the evening hour,
Are the times to water
   Every kind of flower.
Watering at noonday,
   When the sun is high,
Doesn't help the flowers,
   Only makes them die.

Also, when you water,
   Water at the roots;
Flowers keep their mouths where
   We should wear our boots.
Soak the earth around them,
   Then through all the heat
The flowers will have water
   For their thirsty "feet"!

P. A. Ropes

The Postman

Rat-a-tat-tat, Rat-a-tat-tat,
  Rat-a-tat-tat tattoo!
That's the way the Postman goes,
  Rat-a-tat-tat tattoo!
Every morning at half-past eight
You hear a bang at the garden gate,
And Rat-a-tat-tat, Rat-a-tat-tat,
  Rat-a-tat-tat tattoo!

Clive Sansom

If

If I were oh, so very small,
  I'd hide myself away,
And creep into a p eony cup
  To spend the summer's day.

If I were oh, so very tall,
  I'd walk among the trees,
And bend to pick the topmost leaf
  As easy as you please.

P. A. Ropes

Timid Bunnies

See the bunnies sitting there,
Let us give them all a scare,
Clap your hands, ha, ha! they flop
Each beneath a turnip top;
Clap again, see how they run,
White tails bobbing in the sun;
Fathers, sons, and big, big brothers,
Little babies and their mothers;
Helter-skelter, off they go,
To their burrows down below.

Jeannie Kirby

Johnny's Farm

Johnny had a little dove;
   Coo, coo, coo.
Johnny had a little mill;
   Clack, clack, clack.
Johnny had a little cow;
   Moo, moo, moo.
Johnny had a little duck;
   Quack, quack, quack.
Coo, coo; clack, clack; moo, moo; quack, quack;
Down on Johnny's little farm.

Johnny had a little hen;
   Cluck, cluck, cluck.
Johnny had a little crow;
   Caw, caw, caw.
Johnny had a little pig;
   Chook, chook, chook.
Johnny had a little donkey;
   Haw, haw, haw.
Coo, coo; clack, clack; moo, moo; quack, quack;
Cluck, cluck; caw, caw; chook, chook; haw, haw;
Down on Johnny's little farm.

Johnny had a little dog,
   Bow, wow, wow;
Johnny had a little lamb,
   Baa, baa, baa;
Johnny had a little son,
   Now, now, now!
Johnny had a little wife,
   Ha! ha!! ha!!!
Coo, coo; clack, clack; moo, moo; quack, quack;
Cluck, cluck; caw, caw; chook, chook; haw, haw;
Bow-wow; baa, baa; now, now; ha! ha!!
Down on Johnny's little farm.

H. M. Adams

I Saw a Ship A-Sailing

I saw a ship a-sailing,
A-sailing on the sea;
And, oh! it was laden
With pretty things for me.

There were comfits in the cabin,
And apples in the hold;
The sails were made of silk,
And the masts were made of gold.

The four-and-twenty sailors
That stood between the decks,
Were four-and-twenty white mice,
With chains about their necks.

The Captain was a duck,
With a packet on his back,
And when the ship began to move,
The Captain said, "Quack quack!"

If

If I take an acorn
    That's fallen from its cup,
And plant it in the garden
    And never dig it up;
The sun and rain will change it
    To a great big tree,
With lots of acorns on it
    Growing all for me.

I'll plant an orange pippin,
    And see what that will do;
I hope an orange tree will grow,
    I think it will, don't you?
If oranges should really grow,
    And if there should be many,
I'll put them in a basket
    And sell them two a penny.

Alice Todd

Mr. Brown

Mr. Brown
Goes up and down,
And round and round,
And round the town;
Up and down,
Round and round,
Up and down
And round the town.

Rodney Bennett

Little Betty Blue

Little Betty Blue
Has a button on her shoe;
But she's too fat to button it,
So what can Betty do?

She can ask her brother Paul
Who is rather thin and small;
Then he will come and button it
Without a fuss at all!

Agnes Grozier Herbertson

A Little Bird's Song

Sometimes I've seen,
Sometimes I've heard,
Up in the tree
A little bird,
Singing a song,
A song to me,
A little brown bird
Up in the tree.
Sometimes he stays,
Sometimes he sings,
Then to the wind
He spreads his wings,
Flying away,
Away from me,
A little brown bird
Up in the tree.

Margaret Rose

Pussy-Cat and Puppy-Dog

Mee-ow, mee-ow,
Here's a little pussy-cat
With furry, furry fur,
Stroke her very gently
And she'll purr, purr, purr.

Bow-wow, bow-wow,
Here's a little puppy-dog
With a wiggly-waggly tail,
Pat him and he'll wag it
With a wiggy-wag-wag
And a waggy-wag-wag.

Lilian McCrea

My Party

I'm giving a party to-morrow at three,
And these are the people I'm asking to tea.

I'm sure you will know them—they're old friends, not new;
Bo-peep and Jack Horner and Little Boy Blue.

And Little Miss Muffet, and Jack and his Jill
(Please don't mention spiders—nor having a spill).

And Little Red Riding-Hood—Goldilocks too
(When sitting beside them, don't talk of the Zoo).

And sweet Cinderella, and also her Prince
(They're married—and happy they've lived ever since!)

And Polly, and Sukey; who happily settle
On each side the hearth, to look after the kettle.

All these are the people I'm asking to tea;
So please come and meet them to-morrow at three.

Queenie Scott-Hopper

Just Like Me

I went up one pair of stairs
 Just like me.
I went up two pairs of stairs
 Just like me.
I went into a room
 Just like me,
I looked out of a window
 Just like me,
And there I saw a monkey
 Just like me.

Our Mother

Hundreds of stars in the pretty sky,
Hundreds of shells on the shore together,
Hundreds of birds that go singing by,
Hundreds of birds in the sunny weather.

Hundreds of dewdrops to greet the dawn,
Hundreds of bees in the purple clover,
Hundreds of butterflies on the lawn,
But only one mother the wide world over.

There Are Big Waves

There are big waves and little waves,
 Green waves and blue,
Waves you can jump over,
 Waves you dive thro',
Waves that rise up
 Like a great water wall,
Waves that swell softly
 And don't break at all,
Waves that can whisper,
 Waves that can roar,
And tiny waves that run at you
 Running on the shore.

Eleanor Farjeon

79

Just Like This

Action Rhyme

The trees are waving to and fro,
Just like this; just like this;
Branches swaying high and low,
Just like this; just like this.

The waves are tossing up and down,
Just like this; just like this;
On the sand lies seaweed brown,
Just like this; just like this.

The birds are always on the wing,
Just like this; just like this;
Bees are humming in the ling,
Just like this; just like this.

The gnats are darting through the air,
Just like this; just like this;
Dragon-flies flit here and there,
Just like this; just like this.

Squirrels are racing up the trees,
Just like this; just like this;
Rabbits scurry o'er the leas,
Just like this; just like this.

Forest ponies frisk and prance,
Just like this; just like this;
Little children play and dance,
Just like this; just like this.

D. A. Olney

A Finger Play for a Snowy Day

I

This is how snowflakes play about,
Up in cloudland they dance in and out.

This is how they whirl down the street,
Powdering everybody they meet.

This is how they come fluttering down,
Whitening the roads, the fields, and the town.

This is how snowflakes cover the trees,
Each branch and twig bends in the breeze.

This is how snowflakes blow in a heap,
Looking just like fleecy sheep.

This is how they cover the ground,
Cover it thickly, with never a sound.

This is how people shiver and shake
On a snowy morning when first they wake.

This is how snowflakes melt away
When the sun sends out his beams to play.

The Butterfly

I know a little butterfly with tiny golden wings,
He plays among the summer flowers and up and down he
    swings,
He dances on their honey cups so happy all the day,
And then he spreads his tiny wings—and softly flies away.

Margaret Rose

The Washing-up Song

Sing a song of washing-up,
Water hot as hot,
Cups and saucers, plates and spoons,
Dishes such a lot!
Work the dish-mop round and round,
Wash them clean as clean,
Polish with a dry white cloth,
How busy we have been!

Elizabeth Gould

The Clucking Hen

"Will you take a walk with me,
    My little wife, to-day?
There's barley in the barley-field,
    And hay-seed in the hay."

"Thank you," said the clucking hen;
    "I've something else to do;
I'm busy sitting on my eggs,
    I cannot walk with you."

"Cluck, cluck, cluck, cluck,"
    Said the clucking hen;
"My little chicks will soon be hatched,
    I'll think about it then."

The clucking hen sat on her nest,
    She made it in the hay;
And warm and snug beneath her breast
    A dozen white eggs lay.

Crack, crack, went all the eggs,
    Out dropt the chickens small!
"Cluck," said the clucking hen,
    "Now I have you all.

"Come along, my little chicks,
    I'll take a walk with you";
"Hello!" said the barn-door cock,
    "Cock-a-doodle-do!"

Laughter

No one in the garden
Up the mossy path,
Yet I almost certainly
Heard a little laugh.

Light as fluffy thistledown,
Fresh as dew at morning,
Happy as a bird's song
When the day is dawning.

No one in the rockery
As I tiptoe round,
Listening for another laugh,
But scarce a *single sound.*

Nothing but the sound of grass
Rippling in the breeze.
No one in the garden
But the flowers and trees.

Olive Enoch

Over the Fields

Children walk in single file or with partners, reciting poem and keeping time to the rhythm of the verses.

Over the fields where the cornflowers grow,
Over the fields where the poppies blow,
Over the stile there's a way we know—
    Down to a rustling wood!

Over the fields where the daisies grow,
Over the bank where the willows blow,
Over the bridge there's a way we know—
    Down to a rippling brook!

Over the hills where the rainbows go,
Where golden gorse and brambles grow,
Over the hills there's a way we know—
    Down to a rolling sea!

Adeline White

83

In My Garden

A Poem for Dramatisation

In my little garden
  By the apple tree,
Daffodils are dancing—
  One—two—three!

In my little garden
  By the kitchen door,
Daisies red are smiling—
  Two—three—four!

In my little garden
  By the winding drive,
Roses bright are climbing—
  Three—four—five!

In my little garden
  By the pile of bricks,
Hollyhocks are growing—
  Four—five—six!

In my little garden
  Down in sunny Devon,
Violets are hiding—
  Five—six—seven!

In my little garden
  By the cottage gate,
Pansies gay are shining—
  Six—seven—eight!

Daffodils in golden gowns,
  Daisies all in red,
Hollyhocks so very tall
  By the garden shed,
Roses in the sunshine,
  Violets dewy bright,
Pansies smiling gaily—
  What a lovely sight!

84

Gipsy Man

Gipsy man, O gipsy man,
In your yellow caravan,
Up and down the world you go—
Tell me all the things you know!

Sun and moon and stars are bright,
Summer's green and winter's white,
And I'm the gayest gipsy man
That rides inside a caravan.

Dorothy King

A Happy Child

My house is red—a little house,
A happy child am I,
I laugh and play the livelong day,
I hardly ever cry.

I have a tree, a green, green tree,
To shade me from the sun;
And under it I often sit,
When all my work is done.

My little basket I will take,
And trip into the town;
When next I'm there I'll buy some cake,
And spend my bright half-crown.

Kate Greenaway

Haymaking

The farmer is busy, so busy, to-day,
Trying to gather in all his hay,
So off to the hayfield hurry away
And see what you can do.
Will you rake, and toss, and turn the hay?
Will you ride in the cart which takes it away?
Or pile up the rick as high as you may?
Or—will-you-only-*play*?

E. M. Adams

If I Were an Apple

If I were an apple
  And grew upon a tree,
I think I'd fall down
  On a nice boy like me.

I wouldn't stay there,
  Giving nobody joy;
I'd fall down at once,
  And say, "Eat me, my boy."

The King of China's Daughter

The King of China's daughter,
  So beautiful to see
With her face like yellow water, left
  Her nutmeg tree.
Her little rope for skipping
  She kissed and gave it me—
Made of painted notes of singing-birds
  Among the fields of tea.
I skipped across the nutmeg grove,
  I skipped across the sea;
But neither sun nor moon, my dear,
  Has yet caught me.

Edith Sitwell

Haymaking

This is the way we make our hay;
Men cut the grass, then lad and lass,
We take it and shake it, and shake it,
Then into heaps we rake it,
And leave it to the sun to bake it;
And when it is brown we pull it down,
And again we take it and shake it,
And again with our rakes we rake it;
And when we have done, with dance and fun,
Home in our carts we take it.

A. P. Graves

My Little Dog

I helped a little lame dog
  Over such a stile,
He followed me with gratitude
  Many a weary mile.
I shoo-ed at him and chased him,
  But he stuck there, close behind;
(I'm sure his bark was saying,
  "I know that you'll be kind!")
He came into my housie,
  And he wouldn't go away,
So I'll keep my little lame dog
  To myself, if I may.

Pearl Forbes MacEwen

Who's that A-knocking?

Who's that a-knocking,
  A-knocking at the door—
One knock!—two knocks!
  Three knocks!—four!
He's come to the window,
  He's taking a peep
To find out whether
  Baby's asleep.

Emile Jacot

Little Robin Redbreast

Little Robin Redbreast sat upon a tree,
Up went Pussy-cat, and down went he;
Down came Pussy-cat, and away Robin ran;
Says little Robin Redbreast, "Catch me if you can!"

Little Robin Redbreast jumped upon a wall,
Pussy-cat jumped after him, and almost got a fall;
Little Robin chirped and sang, and what did Pussy say?
Pussy-cat said, "Mew!" and Robin jumped away.

How Many Days Has My Baby To Play?

How many days has my baby to play?
Saturday, Sunday, Monday,
Tuesday, Wednesday, Thursday, Friday,
Saturday, Sunday, Monday.

The Wolf and the Lambs

A verse-speaking piece suitable for acting

Wolf:
Little young lambs, oh! why do you stay
Up in the bleak hills amid the snow?
I know a place where the fields are gay,
Where sweet-stalked clovers and daisies grow!
Follow me, little lambs! Follow me, do!
And pleasant pastures I'll show to you!

Lambs:
Oh, Mr. Wolf, how kind you are
To offer us lambs such splendid things!
But, tell us, please, is it very far?
We are lambs, not birds, for we have no wings,
And little legs tire, indeed they do!
So perhaps we had better not go with you!

Wolf:
Little young lambs, it is very near!
Only a dozen steps away!
How cold it is and dreary here,
But there it is sunshine all the day!
Follow me, little lambs! Follow me, do!
And pleasant pastures I'll show to you!

Lambs:
Oh, Mr. Wolf, how kind you are,
But our mother has told us not to go!
She says that such pastures may be too far,
She says there are far worse things than snow!
In fact, Mr. Wolf—we tell you true!—
She says there is nothing worse than you!

Ivy O. Eastwick

Boats Sail on the Rivers

Boats sail on the rivers,
  And ships sail on the seas;
But clouds that sail across the sky
  Are prettier far than these.

There are bridges on the rivers,
  As pretty as you please;
But the bow that bridges heaven,
  And overtops the trees,
And builds a road from earth to sky,
  Is prettier far than these.

Christina Rossetti

Five Little Brothers

Five little brothers set out together
  To journey the live-long day,
In an odd little carriage, all made of leather,
  They hurried away, away—
One big brother and three quite small,
And one wee fellow, no size at all.

The carriage was dark and none too roomy,
  And they could not move about;
The five little brothers grew very gloomy,
  And the wee one began to pout;
Till the biggest one whispered: "What do you say?
Let's leave the carriage and run away."

So out they scampered, the five together,
  And off and away they sped.
When somebody found the carriage of leather,
  Oh, my! how she shook her head!
'Twas her little boy's shoe, as everyone knows,
And the five little brothers were five little toes!

Ella Wheeler Wilcox

We Thank You!

Bus driver,
Tram driver,
Driver of a train:
They take us out,
And bring us back again.
Tram conductor,
Bus conductor,
Train guard too:
They look after us,
Tell us what to do.
Bus men, train men,
Tram men, and motor men:
For all you do for us
WE THANK YOU!

L. E. Cox

The Little Piggies

Child: Where are you going, you little pig?
1st Pig: I'm leaving my mother, I'm growing so big!

Child: So big, young pig!
               So young, so big!
What, leaving your mother, you foolish young pig!
Where are you going, you little pig?

2nd Pig: I've got a new spade, and I'm going to dig.

Child: To dig, little pig!
               A little pig dig!
Well, I never saw a pig with a spade that could dig!
Where are you going, you little pig?

3rd Pig: Why, I'm going to have a nice ride in a gig.

Child: In a gig, little pig!
               What, a pig in a gig!
Well, I never saw a pig ride in a gig!
Where are you going, little pig?

4th Pig: I'm going to the barber's to buy a wig.

Child: A wig, little pig!
                   A pig in a wig!
           Why, whoever before saw a pig in a wig?
           Where are you going, you little pig?

5th Pig: Why, I'm going to the ball to dance a fine jig.

Child: A jig, little pig!
                   A pig dance a jig!
           Well, I never before saw a pig dance a jig!
                                              Thomas Hood

Through Nurseryland

Now, rocking horse! rocking horse! where shall we go?
The world's such a very big place, you must know,
That to see all its wonders, the wiseacres say,
'Twould take us together a year and a day.

Suppose we first gallop to Banbury Cross,
To visit that lady upon a white horse,
And see if it's true that her fingers and toes
Make beautiful music, wherever she goes.

Then knock at the door of the Old Woman's Shoe,
And ask if her wonderful house is on view,
And peep at the children, all tucked up in bed,
And beg for a taste of the broth without bread.

On poor Humpty-Dumpty we'll certainly call,
Perhaps we might help him to get back on his wall;
Spare two or three minutes to comfort the Kits
Who've been kept without pie, just for losing their mits.

A rush to Jack Horner's, then down a steep hill,
Not over and over, like poor Jack and Jill!
So, rocking horse! rocking horse! scamper away,
Or we'll never get back in a year and a day.

My Little House

I have a little house
   With windows and a door,
Two chimneys on the top,
   And a plot of grass before.

I have a little house,
   With curtains and a blind,
Two chimneys on the top,
   And a plot of grass behind.

I have a little house,
   Where I go in and out,
Two chimneys on the top,
   And a garden all about.

J. M. Westrup

Trouble at the Farm

Help! Help!
What's to do?
Dobbin the horse
Has cast a shoe!

Help! Help!
What is the matter?
Porkie the pig
Has eaten the platter!

Help! Help!
What is it now?
Sammie the sheep-dog
Is chasing the cow!

Oh! dear!
What a to-do!
Such muddles and troubles
I never knew!

Ivy O. Eastwick

Off we go to Market

1. We feed the chickens every day,

Action of feeding chickens.

Singing as we go.

Partners take hands and swing across to opposite positions.

We gather up the eggs they lay,

Action of picking up eggs.

Singing as we go.

Partners take hands and swing back to places.

Then off we go to market,
Off we go to market,
Off we go to market,
Singing as we go.

*Still with hands across, all follow the first couple down the room
and back to place.*

2. We plant the turnips in the ground,
   Singing as we go,
   We pull them when they're large and round,
   Singing as we go.
   Then off we go to market,
   Off we go to market,
   Off we go to market,
   Singing as we go.

3. We gather cherries ripe and red,
   Singing as we go.
   We put them in a basket bed,
   Singing as we go,
   Then off we go to market,
   Off we go to market,
   Off we go to market,
   Singing as we go.

Gwen A. Smith

93

O Sailor, Come Ashore

O sailor, come ashore,
  What have you brought for me?
Red coral, white coral,
  Coral from the sea.

I did not dig it from the ground,
  Nor pluck it from a tree;
Feeble insects made it,
  In the stormy sea.

Christina Rossetti

Oh! Look at the Moon

Oh! look at the moon,
She is shining up there;
Oh! Mother, she looks
Like a lamp in the air.

Last week she was smaller,
And shaped like a bow;
But now she's grown bigger,
And round as an O.

Pretty moon, pretty moon,
How you shine on the door,
And make it all bright
On my nursery floor!

You shine on my playthings,
And show me their place,
And I love to look up
At your pretty bright face.

And there is the star
Close by you, and maybe
That small, twinkling star
Is your little baby.

Eliza Lee Follen

Three Dogs

I know a dog called Isaac,
   Who begs for cake at tea;
He's fat and white and most polite,
   And belongs to Timothy.

I know a dog who carries
   His master's walking-stick:
He's old and slow, and his name is Joe,
   And *he* belongs to Dick.

I know a dog called Jacob,
   The best of all the three,
Sedate and wise, with nice brown eyes,
   And *he* belongs to Me.

E. C. Brereton

Making Tens

How many ways can you bring me ten?
Now think fast, my merry little men.

Glad to be first, see Jack's eyes shine,
As he quickly comes to me with one and—

Right on his heels his usual mate
Robert follows with two and—

Next to come is Dick from Devon,
And he has written three and—

Then follows quickly Harold Hicks,
I see he makes it four and—

Last of all comes Mortimer Clive,
But first to think of five and—

M. M. Hutchinson

O Dandelion

"O dandelion, yellow as gold,
What do you do all day?"

"I just wait here in the tall green grass
Till the children come to play."

"O dandelion, yellow as gold,
What do you do all night?"

"I wait and wait till the cool dews fall
And my hair grows long and white."

"And what do you do when your hair is white
And the children come to play?"

"They take me up in their dimpled hands
And blow my hair away!"

Old Mother Goose

Old Mother Goose when
    She wanted to wander,
Would ride through the air
    On a very fine gander.

Mother Goose had a house,
    'Twas built in a wood,
Where an owl at the door
    For sentinel stood.

She had a son Jack,
    A plain-looking lad,
He was not very good,
    Nor yet very bad.

She sent him to market,
    A live goose he bought;
"Here, Mother," says he,
    "It will not go for nought."

Jack's goose and her gander
  Grew very fond,
They'd both eat together,
  Or swim in one pond.

Jack found one morning,
  As I have been told,
His goose had laid him
  An egg of pure gold.

Jack rode to his mother,
  The news for to tell;
She call'd him a good boy,
  And said it was well.

A rogue got the goose,
  Which he vow'd he would kill,
Resolving at once
  His pockets to fill.

Jack's mother came in
  And caught the goose soon,
And mounting its back,
  Flew up to the moon.

A-Hunting

The queen is gone a-hunting in the royal wood,
Between ourselves, at hunting she is not much good—
She will not catch the things she hunts, she doesn't think
  it right,
But in her scarlet hunting robes, she's such a pretty sight.
    Hey ho! derry, derry, in the woods so green
    That's how I'd go hunting if I were a queen.

The king is gone a-hunting in the palace pond,
Of hunting little tadpoles he is very fond.
His robes are wet as anything, his crown is all awry,
He's taken off his shoes and socks and hung them out to
  dry.
    Fee fo! fiddle daddle, let him have his fling,
    That's how I'd go hunting if I were a king.

Jennie Dunbar

Who Likes the Rain?

"I," said the duck. "I call it fun,
For I have my pretty red rubbers on;
They make a little three-toed track
In the soft, cool mud—quack! quack!"

"I," cried the dandelion, "I,
My roots are thirsty, my buds are dry,"
And she lifted a tousled yellow head
Out of her green and grassy bed.

Sang the brook: "I welcome every drop,
Come down, dear raindrops; never stop
Until a broad river you make of me,
And then I will carry you to the sea."

"I," shouted Ted, "for I can run,
With my high-top boots and raincoat on,
Through every puddle and runlet and pool
I find on the road to school."

Mrs. Indiarubber Duck

Mrs. Indiarubber Duck,
I like to see you float
Round and round my bath-tub
Like a tiny sailing boat.

Mrs. Indiarubber Duck,
I like to see you sip
The lovely soapy water
When you take your morning dip.

Mrs. Indiarubber Duck,
I stroke your shining back,
But oh! how splendid it would be
If only you could quack.

D. Carter

Marketing

I am going to market
   To buy a loaf of bread;
But if the buns are shiny ones
   I'll buy some buns instead.

I am going to market
   To buy a Cheddar cheese,
And I shall tell the men who sell,
   "A fresh one, if you please."

I am going to market
   To buy some juicy plums,
The men will say, "They're fresh to-day,"
   To everyone that comes.

I am going to market
   To see what I can see;
I'll look around and spend a pound,
   And come back home for tea.

E. J. Falconer

Little Trotty Wagtail

Little Trotty Wagtail, he went in the rain,
And twittering, tottering sideways he ne'er got straight
   again.
He stooped to get a worm, and looked up to get a fly,
And then he flew away ere his feathers they were dry.

Little Trotty Wagtail, he waddled in the mud,
And left his little footmarks, trample where he would.
He waddled in the water-pudge, and waggle went his tail,
And chirrup up his wings to dry upon the garden rail.

Little Trotty Wagtail, you nimble all about,
And in the dimpling water-pudge you waddle in and out;
Your home is nigh at hand, and in the warm pig-stye,
So, little Master Wagtail, I'll bid you a good-bye.

John Clare

Baby Beds

Little lambs, little lambs,
Where do you sleep?
"In the green meadow,
With mother sheep."

Little birds, little birds,
Where do you rest?
"Close to our mother,
In a warm nest."

Baby dear, Baby dear,
Where do you lie?
"In my warm bed,
With Mother close by."

The Pigeons

Out in the garden,
    Out in the sun,
Two pigeons were talking.
    I listened. Said One:
"I do think it's fine
For the time of the year.
    Don't yo-ou? Don't yo-o-ou?"
And Two, from the branch
Of another tree near,
    Said, "I do-o. I do-o-o."

Number One called:
    "Do come and look,
I've found in this thorn-tree
    The cosiest nook.
I do think a thorn
Is a snug sort of tree.
    Don't you-ou? Don't yo-o-ou?"
And Two, as she flew
Through the garden to see,
    Said, "I do-o. I do-o-o."

Number One said:
  "I've found a twig,
It isn't too little,
  It isn't too big.
I think it is time
We were building a nest.
  Don't you-ou? Don't yo-o-ou?"
And Two said: "My dear,
If you think it is best,
  Yes, I do-o. I do-o-o."

Out in the garden,
  Out in the sun,
They're talking this morning.
  Hush! Listen to One:
"I think that's the finest egg
Ever was laid.
  Don't yo-ou? Don't yo-o-ou?"
And Two, sitting snug
  In the nest they have made,
  Says, "I do-o. They're two-o-o!"

Rodney Bennett

The Muffin-Man's Bell

"Tinkle, tinkle, tinkle": 'tis the muffin-man you see:
  "Tinkle, tinkle," says the muffin-man's bell;
"Any crumpets, any muffins, any cakes for your tea:
  There are plenty here to sell."

"Tinkle," says the little bell, clear and bright:
  "Tinkle, tinkle," says the muffin-man's bell;
We have had bread and milk for supper to-night,
  And some nice plum-cake as well.

"Tinkle, tinkle, tinkle," says the little bell again,
  But it sounds quite far away;
"If you don't buy my muffins and my cakes, it is plain
  I must take them home to-day."

Ann Hawkshawe

101

Mr. Beetle

With a very big yawn
Mr. Beetle awoke.
"Oh dear, oh dear,
I do feel queer!
My neck is stiff,
My legs are as if
I'd slept in a pig-and-a-poke."

He ran to the sunlight,
He bathed in the dew,
He cleaned his teeth
With a grassy sheath,
He shaved and behaved
As gentlemen beetles do.

He lived all alone—
Maria did too,
But he wanted some stitches
In jacket and breeches,
So he called at her house
And made her his spouse.
And they lived, they did,
Under the yew.

Emily Hover

The Moonlight

The moonlight is a gentle thing,
    Through the window it gleams
Upon the snowy pillow where
    The happy infant dreams.

It shines upon the fisher's boat,
    Out on the lovely sea;
Or where the little lambkins lie
    Beneath the old oak tree.

Ann Hawkshawe

Twice

Twice one are two,
And twice two are four,
Say it over carefully
At least once more.

Twice two are four,
And twice three are six,
Say it over carefully
Until it sticks.

Twice three are six,
And twice four are eight,
Write it down on paper, pad,
Or on your slate.

Twice four are eight,
And twice five are ten,
Write it down with pencil
Or with chalk or pen.

Twice five are ten,
And twice six are twelve,
In the number garden
You must delve, delve, delve.

M. M. Hutchinson

Come Here, Little Robin

Come here, little Robin, and don't be afraid,
    I would not hurt even a feather;
Come here, little Robin, and pick up some bread,
    To feed you this very cold weather.

The winter has come, but it will not stay long,
    And summer we soon shall be greeting;
Then remember, dear Robin, to sing me a song
    In return for the breakfast you're eating.

What Piggy-Wig Found

Piggy-wig found he had four little feet,
  And said to his mother one day,
"Mother, I find I have four little feet,
  What shall I do with them, pray?"

  "Run about, run about, Piggy-wig-wig,
  Run on your four little feet and grow big!"

Piggy-wig found he had two little eyes,
  And said to his mother one day,
"Mother, I find I have two little eyes,
  What shall I do with them, pray?"

  "Look about, look about, Piggy-wig-wig,
  Look with your two little eyes, and grow big!"

Piggy-wig found he had one little nose,
  And said to his mother one day,
"Mother, I find I have one little nose,
  What shall I do with it, pray?"

  "Sniff about, sniff about, Piggy-wig-wig,
  Sniff with your one little nose and grow big!"

Piggy-wig found he had one little mouth,
  And said to his mother one day,
"Mother, I find I have one little mouth,
  What shall I do with it, pray?"

  "Eat with it, eat with it, Piggy-wig-wig,
  Eat with your one little mouth and grow big!"

So Piggy-wig ran on his four little toes,
  And looked with his two little eyes,
And ate with his mouth, and sniffed with his nose,
  And soon he grew BIG and WISE!

Enid Blyton

My Garden

I picked fresh mint
For Mary Quint,
Who made it, of course,
Into Canterbury sauce.
She said: "Thank you, Poppet,
And here's for your pains
Gooseberry bushes
And Raspberry canes."

I borrowed a spade
With a speedy blade,
And dug at the soil
With desperate toil;
Then I put them in,
And I hope that it rains
On my Gooseberry bushes
And Raspberry canes.

Time will tell
If I planted well,
But if every shoot
Should be hung with fruit,
And Mary calls
About mid-July,
There'll be Gooseberry pudding
And Raspberry pie!

Norah Hussey

The Weathercock

The moon is like a lamp,
    The sun is like a fire,
The weathercock can see them both;
    He sits upon the spire.

He sits upon the spire
    High above the ground—
I'd like to be a weathercock
    Turning round and round.

Rose Fyleman

Strange Talk

A little green frog lived under a log,
  And every time he spoke.
Instead of saying, "Good morning,"
  He only said, "Croak—croak."

A duck lived by the waterside,
  And little did he lack,
But when we asked, "How do you do,"
  He only said, "Quack-quack."

A rook lived in an elm tree,
  And all the world he saw,
But when he tried to make a speech
  It sounded like, "Caw-caw."

A little pig lived in a sty,
  As fat as he could be,
And when he asked for dinner
  He cried aloud, "Wee-wee."

Three pups lived in a kennel,
  And loved to make a row,
And when they meant, "May we go out?"
  They said, "Bow-wow! Bow-wow!"

If all these animals talked as much
  As little girls and boys,
And all of them tried to speak at once,
  Wouldn't it make a noise?

L. E. Yates

The Muffin Man

The muffin man walked down our street,
And whom do you think he happened to meet?
John and Ann were standing there,
Both with pennies to spend at the fair.
But when they thought about our tea
They bought muffins for you and me!

Ann Croasdell

Three Little Men in a Boat

Three little men,
On a lake afloat,
Three little men
With a leaf for a boat.
One moon shines on them
High overhead,
One shines up
From the lake's deep bed.

Between two moons,
Among lilies afloat,
The little men sail
In their aspen boat,
Till the moons grow pale,
And the stars, and then
Three little men
Sail homeward again.

Rodney Bennett

Who?

Who will feed the dicky-birds on the garden wall?
Winter-time is very big—they are very small!

Who will feed the dicky-birds on the frozen trees?
Every little twitter means, "Feed us, if you please!"

Who will feed the dicky-birds in the frost and snow?
See them on the chimney pot—cuddled in a row!

Who will feed the dicky-birds till the days of spring?
Think of what they do for you and the songs they sing!

I will feed the dicky-birds, and when springtime comes,
Every little song will mean, "Thank you for the crumbs!"

Florence Hoatson

107

Trains

Our garden's very near the trains;
  I think it's jolly fine
That I have just to climb the fence
  To watch the railway line!

I love to see the train that takes
  A minute to the mile;
The engine-man, as he goes past,
  Has only time to smile!

Then comes a train with empty trucks,
  That never goes so fast;
Its driver-man has always time
  To wave as he goes past!

The man who drives the luggage train,
  That passes here at three,
Not only smiles and waves his hand,
  But whistles once for me!

Hope Shepherd

Minnie and Mattie

Minnie and Mattie,
  And fat little May,
Out in the country,
  Spending a day.

Such a bright day,
  With the sun glowing,
And the trees half in leaf,
  And the grass growing.

Pinky white pigling
  Squeals through his snout,
Woolly white lambkin
  Frisks all about.

Cluck! cluck! the nursing hen
  Summons her folk,
Ducklings all downy soft,
  Yellow as yolk.

Cluck! cluck! the mother hen
   Summons her chickens
To peck the dainty bits
   Found in her pickings.

Minnie and Mattie
   And May carry posies,
Half of sweet violets,
   Half of primroses.

Give the sun time enough,
   Glowing and glowing,
He'll rouse the roses
   And bring them blowing.

Don't wait for roses
   Losing to-day,
O Minnie, Mattie,
   And wise little May.

Violets and primroses,
   Blossoms to-day
For Minnie and Mattie
   And fat little May.

Christina Rossetti

Mincemeat

Sing a song of mincemeat,
Currants, raisins, spice,
Apples, sugar, nutmeg,
Everything that's nice,
Stir it with a ladle,
Wish a lovely wish,
Drop it in the middle
Of your well-filled dish,
Stir again for good luck,
Pack it all away
Tied in little jars and pots,
Until Christmas Day.

Elizabeth Gould

Two Little Kittens

Two little kittens,
One stormy night,
Began to quarrel,
And then to fight.

One had a mouse
And the other had none;
And that was the way
The quarrel begun.

"I'll have that mouse,"
Said the bigger cat.
"You'll have that mouse?
We'll see about that!"

"I will have that mouse,"
Said the tortoise-shell;
And, spitting and scratching,
On her sister she fell.

I've told you before
'Twas a stormy night,
When these two kittens
Began to fight.

The old woman took
The sweeping broom,
And swept them both
Right out of the room.

The ground was covered
With frost and snow,
They had lost the mouse,
And had nowhere to go.

So they lay and shivered
Beside the door,
Till the old woman finished
Sweeping the floor.

And then they crept in
As quiet as mice,
All wet with snow
And as cold as ice.

They found it much better
That stormy night,
To lie by the fire,
Than to quarrel and fight.

Jane Taylor

Ten Little Indian Boys

One little Indian boy making a canoe,
Another came to help him and then there were two.

Two little Indian boys climbing up a tree,
They spied another one and then there were three.

Three little Indian boys playing on the shore,
They called another one and then there were four.

Four little Indian boys learning how to dive,
An older one taught them and then there were five.

Five making arrows then from slender shining sticks,
One came to lend a bow and then there were six.

Six little Indian boys wishing for eleven,
One only could they find and then there were seven.

Seven little Indian boys marched along in state,
One joined the growing line and then there were eight.

Eight little Indian boys camping near the pine,
One came with bait for fish and then there were nine.

Nine little Indian boys growing to be men,
Captured another brave and then there were ten.

M. M. Hutchinson

Toad The Tailor

Toad the Tailor lived in a well,
   Croak! Croak! Croak! he would sing.
Instead of a knocker his door had a bell.
   Croak! C-C-C-Croak!

The bell, it was hung with the greatest of care,
   Croak! Croak! Croak! he would sing.
At the top of the steps leading down to him there,
   Croak! C-C-C-Croak!

By the light or a lantern his customers came,
   Croak! Croak! he would sing.
He measured them all by the length of their name.
   Croak! C-C-C-Croak!

But nobody grumbled a bit about that,
   Croak! Croak! Croak! he would sing.
It suited the thin and it suited the fat,
   Croak! C-C-C-Croak!

In time the old Toad grew as rich as could be,
   Croak! Croak! Croak! he would sing.
So he hung out a notice, "All Tailoring Free."
   Croak! C-C-C-Croak!

N. E. Hussey

Little Lucy Lester

Little Lucy Lester was a funny little lady;
Up the grassy meadow she would run with all her might;
When she reached the other end, she'd scamper back so
   gaily,
Right into her little house where lived her cat so white.
"Why for do you run so fast?" said Farmer Giles in
   passing,
"Are you going to catch a train, or is your white cat ill?"
"Neither, thank you kindly," said that little Lucy
   Lester—
"You see, I go by clock-work, and I can't stand still."

M. Steel

112

The Little Old Lady

That little grey-haired lady
  Is as old as old can be,
Yet once she was a little girl,
  A little girl like me.

She liked to skip instead of walk,
  She wore her hair in curls;
She went to school at nine, and played
  With other little girls.

I wonder if, in years and years,
  Some little girl at play,
Who's very like what I am now,
  Will stop to look my way,

And think: "That grey-haired lady
  Is as old as old can be,
Yet once she was a little girl,
  A little girl like me."

Rodney Bennett

Mice

I think mice
Are rather nice.

Their tails are long,
Their faces small,
They haven't any
Chins at all.
Their ears are pink,
Their teeth are white,
They run about
The house at night.
They nibble things
They shouldn't touch
And no one seems
To like them much.

But I think mice
Are nice.

Rose Fyleman

Little Brown Seed

Little brown seed, round and sound,
Here I put you in the ground.

You can sleep a week or two,
Then—I'll tell you what to do:

You must grow some downward roots,
Then some tiny upward shoots.

From those green shoots' folded sheaves
Soon must come some healthy leaves.

When the leaves have time to grow,
Next a bunch of buds must show.

Last of all, the buds must spread
Into blossoms white or red.

There, Seed! I've done my best.
Please to grow and do the rest.

Rodney Bennett

What Is It?

Here's a guessing story,
  Listen and you'll hear,
We have something in our house,
  Very, very queer.

It hasn't any teeth,
It hasn't any hair,
It cannot walk,
It cannot talk,
And yet it's always there.

Here's a guessing story,
Will you give it up?
It's just a little-little-little
Tiny, baby pup!

H. E. Wilkinson

114

The March Wind

The merry March wind is a boisterous fellow,
He tosses the trees; and the daffodils yellow
Dance and sway, as he blows by
To hurry the clouds across the sky.

He plays such pranks with the weather vane,
Turning it round, then back again.
But the game he enjoys the best of all,
Is blowing my bonnet right over a wall.

E. H. Henderson

A Little Finger Game

Here is a house with a pointed door,
"Pointed door." Index fingers and thumbs together.
Windows tall, and a fine flat floor.
*"Windows tall." Fingers of both hands joined at the tips
and stretched apart. "Fine flat floor." Hands held
flat, palms down, side by side on floor or desk.*
Three good people live in the house,
*"Three good people." Three middle fingers of one hand
standing up under shelter of the other.*
One fat cat, and one thin mouse.
*"One fat cat." Right-hand thumb stands up. "One thin
mouse." Right-hand little finger stands up.*
Out of his hole the mousie peeps,
*"Out of his hole." Right-hand little finger peeps through
left hand folded into a fist.*
Out of his corner the pussie-cat leaps!
*"Out of his corner." Right-hand thumb jumps over upon
left-hand fist.*
Three good people say "Oh! oh! oh!"
"Three good people." Fingers stand up as before.
Mousie inside says "No! no! no!"
*"Mousie inside." Little finger draws back inside left-hand
fist.*

E. J. Falconer

The Postman

Bring me a letter, postman!
Bring me a letter, do!
To-morrow at the garden gate
I will wait for you.

Bring one from a fairy
Who says she'll come to tea,
Then I'll put on my party frock,
How lovely that will be.

And please, oh Mr. Postman,
If fairies you know none,
Write me a letter from yourself,
And bring it, just for fun.

Alice Todd

Mrs. Jenny Wren

Mrs. Jenny Wren!
  I have never, never heard
Such a very big voice
  For a very tiny bird.
You sit on a post
  And you sing and you sing,
You're a very bold bird
  For such a tiny little thing,
Jenny Wren.

If I had a voice
  For my size as big as yours,
I should never dare sing
  Without shutting all the doors.
I'd sing very softly
  For fear they should hear,
Or they'd hurry away
  And put a finger in each ear,
Jenny Wren.

Rodney Bennett

Mistress Comfort

Little Mistress Comfort got up early one fine day,
She swept her little porch, and cleaned
The knocker on her door,
She gave her little cat some milk,
Her little cow some hay,
She fed her little cocks and hens,
Then swept her little floor.

She filled a little platter with some porridge, nice and hot,
She ate her little breakfast,
Then she climbed her little stair;
She shook her little pillows up,
She made her little cot
And all her little house so clean
And shining everywhere.

She sat down by her spinning-wheel and spun a little thread,
She made a little loaf for tea.
She mended her red cloak.
As busy as a bee she was,
And ere she went to bed
She set a little crock of cream
For chance-come Fairy Folk.

Then tired Mistress Comfort sweetly slept
The whole night through,
In the morning, when she woke, she found a
SIXPENCE IN HER SHOE.

Elizabeth Gould

Mr. Pennycomequick

There was an old party called Pennycomequick,
Who rode off to town on the back of a stick;
His house was a teapot without any spout,
He just lifted the lid when he wished to look out.

P. M. Stone

117

Noises in the Night

When I'm in bed at night,
All tucked up warm and tight,
All kinds of noises
Go in at my two ears.
Brr . . . go the motor cars
Out on the street.
Whirr . . . sings the wind
As it blows round the house.
Ting-a-ling-ling
Ring the bicycle bells.
And ding-dong, ding-dong,
Sings the Grandfather Clock downstairs.
Then I hear nothing—nothing at all,
Because I'm asleep, sound asleep.

1. *Children pretend to cuddle down in bed.*
2. *They listen to the noises as the teacher tells the story.*
3. *They close their eyes and go fast asleep as the teacher very quietly and slowly says the last two lines.*

Lilian McCrea

Miller, Miller

Miller, Miller,
Meet the farmer
When the weather
Has turned warmer!

Buy his wheat
And stack it till
You shall take it
To the mill.

Windmill, Windmill,
Turn a round!
Never stop
Till the wheat is ground!

Baker, Baker,
Hurry and go
To the bakehouse
And bake your dough!

Oven, Oven,
Cook the bread,
Or else the children
Cannot be fed!

Oven, Oven,
See that you bake
An icy, spicy,
Sugary cake!

A sugary cake
And a loaf of bread,
And so the children
Shall all be fed!

Ivy O. Eastwick

The Little Maid and the Cowslips

"Where art thou wandering, little child?"
    I said to one I met to-day—
She push'd her bonnet up and smil'd,
    "I'm going upon the green to play:
Folks tell me that the May's in flower,
    That Cowslip-peeps are fit to pull,
And I've got leave to spend an hour
    To get this little basket full."

John Clare

Pretty Lady

The prettiest lady that ever I've seen
Came dancing, dancing, over the green.
She wore a hat with a curly feather,
Her dear little shoes were of scarlet leather.

With the tips of her fingers she held up her gown;
She didn't look up, she didn't look down,
She didn't look left, she didn't look right,
Her curls flew out in a stream of light.
My mother called and I looked away—
I never have seen her since that day.

Rose Fyleman

In the Mirror

In the mirror
On the wall,
There's a face
I always see;
Round and pink,
And rather small,
Looking back again
At me.

It is very
Rude to stare,
But she never
Thinks of that,
For her eyes are
Always there;
What can she be
Looking at?

Elizabeth Fleming

The Three Little Kittens

Three little kittens lost their mittens,
   And they began to cry:
      "Oh, Mother dear,
      We very much fear
That we have lost our mittens!"

   "Lost your mittens!
   You naughty kittens!
Then you shall have no pie!"
   "Mee-ow, mee-ow, mee-ow."
"No, you shall have no pie."
   "Mee-ow, mee-ow, mee-ow!"

The three little kittens found their mittens,
   And they began to cry:
      "Oh, Mother dear,
      See here—see here!
See, we have found our mittens!"

120

"Put on your mitte
You silly kittens,
And you may have some pie."
"Purr, purr, purr,
Oh, let us taste the pie!
Purr, purr, purr."

The three little kittens put on their mittens,
And soon ate up the pie;
"Oh, Mother dear,
We greatly fear
That we have soiled our mittens!"

"Soiled your mittens!
You naughty kittens!"
Then they began to sigh:
"Mee-ow, mee-ow, mee-ow!"
Then they began to sigh:
"Mee-ow, mee-ow, mee-ow!"

The three little kittens washed their mittens
And hung them out to dry;
"Oh, Mother dear,
Do you not hear
That we have washed our mittens?"

"Washed your mittens!
Then you're good kittens;
But I smell a rat close by!"
"Hush, hush! Mee-ow, mee-ow!
We smell a rat close by!
Mee-ow, mee-ow, mee-ow!"

The Milkman

Clink, clink, clinkety-clink,
The milkman's on his rounds, I think.
Crunch, crunch, come the milkman's feet
Closer and closer along the street —
Then clink, clink, clinkety-clink,
He's left our bottles of milk to drink.

Clive Sansom

Little Tommy Tiddler

Little Tommy Tiddler
Is going to be a fiddler;
They've given him a fiddle,
And they've given him a bow.
Play, play, play, Tommy Tiddler!
Say, say, say, Tommy Tiddler,
Play a little twiddle
On the middle of your fiddle,
Or we'll go, we'll go, we'll go, go, go,
And take away your fiddle and your bow.

Paul Edmonds

A Summer Shower

"Hurry!" said the leaves;
"Hurry, birds, hurry!
See how the tall trees
Are all in a flurry!"

"Come under, quick,
Grasshoppers, cricket!"
Said the leafy vines
Down in the thicket.

"Come here," said the rose
To bee and spider;
"Ant, here's a place!
Fly, sit beside her!"

"Rest, butterfly,
Here in the bushes,
Close by the robin,
While the rain rushes!"

"Why, there is the sun!
And the birds are singing:
Good-bye, dear leaves,
We'll all be winging."

122

"Bee," said the rose,
  "Thank you for calling.
Come in again
  When the rain is falling."

Dicky-Birds

Two little dicky-birds
Sitting on a twig,
Both very plump
And neither very big.

"Tweet!" said the first one,
"Cheep!" said his brother—
Wasn't that a funny way
To talk to one another?

Down flew one bird
And picked up a crust;
Off went the other
To a little heap of dust;

Plunged into a dust-bath,
All puffed out and fat,
Wouldn't it be very strange
To have a bath like that?

Both little brown birds
At the set of sun
Flew into a big tree
Because the day was done.

Cuddled in a warm nest,
Cosy as could be,
Mustn't it be lovely
Sleeping in a tree?

Natalie Joan

Ten Little Dicky-Birds

Addition in Ones to Ten

1. One little dicky-bird
   Hopped on my shoe;
   Along came another one,
   And that made two.

Chorus:
   Fly to the tree-tops;
   Fly to the ground;
   Fly, little dicky-birds,
   Round and round.

2. Two little dicky-birds,
   Singing in a tree;
   Along came another one,
   And that made three.

   Chorus

3. Three little dicky-birds,
   Came to my door;
   Along came another one,
   And that made four.

   Chorus

4. Four little dicky-birds
   Perched on a hive;
   Along came another one,
   And that made five.

   Chorus

5. Five little dicky-birds
   Nesting in the ricks;
   Along came another one,
   And that made six.

   Chorus

6. Six little dicky-birds
   Flying up to heaven;
   Along came another one,
   And that made seven.

   Chorus

7. Seven little dicky-birds ·
   Sat upon a gate;
   Along came another one,
   And that made eight.

   Chorus

8. Eight little dicky-birds
   Swinging on a line;
   Along came another one,
   And that made nine.

   Chorus

9. Nine little dicky-birds
   Looking at a hen;
   Along came another one,
   And that made ten.

   Chorus

Actions:

Fingers are erected one by one from closed fists, to represent the birds. During the chorus, actions are as follows:
Line 1. "Birds" are held up high.
Line 2. "Birds" are held down low.
Lines 3 and 4. "Birds" are circled round and round.

A. W. I. Baldwin

Love Me—I Love You

Love me—I love you,
   Love me, my baby;
Sing it high, sing it low,
   Sing it as may be.

Mother's arms under you;
   Her eyes above you;
Sing it high, sing it low,
   Love me—I love you.

Christina Rossetti

125

Thank You, Pretty Cow

Thank you, pretty cow, that made
Pleasant milk to soak my bread,
Every day and every night
Warm, and fresh, and sweet, and white.

Do not chew the hemlock rank,
Growing on the weedy bank,
But the yellow cowslip eat,
That will make it very sweet.

Where the purple violet grows,
Where the bubbling water flows,
Where the grass is fresh and fine,
Pretty cow, go there and dine.

Jane Taylor

The Dormouse

The Dormouse felt so sleepy
  Nid-nodding went his head,
He said "Good night" to everyone,
  And cuddled up in bed.

Down fell the icy raindrops,
  The cold wind whistled round;
The Dormouse in his snuggly bed,
  Lay sleeping safe and sound.

There he was found one morning
  By Jeremy and Jane;
They whispered low, then on tip-toe,
  They crept away again.

They filled a bag with acorns,
  And hid it in the brakes,
So that the little Dormouse,
  May find it when he wakes.

Charlotte Druitt Cole

Song for a Ball-Game

Bounce ball! Bounce ball!
  One—two—three.
Underneath my right leg
  And round about my knee.
Bounce ball! Bounce ball!
  Bird—or—bee
Flying from the rose-bud
  Up into the tree.

Bounce ball! Bounce ball!
  Fast—you—go
Underneath my left leg
  And round about my toe.
Bounce ball! Bounce ball!
  Butt—er—fly
Flying from the rosebud
  Up in the sky.

Bounce ball! Bounce ball!
  You—can't—stop.
Right leg and left leg
  Round them both you hop.
Bounce ball! Bounce ball!
  Shy—white—dove,
Tell me how to find him,
  My own true love.

Wilfred Thorley

The Farmyard

One black horse standing by the gate,
Two plump cats eating from a plate;
Three big goats kicking up their heels,
Four pink pigs full of grunts and squeals;
Five white cows coming slowly home,
Six small chicks starting off to roam;
Seven fine doves perched upon the shed,
Eight grey geese eager to be fed;
Nine young lambs full of frisky fun,
Ten brown bees buzzing in the sun.

A. A. Attwood

Ding-Dong!

Ding-dong! Ding-dong!
  All the bells are ringing,
Ding-dong! Ding-dong!
  'Tis a holiday.

Ding-dong! Ding-dong!
  All the birds are singing,
Ding-dong! Ding-dong!
  Let's go out and play.

Kitty

Once there was a little Kitty
  Whiter than snow;
In a barn she used to frolic,
  Long time ago.

In the barn a little mousie
  Ran to and fro;
For she heard the Kitty coming,
  Long time ago.

Two eyes had little Kitty,
  Black as a sloe;
And they spied the little mousie,
  Long time ago.

Four paws had little Kitty,
  Paws soft as dough,
And they caught the little mousie,
  Long time ago.

Nine teeth had little Kitty,
  All in a row;
And they bit the little mousie,
  Long time ago.

When the teeth bit little mousie,
  Little mouse cried "Oh!"
But she got away from Kitty,
  Long time ago.

A Penny Wish

I wish I had an aeroplane
To fetch my oranges from Spain.

I wish I had a motor car
To ride in when I go too far.

I wish I had a little train
To go to town and home again.

And if I had a sailing boat
I'd use it with my sailor coat.

But what's the good of wanting any
When all I have is just a penny!

Irene Thompson

The Pigeon's Story

Where do you think I've been to-day?
    Rooketty coo! rooketty coo!
Off to the town in the farmer's dray,
    Rooketty, rooketty coo!

What do you think I did to-day?
    Rooketty coo! rooketty coo!
Out of the cage I hopped away,
    Rooketty, rooketty coo!

What happened next? I hear you say,
    Rooketty coo! rooketty coo!
Spreading my wings I flew away,
    Rooketty, rooketty coo!

Back to my mate I found my way,
    Rooketty coo! rooketty coo!
Now I am home with you to play,
    Rooketty, rooketty coo!

Jeannie Kirby

The Song of the Engine

Slowly

With snort and pant the engine dragged
　　Its heavy train uphill,
And puffed these words the while she puffed
　　And laboured with a will:

Very slowly

"I think—I can—I think—I can,
　　I've got—to reach—the top,
I'm sure—I can—I will—get there,
　　I sim—ply must—not stop!"

More quickly

At last the top was reached and passed,
　　And then—how changed the song!
The wheels all joined in the engine's joy,
　　As quickly she tore along!

Very fast

"I knew I could do it, I knew I could win,
　　Oh, rickety rackety rack!
And now for a roaring rushing race
　　On my smooth and shining track!"

H. Worsley-Benison

The Paddling Pool

If you find a paddling pool,
Dabble your toes to make them cool.
　　Splash! Splash! Splash!
Kick up your feet and scatter the spray,
Oh what fun for a bright sunny day!
　　Splash! Splash! Splash!

E. M. Adams

Wandering Jack

Listen to the song
Of Wandering Jack.
He carries a bundle
On his back.
What is inside it?
Shall I tell?
He carries inside it
Dreams to sell.
Some cost a penny,
Some cost a pound.
But some cost nothing,
I'll be bound.

Emile Jacot

A Growing Rhyme

A farmer once planted some little brown seeds
With a pit-a-pit, pit-a-pat, pit-a-pat, pat.
He watered them often and pulled up the weeds,
With a tug-tug at this and a tug-tug at that.
The little seeds grew tall and green in the sun,
With a push-push up here, and a push-push up there,
And a beautiful plant grew from every one,
With a hey diddle, holding their heads in the air.

J. M. Westrup

Good Morning

Good morning to you and good morning to you;
Come pull on your stocking and put on your shoe;
There are bees, there are birds, there are flowers in the
sun—

Good morning to you and good morning to you;
Come out of your beds, there is plenty to do.
Come out with a shout and a laugh and a run—
Good morning, good morning to every one.

Rose Fyleman

131

The Two Families

One summer I stayed
On a farm, and I saw
A quaint little sight
I had not seen before.

A cat and her kittens,
And a sow and her troup
Of little pink pigs,
In one family group.

The mother cat came
To be petted by me,
While I looked at her kittens,
So sooty and wee!

Like tiny black smuts,
The two little dears
Contentedly slept
Beside the sow's ears.

Till one kitten woke,
And started to roam
On Mrs. Pig's back
As if quite at home.

And there it sat down
To gaze at its friends,
The little pink pigs
With their queer curly ends!

And old Mother Pig
Snored loudly and deep,
Nor noticed the kittens,
Awake or asleep!

Joyce L. Brisley

The Birdies' Breakfast

Two little birdies, one wintry day,
Began to wonder, and then to say,
"How about breakfast, this wintry day?"

Two little maidens, that wintry day,
Into the garden soon took their way,
Where the snow lay deep, that wintry day.

One with her broom swept the snow away;
One scattered crumbs, then went to play;
So the birdies had breakfast that wintry day.

Pretty Maid Marion

Pretty Maid Marion, where have you been?
Gathering buttercups down on the green.

Pretty Maid Marion, what did you see?
A skylark, a grasshopper-green, and a bee.

Pretty Maid Marion, what did you hear?
A little lark singing high up in the air!

Pretty Maid Marion, what did you do?
I screwed up my mouth—so!—and I whistled too!

Ivy O. Eastwick

Fantasy and Fairyland

We want to go to Fairyland
To dance by the light of the moon

I'd Love to be a Fairy's Child

Children born of fairy stock
Never need for shirt or frock,
Never want for food or fire,
Always get their heart's desire:
Jingle pockets full of gold,
Marry when they're seven years old,
Every fairy child may keep
Two strong ponies and ten sheep;
All have houses, each his own,
Built of brick or granite stone;
They live on cherries, they run wild—
I'd love to be a fairy's child.

Robert Graves

The Fairy Flute

My brother has a little flute
    Of gold and ivory,
He found it on a summer night
    Within a hollow tree,
He plays it every morning
    And every afternoon,
And all the little singing-birds
    Listen to the tune.
He plays it in the meadows,
    And everywhere he walks
The flowers start a-nodding
    And dancing on their stalks.
He plays it in the village,
    And all along the street
The people stop to listen,
    The music is so sweet.
And none but he can play it
    And none can understand,
Because it is a fairy flute
    And comes from Fairyland.

Rose Fyleman

The Faerie Fair

The fairies hold a fair, they say,
Beyond the hills when skies are grey
And daylight things are laid away.

And very strange their marketing,
If we could see them on the wing
With all the fairy ware they bring.

Long strings they sell, of berries bright,
And wet wind-fallen apples light
Blown from the trees some starry night.

Gay patches, too, for tattered wings,
Gold bubbles blown by goblin things,
And mushrooms for the fairy rings.

Fine flutes are there, of magic reed,
Whose piping sets the elves indeed
A-dancing down the dewy mead.

These barter they for bats and moles,
For beaten silver bells and bowls
Bright from the caverns of the Trolls.

And so they show, and sell and buy,
With song and dance right merrily,
Until the morning gilds the sky.

Florence Harrison

Where The Bee Sucks

Where the bee sucks, there suck I:
In a cowslip's bell I lie;
There I couch when owls do cry.
On the bat's back I do fly
After summer merrily.
Merrily, merrily shall I live now
Under the blossom that hangs on the bough.

Shakespeare

137

Hob the Elf

Perhaps, if you
  Are very good,
You'll see a cottage
  In the wood,
Where lies in comfort
  Hob, the elf,
All in the cottage
  By himself.
The cottage small
  Is made of bark.
Inside it is
  So very dark,
That when night comes
  Our little elf
Puts a bright lantern
  On the shelf,
And there he sits
  With glasses round,
Reading his book
  Without a sound.

Norman M. Johnson

Fairy Feet

Nobody lives in the cottage now,
  But birds build under the thatch,
And a trailing rose half hides the door
  And twines itself round the latch.

Nobody walks up the cobble path,
  Where the grass peeps in between,
But fairy feet tread the cobble stones
  And keep them wonderfully clean.

Nobody knows that the raindrops bright
  Which fall on the grey old stones
Are the feet of the fairies dancing for joy
  On the path that nobody owns.

Phyllis L. Garlick

138

The Little Elf-Man

I met a little elf-man once
Down where the lilies blow.
I asked him why he was so small,
And why he didn't grow.

He slightly frowned, and with his eye
He looked me through and through—
"I'm just as big for me," said he,
"As you are big for you!"

J. K. Bangs

About the Fairies

Pray, where are the little bluebells gone,
   That lately blossomed in the wood?
Why, the little fairies have each taken one,
   And put it on for a hood.

And where are the pretty grass-stalks gone,
   That waved in the summer breeze?
Oh, the fairies have taken them, every one,
   To plant in their gardens like trees.

And where are the great big blue-bottles gone,
   That buzzed in their busy pride?
Oh, the fairies have caught them, every one,
   And have broken them in, to ride.

And they've taken the glow-worms to light their halls,
   And the cricket to sing them a song;
And the great red rose leaves to paper their walls,
   And they're feasting the whole night long.

And when Spring comes back, with its soft mild ray,
   And the ripple of gentle rain,
The fairies bring what they've taken away,
   And give it us all again.

Jean Ingelow

139

Bramble Jam

A little old woman,
As old as could be,
Picked the ripe berries
From bush and tree.

Then in a clearing
She made a fire,
Piling the dry sticks
Higher and higher;
And at the top
Of the crackling pile,
She put her gallipot
On to boil,
Sugar and fruit
She boiled for hours,
Till the juice set red
As peony-flowers;
And all the next morning
The Little Folks ran
With pursefuls of money
To buy pots of jam.

Irene F. Pawsey

The Elfin People Fill the Tubes

"I know a solemn secret to keep between ourselves—
I heard it from a sparrow who heard it from the elves—
That always after 2 a.m., before the first cock-crow,
The elfin people fill the Tubes just full to overflow.

"The grown-ups do not know it; they put the trains to bed
And never guess that magic will drive them in their stead;
All day the goblin drivers were hiding in the dark
(If mortals catch a fairy's eye they take it for a spark).

"Elves patter down the subways; they crowd the moving
    stairs;
From purses full of tiddly-winks they pay the clerk their
    fares;
A Brownie checks the tickets and says the proper things:
'Come, pass along the car there!' 'Now, ladies, mind your
    wings!'

140

"They're never dull like mortals who read and dream and
    doze;
The fairies hang head downwards, strap-hanging by their
    toes;
When Puck is the conductor he also acts as host
And sets them playing Leapfrog or Coach or General Post.

"I'd love to travel with them! The sparrow says he thinks
I'd get from here to Golders Green for three red
    tiddly-winks;
Two yellows pay to Euston, four whites to Waterloo;
Perhaps I'll go some moonlight night; the question is—
    will *you*?"

Winifred Letts

Picnics

If you go a-picnicking and throw your scraps about,
You'll never see the little folk go running in and out;
And if you leave your orange-peel all littered on the grass,
You'll never go to Fairy Land or see the fairies pass.
    For empty tins and tangled strings
    And paper bags are not the things
    To scatter where a linnet sings.

So if you go a-picnicking remember you're a guest
Of all the tiny people, and you'll really find it best
To leave their ballroom tidy and to clear away the mess,
And perhaps you'll see a fairy in her newest dancing dress.
    But paper bags and broken combs
    Will really wreck the pixie homes
    And frighten all the tiny gnomes.

But if you go a-picnicking and you are elfin wise,
You'll maybe hear with fairy ears and see with goblin eyes;
The little folk will welcome you, and they will open wide
The hidden doors of Fairy Land, and you will pass inside,
    And maybe see a baby fay
    White cradled in a cherry spray,
    Although it is Bank Holiday.

From "Punch"

The Way to Fairyland

Which is the way to Fairyland,
    To Fairyland, to Fairyland?
We want to go to Fairyland,
    To dance by the light of the moon.

Up the hill and down the lane,
    Down the lane, down the lane,
Up te hill and down the lane,
    You'll get there very soon.

Across the common and through the gate,
    Through the gate, through the gate,
Across the common and through the gate,
    You'll get there very soon.

Over the stile and into the wood,
    Into the wood, into the wood,
Over the stile and into the wood,
    You'll get there very soon.

Here we are in Fairyland,
    In Fairyland, in Fairyland,
Here we are in Fairyland,
    We'll dance by the light of the moon.

Eunice Close

Who'll Help a Fairy?

"Oh! what shall I do?" sobbed a tiny mole,
"A Fairy has tumbled into my hole;
It is full of water and crawling things,
And she can't get out, for she's hurt her wings.

"I did my best to catch hold of her hair,
But my arms are short, and she's still in there.
Oh! help her, white rabbit, your arms are long;
You say you're good, and I know you're strong."

"Don't bother me," the white rabbit said—
She shut up her eyes, and her ears grew red—
"There's lots of mud, and it's sure to stick
On my beautiful fur, so white and thick."

"Oh dear! oh dear!" sobbed the poor little mole,
"Who'll help the Fairy out of the hole?"
A little brown rabbit popped up from the gorse,
"I'm not very strong, but I'll try, of course."

His little tail bobbed as he waddled in,
The muddy water came up to his chin;
But he caught the Fairy tight by the hand,
And helped her to get to Fairyland.

But she kissed him first on his muddy nose,
She kissed his face and his little wet toes;
And when the day dawned in the early light,
The common brown rabbit was silvery white.

The Light-Hearted Fairy

Oh, what is so merry, so merry, heigh-ho!
As the light-hearted fairy? Heigh-ho, heigh-ho!
      He dances and sings
      To the sound of his wings
With a hey and a heigh and a ho!

Oh, who is so merry, so airy, heigh-ho!
As the light-headed fairy? Heigh-ho, heigh-ho!
      His nectar he sips
      From the primroses' lips,
With a hey and a heigh and a ho!

Oh, who is so merry, so merry, heigh-ho!
As the light-footed fairy? Heigh-ho, heigh-ho!
      The night is his noon
      And his sun is the moon
With a hey and a heigh and a ho!

The Yellow Fairy

There lived in a laburnum tree
  A little fairy fellow,
He wore a feather in his cap,
  And he was dressed in yellow.

He sang a song the whole day long
  So merry and so clever,
But when I climbed to peep at him,
  He flew away for ever.

Charlotte Druitt Cole

The Kind Mousie

There once was a cobbler,
  And he was so wee
That he lived in a hole
  In a very big tree.
He had a good neighbour,
  And she was a mouse—
She did his wee washing
  And tidied his house.

Each morning at seven
  He heard a wee tap,
And in came the mouse
  In her apron and cap.
She lighted his fire
  And she fetched a wee broom,
And she swept and she polished
  His little Tree-room.

To take any wages
  She'd always refuse,
So the cobbler said, "Thank you!"
  And mended her shoes;
And the owl didn't eat her,
  And even the cat
Said, "I *never* would catch
  A kind mousie like that!"

Natalie Joan

Bubbles

Out in the garden
When school was done
I blew bubbles
In the sun.

I blew a bubble
Huge as could be!
It hung in the air
For all to see.

Into my bubble
I looked and found
A chining land
That was rainbow round.

It looked like a world
Meant for no one but fairies.
They'd keep little farms there
With cows, chicks, and dairies.
Woods where the pixies
Could picnic for pleasure,
And hide near the rainbows
Their crocks of strange treasure.

Countries were marked there
Plain as could be;
Green for the country,
Blue for the sea.
Purple for heather,
Sunshine like gold,
Bubble-land weather
Could never be cold.

And then came a bee
All furry and fat.
Before I could think
What he would be at
My beautiful bubble
He brushed with his wing,
And all that was left
Was a little damp ring.

L. Nicholson

The Magic Whistle

On my little magic whistle I will play to you all day;
I will play you songs of Summer and the hilltops far away;
I will play you songs of Spring-time when the daffodillies
    bloom
And the wild March horses scamper by across the golden
    broom.

I will play you sweetest music of the silver fluttering trees,
When the raindrops gently falling touch the quivering
    autumn leaves;
I will play to you of castles 'neath a fairy sky of blue;
On my little magic whistle, oh! I'd play it all to you.

Margaret Rose

You Spotted Snakes

You spotted snakes, with double tongue,
    Thorny hedgehogs, be not seen;
Newts and blind-worms, do no wrong;
    Come not near our fairy queen;

    Philomel, with melody,
    Sing in our sweet lullaby;
Lulla, lulla, lullaby; lulla, lulla, lullaby!
    Never harm,
    Nor spell nor charm,
    Come our lovely lady nigh;
    So, good night, with lullaby.

Weaving spiders, come not here;
    Hence, you long-legg'd spinners, hence;
Beetles black, approach not near;
    Worm nor snail, do no offence.

    Philomel, with melody,
    Sing in our sweet lullaby;
Lulla, lulla, lullaby; lulla, lulla, lullaby!
    Never harm,
    Nor spell nor charm,
    Come our lovely lady nigh;
    So, good night, with lullaby.

Shakespeare

Puk-Wudjies

They live 'neath the curtain
        Of fir woods and heather,
And never take hurt in
        The wildest of weather,
But best they love Autumn—she's brown as—themselves—
And they are the brownest of all the brown elves;
        When loud sings the West Wind,
        The bravest and best wind,
And puddles are shining in all the cart ruts,
        They turn up the dead leaves,
        The russet and red leaves,
Where squirrels have taught them to look out for nuts.

The hedge-cutters hear them
        Where berries are glowing,
The scythe circles near them
        At time of the mowing,
But most they love woodlands when Autumn winds pipe,
And all through the cover the beechnuts are ripe,
        And great spiky chestnuts,
        The biggest and best nuts
Blown down in the ditches, fair windfalls lie cast,
        And no tree begrudges
        The little Puk-Wudjies
A pocket of acorns, or handful of mast.

So should you be roaming,
        When branches are sighing,
When up in the gloaming
        The moon-wrack is flying,
And hear through the darkness, again and again,
What's neither the wind nor the spatter of rain—
        A flurry, a flurry,
        A scuffle, a scurry,
A bump like the rabbits that bump on the ground,
        A patter, a bustle,
        Of small things that rustle,
You'll know the Puk-Wudjies are somewhere around.

Patrick R. Chalmers

Jock O' Dreams

When the sun goes down and the world is still,
Then Jock o' Dreams comes over the hill;
Over the hill he quietly slips,
Holding his finger to his lips.

His golden hair is pale as the moon,
He has two bright stars on his velvet shoon;
Soft his step as an elfin dance,
His sea-blue eyes have an elfin glance.

The dreams he carries are light as air,
He tosses them here, he tosses them there,
In at the windows, under the doors,
All the way up to the attic floors.

Through the silent streets he goes walking about
Till the moon drops down and the stars go out;
Then lightly swinging his empty sack,
Softly, softly, he wanders back.

A cold little wind runs over the ground,
A sleepy bird makes a tiny sound,
The sky in the East grows rosily red,
The children murmur and turn in bed.
Over the world the sunlight streams—
But what has become of Jock o' Dreams?

Rose Fyleman

The Dream Ship

I want to go aboard my ship, and sail and sail away—
To see the whales a-spouting and the porpoises at play;
To meet Atlantic rollers with their wild and mighty
    sweep—
I want to know the dangers and the wonders of the deep.

I want to see tall icebergs, all a-sparkle, drifting by
With surf about their buttresses, their spires against the
    sky,
To make my voyage northwards till we're fast amid the floe
Where the white bear prowls around us, hunting seals
    across the snow.

I want to land on coral isles, far in the ocean blue,
To battle round the dreadful Horn as all stout seamen do.
But since I'm not quite old enough I sometimes dream
  instead,
And make myself adventures though they're only in my
  head.

W. K. Holmes

Romance

I saw a ship a-sailing,
  A-sailing on the sea;
Her masts were of the shining gold,
  Her deck of ivory;
And sails of silk, as soft as milk,
  And silvern shrouds had she.

And round about her sailing
  The sea was sparkling white,
The waves all clapped their hands and sang
  To see so fair a sight;
They kissed her twice, they kissed her thrice,
  And murmured with delight.

Then came the gallant captain
  And stood upon the deck,
In velvet coat and ruffles white,
  Without a spot or speck,
And diamond rings and triple strings
  Of pearls about his neck.

And four and twenty sailors
  Were round him bowing low,
On every jacket three times three
  Gold buttons in a row,
And cutlasses down to their knees;
  They made a goodly show.

And then the ship went sailing,
  A-sailing o'er the sea;
She dived beneath the setting sun,
  But never back came she,
For she found the lands of the golden sands,
  Where the pearls and diamonds be.

Gabriel Setoun

Fairy Music

I found a little fairy flute
   Beneath a harebell blue;
I sat me down upon the moss
   And blew a note or two.

And as I blew the rabbits came
   Around me in the sun,
And little mice and velvet moles
   Came creeping, one by one.

A swallow perched upon my head,
   A robin on my thumb,
The thrushes sang in tune with me,
   The bees began to hum.

I loved to see them all around
   And wished they'd always stay,
When down a little fairy flew
   And snatched my flute away!

And then the swallow fluttered off,
   And gone were all the bees,
The rabbits ran, and I was left
   Alone among the trees!

Enid Blyton

Friday

This is the day when the fairy kind
Sit weeping alone for their hopeless lot,
And the wood-maiden sighs to the sighing wind,
And the mermaiden weeps in her crystal grot;
For this is a day that the deed was wrought,
In which we have neither part nor share,
For the children of clay was salvation bought,
But not for the forms of sea or air!
And ever the mortal is most forlorn,
Who meeteth our race on the Friday morn.

Sir Walter Scott

150

Merry Little Men

Down in the grassy hollow
    Live merry little men,
On moonlight nights they frolic—but
    They don't come out till ten.

And I'm in bed by seven,
    And so I don't know when
I'll go and play with them—because
    They don't come out till ten!

Kathleen M. Chaplin

The Rock-a-by Lady

The Rock-a-by Lady from Hush-a-by Street
    Comes stealing; comes creeping;
The poppies they hang from her head to her feet,
And each hath a dream that is tiny and fleet—
She bringeth her poppies to you, my sweet,
    When she findeth you sleeping!

There is one little dream of a beautiful drum—
    "Rub-a-dub!" it goeth:
There is one little dream of a big sugar-plum,
And lo! thick and fast the other dreams come,
Of popguns that bang, and tin tops that hum,
    And a trumpet that bloweth.

And dollies peep out of these wee little drums
    With laughter and singing;
And boats go a-floating on silvery streams,
And the stars peek-a-boo with their own misty gleams.
And up, up, and up, where the mother Moon beams,
    The fairies go winging.

Would you dream of these dreams that are tiny and fleet?
    They'll come to you sleeping:
So shut the two eyes that are weary, my sweet,
For the Rock-a-by Lady from Hush-a-by Street,
With poppies that hang from her head to her feet,
    Comes stealing; comes creeping.

Eugene Field

A Fairy Dream

Two little elves
Were lost one night.
"Where can they be?" said the Queen.
The fairies searched
Till morning light,
But never a trace was seen.

When the sun was up
And the sky was clear,
The wee elves laughed with joy,
They'd whispered a fairy
Dream in the ear
Of the newest baby boy.

Dorothy Gradon

The Dream Fairy

A little fairy comes at night,
Her eyes are blue, her hair is brown,
With silver spots upon her wings,
And from the moon she flutters down.

She has a little silver wand,
And when a good child goes to bed
She waves her wand from right to left
And makes a circle round her head.

And then it dreams of pleasant things,
Of fountains filled with fairy fish,
And trees that bear delicious fruit,
And bow their branches at a wish;

Of arbours filled with dainty scents
From lovely flowers that never fade,
Bright flies that glitter in the sun,
And glow-worms shining in the shade;

And talking birds with gifted tongues
For singing songs and telling tales,
And pretty dwarfs to show the way
Through fairy hills and fairy dales.

Thomas Hood

A Child's Thought

At seven, when I go to bed,
I find such pictures in my head:
Castles with dragons prowling round,
Gardens where magic fruits are found;
Fair ladies prisoned in a tower,
Or lost in an enchanted bower;
While gallant horsemen ride by streams
That border all this land of dreams
I find, so clearly in my head
At seven, when I go to bed.

At seven, when I wake again,
The magic land I seek in vain;
A chair stands where the castle frowned,
The carpet hides the garden ground,
No fairies trip across the floor,
Boots, and not horsemen, flank the door,
And where the blue streams rippling ran
Is now a bath and water-can;
I seek the magic land in vain
At seven, when I wake again.

Robert Louis Stevenson

A Wish

I'd love to give a party
    To all the fairy folk,
With scarlet autumn leaves for plates,
    Oh! it would be a joke!
And every little lady fay
    Should have her acorn cup,
To hold her fragrant rose-leaf tea,
    Until she drank it up;
And every little elf should have
    His acorn pipe to smoke;
I'd love to give a party
    Beneath this grand old oak.

Elizabeth Gould

153

The Little Men

Would you see the little men
Coming down a moonlit glen?—
Gnome and elf and woodland sprite,
Clad in brown and green and white,
Skipping, hopping, never stopping,
Stumbling, grumbling, tumbling, mumbling,
Dancing, prancing, singing, swinging—
Coats of red and coats of brown,
Put on straight or upside down,
Outside in or inside out,
Some with sleeves and some without,
Rustling, bustling, stomping, romping,
Strumming, humming, hear them coming—
You will see the Little Men
If it be a Fairy glen.

Flora Fearne

The Fairies

Come, follow, follow me,
You fairy elves that be
Which circle on the green,
Come, follow Mab, your queen,
Hand in hand let's dance around,
For this place is fairy ground.

When mortals are at rest,
And snoring in their rest,
Unheard and unespied
Through keyholes we do glide;
Over tables, stools and shelves,
We trip it with our fairy elves.

Upon a mushroom's head
Our table-cloth we spread;
A grain of rye or wheat
Is manchet, which we eat;
Pearly drops of dew we drink
In acorn-cups fill'd to the brink.

The grasshopper, gnat and fly,
Serve for our minstrelsy;
Grace said, we dance awhile,
And so the time beguile;
And if the moon doth hide her head,
The glow-worm lights us home to bed.

On tops of dewy grass
So nimbly do we pass,
The young and tender stalk
Ne'er bends when we do walk;
Yet in the morning may be seen
Where we the night before have been.

Mrs. Brown

As soon as I'm in bed at night
   And snugly settled down,
The little girl I am by day
Goes very suddenly away,
   And then I'm Mrs. Brown.

I have a family of six,
   And all of them have names,
The girls are Joyce and Nancy Maud,
The boys are Marmaduke and Claude
   And Percival and James.

We have a house with twenty rooms
   A mile away from town;
I think it's good for girls and boys
To be allowed to make a noise,
   And so does Mr. Brown.

We do the most exciting things,
   Enough to make you creep,
And on and on and on we go,
I sometimes wonder if I know
   When I have gone to sleep.

Rose Fyleman

The Fairy Cobbler

What do you think I saw to-day
  When I walked forth to take the air?
I saw a little house of hay,
  All in a pasture fair.

And just within the green grass door
  I saw a little cobbler sit:
He sat crossed-legged upon the floor,
  And tapped, tip-tit, tip-tit!

"What are you making there so neat?"
  "Gaiters for glow-worms," he made reply,
"And thistledown slippers for fairy feet,
  And garden boots for a butterfly."

"What do they pay you, my busy mite?"
  "Some bring me honey and some bring dew
And the glow-worms visit me every night
  And light my chamber through."

A. Neil Lyons

Child's Song

I know the sky will fall one day,
The great green trees will topple down,
The spires will wither far away
Upon the battlemented town;
When winds and waves forget to flow
And the wild song-birds cease from calling,
Then shall I take my shoes and go
To tell the King the sky is falling.

There's lots of things I've never done,
And lots of things I'll never see;
The nearest rainbow ever spun
Is much too far away from me;
But when the dark air's lost in snow
And the long quiet strikes appalling,
I learn how it will feel to go
To tell the King the sky is falling.

Gerald Gould

156

The Fairy Ring

Let us dance and let us sing,
Dancing in a merry ring;
We'll be fairies on the green,
Sporting round the Fairy Queen.

Like the seasons of the year,
Round we circle in a sphere;
I'll be Summer, you'll be Spring;
Dancing in a fairy ring.

Spring and summer glide away,
Autumn comes with tresses gray,
Winter hand in hand with Spring,
Dancing in a fairy ring.

Faster, faster, round we go,
While our cheeks with roses glow,
Free as birds upon the wing,
Dancing in a fairy ring.

An Elfin Knight

He put his acorn helmet on;
It was plumed of the silk of the thistle down;
The corselet plate that guarded his breast
Was once the wild bee's golden vest;
His cloak, of a thousand mingled dyes,
Was formed of the wings of butterflies;
His shield was the shell of a ladybird green,
Studs of gold on a ground of green;
And the quivering lance which he brandished bright,
Was the sting of a wasp he had slain in fight.

Swift he bestrode his firefly steed;
He bared his blade of the bent-grass blue;
He drove his spurs of the cockle-seed,
And away like a glance of thought he flew,
To skim the heavens, and follow far
The fiery trail of the rocket star.

John Rodman Drake

157

The Rainbow Fairies

Two little clouds, one summer's day,
　　Went flying through the sky;
They went so fast they bumped their heads,
　　And both began to cry.

Old Father Sun looked out and said:
　　"Oh, never mind, my dears,
I'll send my little fairy folk
　　To dry your falling tears."

One fairy came in violet,
　　And one wore indigo;
In blue, green, yellow, orange, red,
　　They made a pretty row.

They wiped the cloud-tears all away,
　　And then from out the sky,
Upon a line the sunbeams made,
　　They hung their gowns to dry.

Little Kings and Queens of the May

Little Kings and Queens of the May,
Listen to me,
If you want to be
Every one of you very good
In that beautiful, beautiful, beautiful wood,
Where the little birds' heads get so turned with delight
That some of them sing all night,
Whatever you pluck,
Leave some for good luck,
Picked from the stalk, or pulled by the root,
From overhead or from underfoot,
Water wonders of ponds or brook,
Wherever you look
And whatever you find,
Leave something behind;
Some for the Naiads,
Some for the Dryads,
And a bit for the Nixies and the Pixies.

Juliana Horatia Ewing

Sea Fairies

They're hiding by the pebbles,
    They're running round the rocks.
Each of them, and all of them
    In dazzling sea-green frocks.

They're gathering strips of sea-weed,
    The ribands fair that lie
Along the winding water mark
    The tide has left so high.

They're flying with the sand,
    They're singing in the caves,
And dancing in the white foam
    They toss from off the waves.

But if you try to catch them
    They're always out of reach—
Not everywhere and anywhere,
    But somewhere on the beach.

Eileen Mathias

Rufty and Tufty

Rufty and Tufty were two little elves
    Who lived in a hollow oak tree.
They did all the cooking and cleaning themselves
    And often asked friends in to tea.

Rufty wore blue, and Tufty wore red,
    And each had a hat with a feather.
Their best Sunday shoes they kept under the bed—
    They were made of magic green leather.

Rufty was clever and kept the accounts,
    But Tufty preferred to do cooking.
He could make a fine cake without weighing amounts—
    And eat it when no one was looking!

Isabell Hempseed

The Fairy Sleep and Little Bo-Peep

Little Bo-Peep,
Had lost her sheep,
And didn't know where to find them,
All tired she sank
On a grassy bank,
And left the birds to mind them.

Then the fairy, Sleep,
Took little Bo-Peep,
In a spell of dreams he bound her,
And silently brought
The flock she sought,
Like summer clouds around her.

When little Bo-Peep—
In her slumber deep—
Saw lambs and sheep together,
All fleecy and white,
And soft and light,
As clouds in July weather;

Then little Bo-Peep
Awoke from her sleep,
And laughed with glee to find them
Coming home once more,
The old sheep before,
And the little lambs behind them.

A Fairy Went A-Marketing

A fairy went a-marketing—
She bought a little fish;
She put it in a crystal bowl
Upon a golden dish.
An hour she sat in wonderment
And watched its silver gleam,
And then she gently took it up
And slipped it in a stream.

A fairy went a-marketing—
    She bought a coloured bird;
It sang the sweetest, shrillest song
    That ever she had heard,
She sat beside its painted cage
    And listened half the day,
And then she opened wide the door
    And let it fly away.

A fairy went a-marketing—
    She bought a winter gown
All stitched about with gossamer
    And lined with thistledown.
She wore it all the afternoon
    With prancing and delight,
Then gave it to a little frog
    To keep him warm at night.

A fairy went a-marketing—
    She bought a gentle mouse
To take her tiny messages,
    To keep her little house.
All day she kept its busy feet
    Pit-patting to and fro,
And then she kissed its silken ears,
    Thanked it, and let it go.

                                    Rose Fyleman

If You See a Fairy Ring

If you see a fairy ring
    In a field of grass,
Very lightly step around,
    Tiptoe as you pass;
Last night fairies frolicked there,
And they're sleeping somewhere near.

If you see a tiny fay
    Lying fast asleep,
Shut your eyes and run away,
    Do not stay to peep;
And be sure you never tell,
Or you'll break a fairy spell.

A Fairy Song

Over hill, over dale,
  Thorough bush, thorough brier,
Over park, over pale,
  Thorough flood, thorough fire!
I do wander everywhere,
Swifter than the moon's sphere;
And I serve the fairy queen,
To dew her orbs upon the green;
The cowslips tall her pensioners be;
In their gold coats spots you see;
Those be rubies, fairy favours,
In those freckles live their savours:
I must go seek some dewdrops here,
And hang a pearl in every cowslip's ear.

Shakespeare

Pigwiggen

Pigwiggen arms him for the field,
A little cockle-shell his shield,
Which he could very bravely wield,
  Yet could it not be piercèd.
His spear abent both stiff and strong,
And well-near of two inches long;
The pile was of a horse-fly's tongue,
  Whose sharpness nought reversèd.

And puts him on a coat of mail,
Which was of a fish's scale,
That when his foe should him assail,
  No point should be prevailing.
His rapier was a hornet's sting;
It was a very dangerous thing,
For if he chanc'd to hurt the king
  It would be long in healing.

His helmet was a beetle's head,
Most horrible and full of dread,
That able was to strike one dead,
  Yet it did well become him;
And for a plume a horse's hair
Which, being tossèd with the air,
Had force to strike his foe with fear,
  And turn his weapon from him.

Himself he on an earwig set,
Yet scarce be on his back could get,
So oft and high he did curvet
    Ere he himself could settle.
He made him turn, and stop, and bound,
To gallop and to trot the round;
He scarce could stand on any ground,
    He was so full of mettle.

Michael Drayton

The Urchin's Dance

By the moon we sport and play,
With the night begins our day:
As we dance the dew doth fall:
Trip it, little urchins all!
Lightly as the little bee,
Two by two, and three by three,
And about go we, and about go we!

John Lyly

The Goblin

A goblin lives in our house, in our house, in our house,
A goblin lives in our house all the year round.

He bumps
And he jumps
And he thumps
And he stumps.
He knocks
And he rocks
And he rattles at the locks.

A goblin lives in our house, in our house, in our house,
A goblin lives in our house all the year round.

Rose Fyleman

Found in the Woods

I found a little brown purse
    The fairies left for me,
It was stitch'd with green and yellow,
    As pretty as could be.
It was full of fairy-money,
    As full as it could be,
So I bought a pot of honey,
    And had it for my tea.

Irene F. Pawsey

From The Merman

Who would be
A merman bold,
Sitting alone,
Singing alone
Under the sea,
With a crown of gold,
On a throne?

I would be a merman bold,
I would sit and sing the whole of the day;
I would fill the sea-halls with a voice of power;
But at night I would roam abroad and play
With the mermaids in and out of the rocks,
Dressing their hair with the white sea-flower;
And holding them back by their flowing locks
I would kiss them often under the sea,
And kiss them again till they kiss'd me
    Laughingly, laughingly;
And then we would wander away, away
To the pale-green sea-groves straight and high,
    Chasing each other merrily.

Lord Tennyson

From The Mermaid

Who would be
A mermaid fair,
Singing alone,
Combing her hair
Under the sea,
In a golden curl
With a comb of pearl,
On a throne?

I would be a mermaid fair;
I would sing to myself the whole of the day;
With a comb of pearl I would comb my hair;
And still as I comb'd I would sing and say,
"Who is it loves me? who loves not me?"
I would comb my hair till my ringlets would fall.

Lord Tennyson

Toadstools

It's not a bit windy,
  It's not a bit wet,
The sky is as sunny
  As summer, and yet
Little umbrellas are
  Everywhere spread,
Pink ones, and brown ones,
  And orange, and red.

I can't see the folks
  Who are hidden below;
I've peeped, and I've peeped
  Round the edges, but no!
They hold their umbrellas
  So tight and so close
That nothing shows under,
  Not even a nose!

Elizabeth Fleming

The Fairy Shoemaker

Tiny shoes so trim and neat,
Fairy shoes for dancing feet;
See the elfin cobbler's shelves
Filled with shoes for tiny elves.

And sitting there he hammers,
And hammering he sings. . . .

"This small shoe of silver,
This small shoe of gold,
This small shoe of diamonds bright—
Will none of them grow old.

"This small shoe will hurry,
This small shoe will skip,
This small shoe will dance all night,
Tipperty, tip, tip, tip.

"This small shoe will twinkle,
This small shoe will shine,
This small shoe will bring me home,
For I shall make it mine."

And sitting there he hammers,
And hammering he dreams. . . .

Tiny shoes so trim and neat,
Fairy shoes for dancing feet,
See the elfin cobbler smile
As he sits and rests awhile.

Phyllis Garlick

The Elfin Pedlar

Lady and gentlemen fays, come buy!
No pedlar has such a rich packet as I.

Who wants a gown
Of purple fold,
Embroidered down
The seams with gold?

See here!—A Tulip richly laced
To please a royal fairy's taste!

Who wants a cap
Of crimson grand?
By great good hap
I've one on hand;
Look, sir!—a Cockscomb, flowering red,
'Tis just the thing, sir, for your head!

Who wants a frock
Of vestal hue?
Or snowy smock?—
Fair maid, do you?
O me!—a Ladysmock so white!
Your bosom's self is not more bright!

Who wants to sport
A slender limb?
I've every sort
Of hose for him:
Both scarlet, striped, and yellow ones,
This Woodbine makes such pantaloons.

Who wants—(hush! hush!)
A box of paint?
'Twill give a blush
Yet leave no taint:
This Rose with natural rouge is fill'd,
From its own dewy leaves distill'd.

Then, lady and gentlemen, come buy!
You never will meet such a merchant as I!

George Darley

The Seasons

Therefore all seasons shall be sweet to thee

Slow Spring

O Year, grow slowly. Exquisite, holy,
    The days go on.
With almonds showing, the pink stars blowing,
    And birds in the dawn.

Grow slowly, year, like a child that is dear,
    Or a lamb that is mild,
By little steps, and by little skips,
    Like a lamb or a child.

Katharine Tynan

Round the Year

The Crocus, while the days are dark,
    Unfolds its saffron sheen;
At April's touch, the crudest bark
    Discovers germs of green.

Then sleep the seasons, full of might;
    While swells the pod
And rounds the peach, and in the night
    The mushroom bursts the sod.

The winter falls; the frozen rut
    Is bound with silver bars,
The snowdrift heaps against the hut
    And night is pierced with stars.

Coventry Patmore

Winter and Spring

But a little while ago
All the ground was white with snow;
Trees and shrubs were dry and bare,
Not a sign of life was there;
Now the buds and leaves are seen,
Now the fields are fresh and green,
Pretty birds are on the wing,
With a merry song they sing!
There's new life in everything!
How I love the pleasant spring!

A Chanted Calendar

First came the primrose,
On the bank high,
Like a maiden looking forth
From the window of a tower
When the battle rolls below,
So look'd she,
And saw the storms go by.

Then came the wind-flower
In the valley left behind,
As a wounded maiden, pale
With purple streaks of woe,
When the battle has roll'd by
Wanders to and fro,
So totter'd she,
Dishevell'd in the wind.

Then came the daisies,
On the first of May,
Like a banner'd show's advance
While the crowd runs by the way,
With ten thousand flowers about them they came
        trooping through the fields,
As a happy people come,
So came they,
As a happy people come
When the war has roll'd away,
With dance and tabor, pipe and drum,
And all make holiday.

Then came the cowslip,
Like a dancer in the fair,
She spread her little mat of green,
And on it danced she.
With a fillet bound about her brow,
A fillet round her happy brow,
A golden fillet round her brow,
And rubies in her hair.

Sydney Dobell

Before Spring

Jonquils and violets smelling sweet
In this grey, unblossoming street—
These to our midwinter bring
The first frail beauty of the Spring.

Sixpence—sixpence for the Spring—
For south wind and bird on wing—
Pennies for a priceless thing!

Glory of flower cups, flower eyes,
Wild, soft grace under iron skies,
Deathless in the gift they bring,
Though they die at evening.

Sixpence—sixpence for the Spring!

P. A. Ropes

February

To-day, I saw the catkins blow,
Altho' the hills are white with snow

White throstles sang "The sun is good";
They waved their banners in the wood.

They come to greet the lurking Spring
As messengers from Winter's King.

And thus they wave while Winter reigns,
While his cold grip still holds the plains.

Oh, tho' the hills are white with snow,
To-day I saw the catkins blow.

Dorothy Una Ratcliffe

A Change in the Year

It is the first mild day of March:
    Each minute sweeter than before,
The redbreast sings from the tall larch
    That stands beside our door.

There is a blessing in the air,
    Which seems a sense of joy to yield
To the bare trees, and mountains bare;
    And grass in the green field.

William Wordsworth

First Spring Morning

Look! look! the spring is come:
    O feel the gentle air,
That wanders thro' the boughs to burst
    The thick buds everywhere!
    The birds are glad to see
    The high unclouded sun:
Winter is fled away, they sing,
    The gay time is begun.

Adown the meadows green
    Let us go dance and play,
And look for violets in the lane,
    And ramble far away
    To gather primroses,
    That in the woodland grow,
And hunt for oxlips, or if yet
    The blades of bluebells show.

There the old woodman gruff
    Hath half the coppice cut,
And weaves the hurdles all day long
    Beside his willow hut.
    We'll steal on him, and then
    Startle him, all with glee
Singing our song of winter fled
    And summer soon to be.

Robert Bridges

Welcome to Spring

I have heard a mother bird
   Singing in the rain—
Telling all her little ones
   Spring has come again!

I have seen a wave of green
   Down a lovely lane—
Making all the hedges glad
   Spring has come again!

I have found a patch of ground
   Golden in the sun;
Crocuses are calling out
   Spring has just begun!

Irene Thompson

Spring Has Come

Hark! the tiny cowslip bell
   In the breeze is ringing;
Birds in every woodland dell
   Songs of joy are singing.
Winter is o'er, Spring once more
   Spreads abroad her golden store;
Hark! the tiny cowslip bell
   In the breeze is ringing.

Spring has come to make us glad,
   Let us give her greeting;
Winter days were cold and sad,
   Winter's reign is fleeting;
Hearts are gay, blithe as May,
   Dance and sport the livelong day;
Spring has come to make us glad,
   Let us give her greeting.

A Seventeenth-century Song

Now that the Winter's Gone

Now that the winter's gone, the earth hath lost
Her snow-white robes; and no more the frost
Candies the grass, or casts an icy cream
Upon the silver lake or crystal stream;
But the warm sun thaws the benumbed earth,
And makes it tender; gives a sacred birth
To the dead swallow; wakes in hollow tree
The drowsy cuckoo and the bumble-bee.
Now do a choir of chirping minstrels bring
In triumph to the world, the youthful Spring:
The valleys, hills and woods, in rich array,
Welcome the coming of the long'd-for May.

Thomas Carew

To Spring

O thou, with dewy locks who lookest down
Thro' the clear windows of the morning, turn
Thine angel eyes upon our western isle,
Which in full choir hails thy approach, O Spring!

William Blake

Spring, the Travelling Man

Spring, the Travelling Man, has been here,
Here in the glen;
He must have passed by in the grey of the dawn,
When only the robin and wren
Were awake,
Watching out with their bright little eyes
In the midst of the brake.
The rabbits, maybe, heard him pass,
Stepping light on the grass,
Whistling careless and gay at the break o' the day.
Then the blackthorn to give him delight
Put on raiment of white;
And, all for his sake,
The gorse on the hill, where he rested an hour,
Grew bright with a splendour of flower.

Winifred M. Letts

175

In Springtime

All Nature seems at work. Slugs leave their lair—
  The bees are stirring—birds are on the wing—
And Winter, slumbering in the open air,
  Wears on his smiling face a dream of Spring!

S. T. Coleridge

The Barrel Organ

Go down to Kew in lilac-time, in lilac-time, in lilac-time,
Go down to Kew in lilac-time (it isn't far from London!);
And you shall wander hand in hand with love in summer's
    wonderland;
Go down to Kew in lilac-time (it isn't far from London!).

The cherry trees are seas of bloom and soft perfume and
    sweet perfume,
The cherry trees are seas of bloom (and oh! so near to
    London!);
And there they say, when dawn is high, and all the world's
    a blaze of sky,
The cuckoo, though he's very shy, will sing a song for
    London.

The nightingale is rather rare and yet they say you'll
    hear him there,
At Kew, at Kew, in lilac-time (and oh! so near to
    London!);
The linnet and the throstle, too, and after dark the long
    halloo,
And golden-eyed tu-whit, tu-whoo of owls that ogle
    London.

For Noah hardly knew a bird of any kind that isn't heard
At Kew, at Kew, in lilac-time (and oh! so near to
    London!);
And when the rose begins to pout, and all the chestnut
    spires are out,
You'll hear the rest without a doubt, all chorusing for
    London:

Come down to Kew in lilac-time, in lilac-time, in lilac-time,
Come down to Kew in lilac-time (it isn't far from
　　London!);
And you shall wander hand in hand with love in summer's
　　wonderland;
Come down to Kew in lilac-time (it isn't far from
　　London!).

Alfred Noyes

Spring Morning

Now the moisty wood discloses
Wrinkled leaves of primèroses,
While the birds, they flute and sing:
Build your nests, for here is Spring.

All about the open hills
Daisies shew their peasant frills,
Washed and white and newly spun
For a festival of sun.

Like a blossom from the sky,
Drops a yellow butterfly,
Dancing down the hedges grey
Snow-bestrewn till yesterday.

Squirrels skipping up the trees
Smell how Spring is in the breeze,
While the birds, they flute and sing:
Build your nests, for here is Spring.

Frances Cornford

Spring Work at the Farm

What does the farmer in the spring?
He sows the seed that harvests bring;
But first he wakes the earth from sleep
By ploughing it well and harrowing it deep.

And busy must be the farmer's boy!
To care for the lambs that leap for joy.
To feed the calves so tender and young
He rises as soon as the day's begun.

And then the farmer's wife so kind,
Food for the ducklings and chicks will find.
And hark! what the queer little piggy-wigs say,
"Don't forget me, I'm hungry to-day."

Thirza Wakley

Spring Goeth All in White

Spring goeth all in white,
    Crowned with milk-white may:
In fleecy flocks of light
    O'er heaven the white clouds stray:

White butterflies in the air;
    White daisies prank the ground:
The cherry and hoary pear
    Scatter their snow around.

Robert Bridges

The Green Lady

A lovely Green Lady
    Embroiders and stitches
Sweet flowers in the meadows,
    On banks and in ditches.

All day she is sewing,
    Embroidering all night;
For she works in the darkness
    As well as the light.

She makes no mistake in
    The silks which she uses,
And all her gay colours
    She carefully chooses.

She fills nooks and corners
    With blossoms so small,
Where none but the fairies
    Will see them at all.

She sews them so quickly,
    She trims them so neatly,
Though much of her broidery
    Is hidden completely.

She scatters her tapestry
    Scented and sweet,
In the loneliest places,
    Or 'neath careless feet;
For bee, or for bird folk,
    For children like me,
But the lovely Green Lady,
    No mortal may see.

Charlotte Druitt Cole

Spring

Sound the flute!
Now 'tis mute;
Birds delight
Day and night
Nightingale
In the dale;
Lark in the sky
Merrily,
Merrily, merrily to welcome in the year.

Little boy,
Full of joy;
Little girl,
Sweet and small;
Cock does crow,
So do you;
Merry voice
Infant noise;
Merrily, merrily to welcome in the year.

Little lamb,
Here I am;
Come and lick
My white neck;
Let me pull
Your soft wool;
Let me kiss
Your soft face;
Merrily, merrily we welcome in the year.

William Blake

179

My Lady Spring

My Lady Spring is dressed in green,
   She wears a primrose crown,
And little baby buds and twigs
   Are clinging to her gown;
The sun shines if she laughs at all,
But if she weeps the raindrops fall.

Spring Quiet

Gone were but the Winter,
   Come were but the Spring,
I would go to a covert
   Where the birds sing.

Where in the whitethorn
   Singeth a thrush,
And a robin sings
   In the holly-bush.

Full of fresh scents
   Are the budding boughs
Arching high over
   A cool green house:

Full of sweet scents,
   And whispering air
Which sayeth softly:
   "We spread no snare;

"Here dwell in safety,
   Here dwell alone,
With a clear stream
   And a mossy stone.

"Here the sun shineth
   Most shadily;
Here is heard an echo
   Of the far sea,
     Though far off it be."

Christina Rossetti

The Magic Piper

There piped a piper in the wood
  Strange music—soft and sweet—
And all the little wild things
  Came hurrying to his feet.

They sat around him on the grass,
  Enchanted, unafraid,
And listened, as with shining eyes
  Sweet melodies he made.

The wood grew green, and flowers sprang up,
  The birds began to sing;
For the music it was magic,
  And the piper's name was—Spring!

E. L. Marsh

Promise

There's a black fog hiding London
  And every tree looks dead,
But I've seen a purple crocus and a jonquil's golden head.
  The shallow ponds are frozen
  And there's snow upon the hills,
But they're selling scarlet tulips now and yellow daffodils.

A bitter wind is blowing,
  The rivers are abrim,
But I toss my head at Winter, I am not afraid of him.
  Although the sun is shrouded
  Spring is just across the sea,
For I've seen a spray of lilac and a red anemone.

Florence Lacey

Spring

Now daisies pied, and violets blue,
  And lady-smocks all silver white,
And cuckoo-buds of yellow hue
  Do paint the meadows with delight,
The cuckoo now on every tree
  Sings cuckoo, cuckoo.

Shakespeare

Slumber in Spring

Grey pussy-willows
For fairy pillows,
So soft for fairy's head;
Cherry-petals sweet
For a cool, clean sheet,
Green moss for a fairy bed.
Fragrant violet for a coverlet.
And hush! down the hill's green sweep,
Comes the wind's soft sigh
For a lullaby;
Sound, sound will a fairy sleep.

Elizabeth Gould

Written in March

The cock is crowing,
The stream is flowing,
The small birds twitter,
The lake doth glitter,
The green field sleeps in the sun;

The oldest and youngest
Are at work with the strongest,
The cattle are grazing,
Their heads never raising;
There are forty feeding like one!

Like an army defeated
The snow hath retreated,
And now doth fare ill
On the top of the bare hill;
The plough-boy is whooping—anon—anon;

There's joy in the mountains;
There's life in the fountains;
Small clouds are sailing,
Blue sky prevailing;
The rain is over and gone.

William Wordsworth

In February

The frozen ground is broken
   Where snowdrops raise their heads,
And nod their tiny greeting
   In glades and garden beds.

The frozen stream is melted,
   The white brook turns to brown,
And foaming through the coppice
   Flows helter skelter down.

The frozen air is golden
   With February sun,
The winter days are over,
   Oh, has the Spring begun?

P. A. Ropes

A Spring Song

See the yellow catkins cover
All the slender willows over;
And on mossy banks so green
Star-like primroses are seen;
And their clustering leaves below,
White and purple violets grow.

Hark! the little lambs are bleating,
And the cawing rooks are meeting
In the elms—a noisy crowd;
And all birds are singing loud,
There, the first white butterfly
In the sun goes flitting by.

Mary Howitt

Spring Prayer

For flowers that bloom about our feet;
For tender grass, so fresh, so sweet;
For song of bird, and hum of bee;
For all things fair we hear or see,
Father in heaven, we thank Thee!

For blue of stream and blue of sky;
For pleasant shade of branches high;
For fragrant air and cooling breeze;
For beauty of the blooming trees,
Father in heaven, we thank Thee!

Ralph W. Emerson

Snowflakes

I heard the snowflakes whisper in the still dark night,
And when I peeped at bedtime, all the roofs were white.
Although the pussy willows their mittened buds unfold,
Although the hazel catkins are waving tails of gold,
Although the buds are bursting on the chestnuts by
    the gate,
And spring is in the countryside—the snow came late.

I saw it in the twilight, and I looked for it at dawn,
But all I found were thrushes on the smooth green lawn,
All the roofs were twinkling and sparkling in the sun,
And myriad buds were waking and opening one by one,
And all that could remind me of snowflakes on the beds
Were clusterings of snowdrops, with whitely drooping
    heads.

Ruth M. Arthur

A Walk in Spring

What could be nicer than the spring,
When little birds begin to sing?
When for my daily walk I go
Through fields that once were white with snow?
When in the green and open spaces
Lie baby lambs with sweet black faces?
What could be finer than to shout
That all the buds are bursting out—
And oh, at last beneath the hill,
To pick a yellow daffodil?

K. C. Lart

184

Night of Spring

Slow, horses, slow,
As through the wood we go—
We would count the stars in heaven,
Hear the grasses grow:

Watch the cloudlets few
Dappling the deep blue.
In our open palms outspread
Catch the blessed dew.

Slow, horses, slow,
As through the wood we go—
All the beauty of the night
We would learn and know!

Thomas Westwood

April

April, April,
Laugh thy girlish laughter;
Then, the moment after,
Weep thy girlish tears!
April, that mine ears
Like a lover greetest,
If I tell thee, sweetest,
All my hopes and fears,
April, April,
Laugh thy golden laughter,
But, the moment after,
Weep thy golden tears.

Sir William Watson

In the April Rain

Listen! In the April rain,
Brother Robin's here again;
Songs, like showers, come and go;
He's house-building, that I know.

185

Though he finds the old pine tree
Is not where it used to be,
And the nest he made last year
Torn and scattered far and near,

He has neither grief nor care,
Building sites are everywhere;
If one nest is blown away,
Fields are full of sticks and hay.

Listen! In the April rain,
Brother Robin sings again,
Sings so full of joy and glee,
He's house-building, don't you see?

Mary Anderson

April Rain

It isn't raining rain to me,
   It's raining daffodils;
In every dimpled drop I see
   Wild flowers on the hills.
The clouds of grey engulf the day
   And overwhelm the town—
It isn't raining rain to me,
   It's raining roses down.

It isn't raining rain to me,
   But fields of clover bloom
Where any buccaneering bee
   May find a bed and room.
A health unto the happy,
   A fig for him who frets—
It isn't raining rain to me,
   It's raining violets.

Robert Loveman

Old May Song

All in this pleasant evening, together come are we,
For the summer springs so fresh, green, and gay;
We tell you of a blossoming and buds on every tree,
Drawing near unto the merry month of May.

May

I feel a newer life in every gale;
    The winds, that fan the flowers,
And with their welcome breathings fill the sail,
    Tell of serener hours—
        Of hours that glide unfelt away
        Beneath the sky of May.

The spirit of the gentle south-wind calls
    From his blue throne of air,
And where his whispering voice in music falls,
    Beauty is budding there;
        The bright ones of the valley break
        Their slumbers, and awake.

The waving verdure rolls along the plain,
    And the wide forest weaves,
To welcome back its playful mates again,
    A canopy of leaves;
        And from its darkening shadows floats
        A gush of trembling notes.

Fairer and brighter spreads the reign of May;
    The tresses of the woods
With the light dallying of the west-wind play;
    And the full-brimming floods,
        As gladly to their goal they run,
        Hail the returning sun.

J. G. Percival

May-Time

There is but one May in the year,
　And sometimes May is wet and cold;
There is but one May in the year,
　But before the year grows old.

Yet, though it be the chilliest May
　With least of sun, and most of showers,
Its wind and dew, its night and day,
　Bring up the flowers.

In May

In May I go a-walking to hear the linnet sing,
The blackbird and the throstle, a-praising God the King;
It cheers the heart to hear them, to see the leaves unfold,
And the meadows scattered over with buttercups of gold.

Summer is Nigh

Summer is nigh!
How do I know?
Why, this very day
A robin sat
On a tilting spray,
And merrily sang
A song of May.
Jack Frost has fled
From the rippling brook;
And a trout peeped out
From his shady nook.
A butterfly too
Flew lazily by,
And the willow catkins
Shook from on high
Their yellow dust
As I passed by:
And so I know
That summer is nigh.

June

Month of leaves,
Month of roses;
Gardens full
Of dainty posies;
   Skies of blue,
   Hedgerows gay,
   Meadows sweet
   With the new-mown hay.

Flowery banks,
A-drone with bees,
Dreaming cattle
Under trees:
   Song-birds pipe
   A merry tune—
   This is summer,
   This is June.

Irene F. Pawsey

A Summer Day

Not by the city bells that chime the hours
   I'll tell this day,
But by the bloom and fall of things in flowers
   And the slow way
Of cloud shadows, and swathing sunshine wrapping
   The gorse-gilt plain;
And little lifted leaves, and water lapping,
   And maybe rain.

A shaken bough, a circle on the water,
   A rose a-blush,
A yellow iris crowned like a king's daughter,
   A piping thrush.
Swift fiery dragon-flies, and brown bees humming,
   And tiny things
Making strange music, and the twilight coming
   On measureless wings.

Florence Harrison

Midsummer Night

The sun goes down,
　The stars peep out,
And long slim shadows
　Flit about.

In velvet shoes
　The quiet dark
Comes stepping soft
　O'er wood and park.

And now the world
　Is fast asleep;
And fays and elves
　Their revels keep.

They fly on the backs of the grey-winged moths,
　They skim on the dragon-flies green and gold.
On shimmering dew-wet grass they alight,
　Tiny petal-skirts whirl, gauzy wings unfold.

The fairies are dancing beneath the moon.
Hush! See the shimmer of their twinkling shoon!
Elizabeth Gould

Hay-Time

Come out, come out, this sunny day,
The fields are sweet with new-mown hay,
The birds are singing loud and clear,
For summer-time once more is here;
So bring your rakes and come and play,
And toss and tumble in the hay.
The sweet wild roses softly blow,
All pink and white the roses grow;
The nodding daisies in the grass,
Lift up their heads to hear you pass
Upon this happy, sunny day,
When you come out to make the hay.
C. M. Lowe

Haytime

It's Midsummer Day
And they're cutting the hay
Down in the meadow just over the way,
The children all run
For a frolic, and fun—
For haytime is playtime out in the sun.

It's Midsummer Day,
And they're making the hay
Down in the meadow all golden and gay,
They're tossing it high
Beneath the June sky,
And the hay rakes are spreading it out to dry.

Irene F. Pawsey

Summer Evening

Crows crowd croaking overhead,
Hastening to the woods to bed.
Cooing sits the lonely dove,
Calling home her absent love.
With "Kirchup! Kirchup!" 'mong the wheats
Partridge distant partridge greets.

Bats fly by in hood and cowl; .
Through the barn-hole pops the owl;
From the hedge, in drowsy hum,
Heedless buzzing beetles hum,
Haunting every bushy place,
Flopping in the labourer's face.

Flowers now sleep within their hoods;
Daisies button into buds;
From soiling dew the buttercup
Shuts his golden jewels up;
And the rose and woodbine they
Wait again the smiles of day.

John Clare
191

A Night in June

The sun has long been set,
    The stars are out by twos and threes,
The little birds are piping yet
    Among the bushes and the trees;
There's a cuckoo, and one or two thrushes,
And a far-off wind that rushes,
And a sound of water that gushes,
And the cuckoo's sovereign cry
Fills all the hollow of the sky.

William Wordsworth

June

The greenest of grass in the long meadow grows;
    And the stream, how the stream is dancing!
How cool is its kiss on the little brown toes
    That find it a playmate entrancing!
        Forgotten the bad days—
        The weary and sad days,
        Or time all unheeding
        That bright hours are speeding,
Forgotten is "bed" by the children in June.

Jane G. Stewart

Lanes in Summer

I love the little winding lanes,
In the sweet days when summer reigns;
The eglantine and hawkweed's plume;
The dog-rose and the bramble bloom,
Like stars from heaven gone astray;
The fragrant scent of new-mown hay;
The poppies in the green-aisled wheat;
The bees that find that clover sweet;
The last song of the wren and thrush
Breaking through the drowsy hush—
If kindly peace be anywhere
'Tis surely there, 'tis surely there.

Malcolm Hemphrey

192

In the Fair Forest

In Summer when the woods are green
  And leaves are large and long,
Full merry it is in the fair forest
  To hear the small birds' song.

To see the red deer seek the dale
  And leave the hills so high,
To shade themselves among the glades
  Under the greenwood tree.

Old Ballad

Song of Summer Days

Sing a song of hollow logs,
Chirp of cricket, croak of frogs,
Cry of wild bird, hum of bees,
Dancing leaves and whisp'ring trees;
Legs all bare, and dusty toes,
Ruddy cheeks and freckled nose,
Splash of brook and swish of line,
Where the song that's half so fine?

Sing a song of summer days,
Leafy nooks and shady ways,
Nodding roses, apples red,
Clover like a carpet spread;
Sing a song of running brooks,
Cans of bait and fishing hooks,
Dewy hollows, yellow moons,
Birds a-pipe with merry tunes.

Sing a song of skies of blue,
Eden's garden made anew,
Scarlet hedges, leafy lanes,
Vine-embowered sills and panes;
Stretch of meadows, splash'd with dew,
Silver clouds with sunlight through,
Call of thrush and pipe of wren,
Sing and call it home again.

J. W. Foley

The Four Sweet Months

First, April, she with mellow showers
Opens the way for early flowers;
Then after her comes smiling May,
In a more sweet and rich array;
Next enters June, and brings us more
Gems than those two that went before:
Then, lastly, July comes, and she
More wealth brings in than all those three.

Robert Herrick

August

The wind sang to the cornfields
    A happy little song,
And this is what he whispered.
    "The harvest won't be long."

The wind sang to the windmill
    A merry little tune.
The windmill answered gaily,
    "The harvest's coming soon."

The whispering of the poppies
    Through the cornfields steals along,
They are joining with the fairies
    Singing harvest's merry song.

Eunice Fallon

Harvest Song

The boughs do shake and the bells do ring,
So merrily comes our harvest in,
Our harvest in, our harvest in,
So merrily comes our harvest in.

We have ploughed, we have sowed,
We have reaped, we have mowed,
We have brought home every load,
Hip, hip, hip, harvest home!

The Harvest

The silver rain, the shining sun,
The fields where scarlet poppies run,
And all the ripples of the wheat
Are in the bread that I do eat.

So when I sit for every meal
And say a grace, I always feel
That I am eating rain and sun,
And fields where scarlet poppies run.

Alice C. Henderson

Harvest

I saw the farmer plough the field,
And row on row
The furrows grow.
I saw the farmer plough the field,
And hungry furrows grow.

I saw the farmer sow the wheat,
The golden grain,
In sun and rain.
I saw the farmer sow the wheat,
In shining sun and rain.

I saw at first a silvery sheen,
Then line on line
Of living green.
I saw at first a silvery sheen,
Then lines of living green.

The living green then turned to gold,
In thirty—fifty—
Hundred fold.
The living green then turned to gold
In mercies manifold.

M. M. Hutchinson

195

Story of the Corn

The grains of corn were planted
　Where plough and rake had been,
And soon, through brown earth pushing
　The young green shoots were seen.

Cleared of weeds by harrow,
　And watered by the rain,
Aided by the sunshine,
　Appears the ripening grain.

The fields of bearded barley,
　The graceful hanging oats,
And ears of wheat packed closely,
　The cheerful reaper notes.

He sees the cornfields waving,
　Yellow and ripe and strong,
And so, his heart rejoicing,
　He sings his harvest song.

K. Fisher

Autumn

I love the fitful gust that shakes
　The casement all the day,
And from the glossy elm tree takes
　The faded leaves away,
Twirling them by the window pane
With thousand others down the lane.

I love to see the shaking twig
　Dance till shut of eve,
The sparrow on the cottage rig,
　Whose chirp would make believe
That Spring was just now flirting by
In Summer's lap with flowers to lie.

I love to see the cottage smoke
   Curl upwards through the trees;
The pigeons nestled round the cote
   On November days like these;
The cock upon the dunghill crowing,
The mill sails on the heath a-going.

John Clare

Autumn

Yellow the bracken,
   Golden the sheaves,
Rosy the apples,
   Crimson the leaves;
Mist on the hillside,
   Clouds grey and white.
Autumn, good morning!
   Summer, good night!

Florence Hoatson

Red in Autumn

Tipperty-toes, the smallest elf,
Sat on a mushroom by himself,
Playing a little tinkling tune
Under the big round harvest moon;
And this is the song that Tipperty made
To sing to the little tune he played.

"Red are the hips, red are the haws,
Red and gold are the leaves that fall,
Red are the poppies in the corn,
Red berries on the rowan tall;
Red is the big round harvest moon,
And red are my new little dancing shoon."

Elizabeth Gould

197

September

There are twelve months throughout the year,
  From January to December—
And the primest month of all the twelve
  Is the merry month of September!
      Then apples so red
      Hang overhead,
      And nuts ripe-brown
      Come showering down
In the bountiful days of September!

There are flowers enough in the summer-time,
  More flowers than I can remember—
But none with the purple, gold, and red
  That dye the flowers of September!
  The gorgeous flowers of September!
      And the sun looks through
      A clearer blue,
      And the moon at night
      Sheds a clearer light
On the beautiful flowers of September!

The poor too often go scant and bare,
  But it glads my soul to remember
That 'tis harvest-time throughout the land
  In the bountiful month of September!
  Oh! the good, kind month of September!
      It giveth the poor
      The growth of the moor;
      And young and old
      'Mong sheaves of gold
Go gleaning in rich September!

Mary Howitt

October

I love to wander through the woodlands hoary,
  In the soft light of an autumnal day,
When summer gathers up her robes of glory,
  And, like a dream of beauty, glides away.

S. W. Whitman

An Autumn Morning

It seems like a dream
  In the garden to-day;
The trees, once so green,
  With rich colours are gay.

The oak is aglow
  With a warm, crimson blush;
The maple leaves show
  A deep purple flush.

The elm tree with bold
  Yellow patches is bright,
And with pale gleaming gold
  The beech seems alight.

And the creeper leaves flare
  Like red flame on the wall;
Their dazzle and glare
  Is the brightest of all.

The big chestnut trees
  Are all russet and brown,
And everywhere leaves
  One by one flutter down.

And all the leaves seem
  To be dressed up so gay,
That it seems like a dream
  In the garden to-day.

Autumn Morning

The south-west wind is blowing,
  A red fox hurries by;
A lake of silver water
  Reflects a rainbow sky!

The morning sun is shining
  Upon the golden corn;
An early blackbird wakens
  And sings to greet the dawn!

Adeline White

Autumn Song

October is a piper,
  Piping down the dell—
Sad sweet songs of sunshine—
  Summer's last farewell,
He pipes till grey November
  Comes in the mist and rain,
And then he puts his pipe away
  Till Autumn comes again.

Margaret Rose

Colour

The world is full of colour!
  'Tis Autumn once again
And leaves of gold and crimson
  Are lying in the lane.

There are brown and yellow acorns,
  Berries and scarlet haws,
Amber gorse and heather
  Purple across the moors!

Green apples in the orchard,
  Flushed by a glowing sun;
Mellow pears and brambles
  Where coloured pheasants run!

Yellow, blue and orange,
  Russet, rose and red—
A gaily-coloured pageant—
  An Autumn flower bed.

Beauty of light and shadow,
Glory of wheat and rye,
Colour of shining water
Under a sunset sky!

Adeline White

October's Party

October gave a party,
The leaves by hundreds came—
The Chestnuts, Oaks and Maples,
And leaves of every name.
The sunshine spread a carpet,
And everything was grand,
Miss Weather led the dancing,
Professor Wind the band.

The Chestnuts came in yellow,
The Oaks in crimson dressed;
The lovely Misses Maple
In scarlet looked their best;
All balanced to their partners,
And gaily fluttered by;
The sight was like a rainbow
New fallen from the sky.

Then, in the rustic hollow,
At hide-and-seek they played,
The party closed at sundown,
And everybody stayed.
Professor Wind played louder;
They flew along the ground;
And then the party ended
In jolly "hands around."

George Cooper

To Autumn

Season of mists and mellow fruitfulness!
   Close bosom-friend of the maturing sun;
Conspiring with him how to load and bless
   With fruit the vines that round the thatch-eaves run;
To bend with apples the moss'd cottage-trees,
   And fill all fruit with ripeness to the core;
     To swell the gourd, and plump the hazel shells
   With a sweet kernel; to set budding more,
And still more, later flowers for the bees,
Until they think warm days will never cease,
     For Summer has o'er-brimmed their clammy cells.

Who hath not seen thee oft amid thy store?
   Sometimes whoever seeks abroad may find
Thee sitting careless on a granary floor,
   Thy hair soft-lifted by the winnowing wind;
Or on a half-reap'd furrow sound asleep,
   Drowsed with the fumes of poppies, while thy hook
     Spares the next swath and all its twinèd flowers;
And sometime like a gleaner thou dost keep
   Steady thy laden head across a brook;
   Or by a cider-press, with patient look,
     Thou watchest the last oozings, hours by hours.

Where are the songs of Spring? Ay, where are they?
   Think not of them, thou hast thy music too—
While barred clouds bloom the soft-dying day,
   And touch the stubble-plains with rosy hue:
Then in a wailful choir, the small gnats mourn
   Among the river sallows, borne aloft
     Or sinking as the light wind lives or dies;
And full-grown lambs loud bleat from hilly bourn;
   Hedge-crickets sing; and now with treble soft
   The redbreast whistles from a garden-croft,
     And gathering swallows twitter in the skies.

J. Keats

202

October

I've brought you nuts and hops;
   And when the leaf drops, why, the walnut drops.
Crack your first nut and light your first fire,
   Roast your first chestnut crisp on the bar;
Make the logs sparkle, stir the blaze higher,
    Logs are as cheery as sun or as star,
    Logs we can find wherever we are.
    Spring one soft day will open the leaves,
Spring one bright day will lure back the flowers;
    Never fancy my whistling wind grieves,
    Never fancy I've tears in my showers:
Dance, night and days! and dance on, my hours!

Christina Rossetti

Rich Days

Welcome to you, rich Autumn days,
   Ere comes the cold, leaf-picking wind;
When golden stocks are seen in fields,
   All standing arm-in-arm entwined;
   And gallons of sweet cider seen
   On trees in apples red and green.

With mellow pears that cheat our teeth,
Which melt that tongues may suck them in,
With blue-black damsons, yellow plums,
   And woodnuts rich, to make us go
   Into the loneliest lanes we know.

W. H. Davies

November

November is a spinner
   Spinning in the mist,
Weaving such a lovely web
   Of gold and amethyst.
In among the shadows
   She spins till close of day,
Then quietly she folds her hands
   And puts her work away.

Margaret Rose

In the Wood

Cold winter's in the wood,
  I saw him pass
Crinkling up fallen leaves
  Along the grass.

Bleak winter's in the wood,
  The birds have flown
Leaving the naked trees
  Shivering alone.

King Winter's in the wood,
  I saw him go
Crowned with a coronet
  Of crystal snow.

Eileen Mathias

A Greenland Winter

Such a wide, still landscape, all cold and white!
And the stars look down through the endless night;
And it's ever so lonely over there,
Where the white bear sleeps in his hidden lair!
There is never the sound of a sea-bird's cry,
No murmuring waters go rippling by,
No breakers roll up to the rocky beach;
There is ice as far as the eye can reach—
A desolate waste, where the foxes roam,
And the seal and the walrus have their home.
If anyone strange came wandering here,
Would they ever guess that our homes are near?
So sheltered and hidden the igloos lie,
Like hillocks of snow 'neath the Arctic sky.

Lucy Diamond

Winter's Song

Drop down, drop down, white snowflakes!
We shall hide ourselves in fur coats
And when the blizzard comes
We shall put on fur caps,
We shall harness our golden sleighs,
We shall drive down from our hillside
And if we fall into a snowdrift
We hope that the wind will not cover us,
So that we can drive back quickly
For the fairy tales which grandfather will tell us.

Translation from the Bohemian

White Fields

In winter-time we go
Walking in the fields of snow;

Where there is no grass at all;
Where the top of every wall,

Every fence, and every tree,
Is as white as white can be.

Pointing out the way we came—
Every one of them the same—

All across the fields there be
Prints in silver filigree;

And our mothers always know,
By the footprints in the snow,

Where it is the children go.

James Stephens

Winter

O Winter's a beautiful time of the year.
There's frost on the hills,
There's snow in the air.
The buds are all still,
The boughs are all bare.

This little maid of long ago
Is warmly dressed from top to toe.
Her hands are hidden in her muff,
I wonder if she's warm enough!

Enid Blyton

Winter

Sweet blackbird is silenced with chaffinch and thrush,
Only waistcoated robin still chirps in the bush:
Soft sun-loving swallows have mustered in force,
And winged to the spice-teeming southlands their course.

Plump housekeeper dormouse has tucked himself neat,
Just a brown ball in moss with a morsel to eat:
Armed hedgehog has huddled him into the hedge,
While frogs scarce miss freezing deep down in the sedge.

Soft swallows have left us alone in the lurch,
But robin sits whistling to us from his perch:
If I were red robin, I'd pipe you a tune,
Would make you despise all the beauties of June.

But, since that cannot be, let us draw round the fire,
Munch chestnuts, tell stories, and stir the blaze higher:
We'll comfort pinched robin with crumbs, little man,
Till he'll sing us the very best song that he can.

Christina Rossetti

Jack Frost

The door was shut, as doors should be,
 Before you went to bed last night;
But Jack Frost has got in, you see,
 And left your window silver white.

He must have waited till you slept;
 And not a single word he spoke,
But pencilled o'er the panes and crept
 Away again before you woke.

And now you cannot see the hills
 Nor fields that stretch beyond the lane
But there are fairer things than these
 His fingers traced on every pane.

Rocks and castles towering high;
 Hills and dales and streams and fields;
And knights in armour riding by,
 With nodding plumes and shining shields.

And here are little boats, and there
 Big ships with sails spread to the breeze;
And yonder, palm trees waving fair
 On islands set in silver seas.

And butterflies with gauzy wings;
 And herds of cows and flocks of sheep
And fruit and flowers and all the things
 You see when you are sound asleep.

For creeping softly underneath
 The door, when all the lights are out,
Jack Frost takes every breath you breathe
 And knows the things you think about.

He paints them on the window pane,
 In fairy lines with frozen steam;
And when you wake you see again
 The lovely things you saw in dream.

Gabriel Setoun

Jack Frost in the Garden

Jack Frost was in the garden;
  I saw him there at dawn;
He was dancing round the bushes
  And prancing on the lawn.
He had a cloak of silver,
  A hat all shimm'ring white,
A wand of glittering star-dust,
  And shoes of sunbeam light.

Jack Frost was in the garden,
  When I went out to play
He nipped my toes and fingers
  And quickly ran away.
I chased him round the wood-shed,
  But, oh! I'm sad to say
That though I chased him everywhere
  He simply wouldn't stay.

Jack Frost was in the garden:
  But now I'd like to know
Where I can find him hiding;
  I've hunted high and low—
I've lost his cloak of silver,
  His hat all shimm'ring white,
His wand of glittering star-dust,
  His shoes of sunbeam light.

John P. Smeeton

Snow

Out of the bosom of the air,
Out of the cloudfolds of her garment shaken,
Over the woodlands, brown and bare,
Over the harvest-fields forsaken,
Silent, and soft, and slow
Descends the snow.

H. W. Longfellow

The Snow

The snow, in bitter cold,
  Fell all the night;
And we awoke to see
  The garden white.

And still the silvery flakes
  Go whirling by,
White feathers fluttering
  From a grey sky.

Beyond the gate, soft feet
  In silence go,
Beyond the frosted pane
  White shines the snow.

F. Ann Elliott

Outside

King Winter sat in his Hall one day,
  And he said to himself, said he,
"I must admit I've had some fun,
I've chilled the Earth and cooled the Sun,
  And not a flower or tree
But wishes that my reign were done,
And as long as Time and Tide shall run,
I'll go on making everyone
  As cold as cold can be."

There came a knock at the outer door:
  "Who's there?" King Winter cried;
"Open your Palace Gate," said Spring
"For you can reign no more as King,
  Nor longer here abide;
This message from the Sun I bring,
'The trees are green, the birds do sing;
The hills with joy are echoing':
  So pray, Sir—step outside!"

Hugh Chesterman

There's Snow on the Fields

There's snow on the fields,
  And cold in the cottage,
While I sit in the chimney nook
  Supping hot pottage.

My clothes are soft and warm,
  Fold upon fold,
But I'm so sorry for the poor
  Out in the cold.

Christina Rossetti

The North Wind

The north wind doth blow,
And we shall have snow,
And what will poor robin do then, poor thing?
  O, he'll go to the barn,
  And to keep himself warm
He'll hide his head under his wing, poor thing.

The north wind doth blow,
And we shall have snow,
And what will the swallow do then, poor thing?
  O, do you not know,
  He's gone long ago
To a country much warmer than ours, poor thing?

The north wind doth blow,
And we shall have snow,
And what will the dormouse do then, poor thing?
  Rolled up in a ball,
  In his nest snug and small,
He'll sleep till the winter is past, poor thing.

The north wind doth blow,
And we shall have snow,
And what will the children do then, poor things?
  O, when lessons are done,
  They'll jump, skip, and run,
And play till they make themselves warm, poor things.

Winter Joys

White stars falling gently,
　　Softly down to earth,
Red fires burning brightly
　　In the warm and cosy hearth.

White trees changed to elfin-land,
　　By red sun's dazzling glow,
Little robin redbreasts
　　Hopping in the snow.

Happy children's voices,
　　Shouting loud with glee,
Oh! the joys of winter
　　Are wonderful to me.

Dorothy Gradon

Jack Frost

Look out! look out!
Jack Frost is about!
He's after our fingers and toes;
　　And, all through the night,
　　The gay little sprite
Is working where nobody knows.

　　He'll climb each tree,
　　So nimble is he,
His silvery powder he'll shake;
　　To windows he'll creep,
　　And while we're asleep,
Such wonderful pictures he'll make.

　　Across the grass
　　He'll merrily pass,
And change all its greenness to white;
　　Then home he will go,
　　And laugh, "Ho! ho! ho!
What fun I have had in the night!"

Cecily E. Pike

211

The North Wind

The Snow Queen comes on dazzling feet
  And brings the sparkling snows,
The clouds fly fast with icy sleet,
  And the North Wind blows.

Robin is singing a brave little song,
  The sweetest song he knows,
But winter nights are dark and long
  And the North Wind blows.

Squirrels are sleeping in hollow tree:
  Seeds are asleep below;
Baby is cosy as cosy can be;
  Let the North Wind blow!

Dorothy Gradon

New Year's Days

The New Year's days are white with snow,
The winds are laughing as they blow.
Across the ponds and lakes we glide,
And o'er the drifting snow we ride,
And down the hills we gaily slide,
  For it is winter weather.

Each rushing stream is warmly dress'd,
An icy coat upon its breast,
And on each branch of every tree,
Packed in as close as close can be,
The next year's leaflets we can see,
  All nestled close together.

Celia Standish

Winter

Summer has doft his latest green,
And Autumn ranged the barley-mows.
So long away when have you been?
And are you coming back to close
The year? It sadly wants repose.

W. D. Landor

All Seasons Shall Be Sweet

Therefore all seasons shall be sweet to thee,
Whether the summer clothe the general earth
With greenness, or redbreast sit and sing
Betwixt the tufts of snow on the bare branch
Of mossy apple-tree, while the nigh thatch
Smokes in the sun-thaw; whether the eve-drops fall
Heard only in the trances of the blast,
Or if the secret ministry of frost
Shall hang them up in silent icicles,
Quietly shining to the quiet moon.

S. T. Coleridge

Flowers and Trees

There is nothing I know of to compare
With apple blossoms falling through the air

The Aconite

Earth has borne a little son,
He is a very little one,
He wears a bib all frilled with green
Around his neck to keep him clean.
Though before another Spring
A thousand children Earth may bring
Forth to bud and blossoming—
Lily daughters, cool and slender,
Roses, passionate and tender,
Tulip sons as brave as swords,
Hollyhocks, like laughing lords,
Yet she'll never love them quite
As much as she loves Aconite:
Aconite, the first of all,
Who is so very, very small,
Who is so golden-haired and good,
And wears a bib, as babies should.

A. M. Graham

Apple Blossoms

Is there anything in Spring so fair
As apple blossoms falling through the air?

When from a hill there comes a sudden breeze
That blows freshly through all the orchard trees.

The petals drop in clouds of pink and white,
Noiseless like snow and shining in the light.

Making beautiful an old stone wall,
Scattering a rich fragrance as they fall.

There is nothing I know of to compare
With apple blossoms falling through the air.

Helen Adams Parker

Pink Almond

So delicate, so airy,
  The almond on the tree,
Pink stars that some good fairy
  Has made for you and me.

A little cloud of roses,
  All in a world of grey,
The almond flower uncloses
  Upon the wild March day.

A mist of roses blowing
  The way of fog and sleet,
A dust of roses showing
  For grey dust in the street.

Pink snow upon the branches,
  Pink snowflakes falling down
In rosy avalanches,
  Upon the dreary town.

A rain, a shower of roses,
  All in a roseless day,
The almond tree uncloses
  Her roses on the grey.

Katharine Tynan

Roses

You love the roses—so do I. I wish
The sky would rain down roses, as they rain
From off the shaken bush. Why will it not?
Then all the valley would be pink and white
And soft to tread on. They would fall as light
As feathers, smelling sweet: and it would be
Like sleeping and yet waking, all at once.

George Eliot

Marigolds

Do you like marigolds?
  If you do
Then my garden is
  Gay for you!

I've been cutting their
  Fragrant stalks
Where they lean on
  The garden walks.

The head's too heavy for
  The brittle stem,
A careless touch and
  You've broken them

Each one shines like a
  Separate star
Set in some heaven where
  Gardens are.

My hands smell of the
  Herb-like scent,
Telling what garden
  Way I went.

Pungent, vivid and
  Strong, they stay
Long after Summer has
  Gone away.

Do you like marigolds?
  Here's a pledge
To meet the frost with
  A golden edge—

To go as far as
  A weak thing may
Linking to-morrow with
  Yesterday.

Louise Driscoll

Larch Wood Secrets

In Larch Wood
Is a little grey pool;
I go there
When the day is cool.
And when I see the sea-gulls
Come flying down the sky,
Then I know that Winter
And the cold days are nigh.

In Larch Wood
There are growing seven larches,
One green hazel
And two silver birches;
And when I hear the squirrel
Chitter-chattering to the sky,
Then I know that Maytime
And the warm days are nigh.

Ivy O. Eastwick

The Stately Lady

I saw a stately lady
   In a green gown,
When the moon was shooting
   Silver arrows down.
And the stately lady
   In her gown of green
Made the sweetest curtsy
   I have ever seen.

"Little lovely lady,
   You must be a queen,
In your yellow satin
   And your gown of green."
But the stately lady
   Bowed her gracious head;
"I was made a tulip,
   Not a Queen," she said.

Flora Sandstrom
219

Wild Flower's Song

As I wandered in the forest
    The green leaves among,
I heard a wild flower
    Singing a song.

I slept on the earth
    In the silent night:
I murmured my thought,
    And I felt delight.

In the morning I went,
    As rosy as morn,
To seek for fresh joy
    But I met with scorn.

William Blake

Child's Song in Spring

The silver birch is a dainty lady,
    She wears a satin gown;
The elm-tree makes the churchyard shady,
    She will not live in town.

The English oak is a sturdy fellow;
    He gets his green coat late;
The willow is smart in a suit of yellow,
    While brown the beech trees wait.

Such a gay green gown God gives the larches—
    As green as He is good!
The hazels hold up their arms for arches
    When Spring rides through the wood.

The chestnut's proud, and the lilac's pretty,
    The poplar's gentle and tall,
But the plane tree's kind to the poor dull city—
    I love him best of all!

E. Nesbit

Bluebells

In the bluebell forest
  There is scarce a sound,
Only bluebells growing
  Everywhere around.

I can't see a blackbird
  Or a thrush to sing,
I think I can almost
  Hear the bluebells ring.

Ah! there is a bunny,
  And he's listening too,
Or perhaps he's thinking—
  What a sea of blue!

O. Enoch

Snowdrops

Little ladies, white and green,
  With your spears about you,
Will you tell us where you've been
  Since we lived without you?

You are sweet, and fresh, and clean,
  With your pearly faces;
In the dark earth where you've been
  There are wondrous places:

Yet you come again, serene,
  When the leaves are hidden;
Bringing joy from where you've been
  You return unbidden—

Little ladies, white and green,
  Are you glad to cheer us?
Hunger not for where you've been,
  Stay till Spring be near us!

L. Alma Tadema

221

Cherry Tree

The Chaffinch flies fast
　　To the red cherry tree,
And sings as he goes:
　　"All for me! All for me!"

The Speckled Brown Thrush
　　Upon fluttering wing
Goes flying and scolds:
　　"Greedy thing! Greedy thing!"

The chattering Starling
　　He visits there, too,
And cries as he flies:
　　"Leave a few! Leave a few!"

But the Blackbird retreats
　　As the others advance,
And calls to them, laughing:
　　"Not a chance! Not a chance!"

Ivy O. Eastwick

The Poppies in the Garden

The poppies in the garden, they all wear frocks of silk,
Some are purple, some are pink, and others white as milk,
Light, light, for dancing in, for dancing when the breeze
Plays a little two-step for the blossoms and the bees.
Fine, fine, for dancing in, all frilly at the hem,
Oh, when I watch the poppies dance I long to dance
　　like them!

The poppies in the garden have let their silk frocks fall
All about the border paths, but where are they at all?
Here a frill and there a flounce—a rag of silky red,
But not a poppy-girl is left—I think they've gone to bed.
Gone to bed and gone to sleep; and weary they must be,
For each has left her box of dreams upon the stem for me.

ffrida Wolfe

Crocuses

A kind voice calls, "Come, little ones,
  'Tis time to wake from sleeping!"
And out of bed without a word
  The drowsy folk come creeping,
And soon above the chilly earth
  Their tiny heads are peeping.

They bravely face the wind of March,
  Its bite and bluster scorning
Like little soldiers—till, oh joy!
  With scarce a word of warning
The crocuses slip off their caps
  And give us gay good morning.

Anna M. Platt

Violets

Under the green hedges, after the snow,
There do the dear little violets grow;
Hiding their modest and beautiful heads
Under the hawthorn in soft mossy beds.

Sweet as the roses and blue as the sky,
Down there do the dear little violets lie;
Hiding their heads where they scarce may be seen,
By the leaves you may know where the violet hath been.

John Moultrie

The Beanfield

A beanfield in blossom smells as sweet
As araby, or groves of orange flowers;
Black-eyed and white, and feathered to one's feet,
How sweet they smell in morning's dewy hours.
When soothing night is left upon the flowers,
Another morn's sun shines brightly o'er the field,
And bean bloom glitters in the gems of showers,
And sweet the fragrance which the union yields
To battered footpaths crossing o'er the fields.

John Clare

From The Daisy

There is a flower, a little flower,
    With silver crest and golden eye,
That welcomes every changing hour,
    And weathers every sky.

It smiles upon the lap of May,
    To sultry August spreads its charms,
Lights pale October on his way,
    And twines December's arms.

But this bold flowerlet climbs the hill,
    Hides in the forest, haunts the glen,
Plays on the margin of the rill,
    Peeps round the fox's den.

On waste and woodland, rock and plain,
    Its humble buds unheeded rise;
The Rose has but a summer reign,
    The Daisy never dies.

James Montgomery

A Buttercup

A little yellow buttercup
    Stood laughing in the sun;
The grass all green around it,
    The summer just begun;
Its saucy little head abrim
    With happiness and fun.

Near by—grown old, and gone to seed—
    A dandelion grew;
To right and left with every breeze
    His snowy tresses flew.
He shook his hoary head, and said:
    "I've some advice for you.

"Don't think because you're yellow now
    That golden days will last;
I was as gay as you are once,
    But now my youth is past.
This day will be my last to bloom;
    The hours are going fast.

"Perhaps your fun may last a week,
    But then you'll have to die."
The dandelion ceased to speak —
    A breeze that capered by
Snatched all the white hairs from his head
    And wafted them on high.

His yellow neighbour first looked sad,
    Then, cheering up, he said:
"If one's to live in fear of death,
    One might as well be dead."
The little buttercup laughed on,
    And waved his golden head.

Buttercups and Daisies

Buttercups and daisies,
    Oh, the pretty flowers;
Coming ere the spring-time,
    To tell of sunny hours,
While the trees are leafless,
    While the fields are bare,
Buttercups and daisies
    Spring up here and there.

Ere the snowdrop peepeth,
    Ere the crocus bold,
Ere the early primrose
    Opes its paly gold —
Somewhere on the sunny bank
    Buttercups are bright;
Somewhere 'mong the frozen grass
    Peeps the daisy white.

Mary Howitt
225

Bluebells

The breeze is on the bluebells,
　　The wind is on the lea;
Stay out! Stay out! my little lad,
　　And chase the wind with me.
If you will give yourself to me
　　Within the fairy ring,
　　　At dead midnight,
　　　When stars are bright,
You'll hear the bluebells sing.

Juliana Horatia Ewing

The Dandelions

Some young and saucy dandelions
　　Stood laughing in the sun;
They were brimming full of happiness,
　　And running o'er with fun.

They stretched their necks so slender
　　To stare up to the sky;
They frolicked with the bumble-bee,
　　And teased the butterfly.

At length they saw beside them
　　A dandelion old;
His form was bent and withered,
　　Gone were his looks of gold.

"Oh, oh!" they cried, "just see him;
　　"Old greybeard, how d'ye do?
We'd hide our heads in the grasses,
　　If we were as bald as you."

So they mocked the poor old fellow,
　　Till night came on apace;
Then a cunning little green night-cap
　　Hid each tiny little face.

But lo! when dawned the morning,
   Up rose each tiny head,
Decked not with golden tresses,
   But long grey locks instead.

The Jungle Trees

The golden trees of England
   They dance on every hill.
The giants of the jungle
   Are terrible and still.

The trees that live in England
   They wave their arms about,
And little paths of greeting
   Run gaily in and out.

But trees that make the jungle
   Are fortified and great;
And he shall find no welcome
   Who enters by their gate.

And I have seen them watching,
   And I have heard them say,
"Our beasts are fierce and hungry,
   And tangled is the way;

"And when behind our branches
   Burns out the sunset flame,
No wanderer who ventures
   Returns the way he came.

"Go back where softer sunlight
   Its sprinkled shadow spills—
Where elm and fir are holding
   High welcome on the hills."

Marjorie Wilson

Poppies

The strange, bright dancers
Are in the garden.
The wind of summer
Is a soft music.
Scarlet and orange,
Flaming and golden,
The strange, bright dancers
Move to the music.
And some are whiter
Than snow in winter,
And float like snowflakes
Drifting the garden.
Oh, have you seen them,
The strange, bright dancers,
Nodding and swaying
To the wind's music?

P. A. Ropes

I Wandered Lonely

I wandered lonely as a cloud
That floats on high o'er vales and hills,
When all at once I saw a crowd,
A host of golden daffodils;
Beside the lake, beneath the trees,
Fluttering and dancing in the breeze.

Continuous as the stars that shine
And twinkle on the milky way,
They stretched in never-ending line
Along the margin of a bay:
Ten thousand saw I at a glance,
Tossing their heads in sprightly dance.

The waves beside them danced; but they
Out-did the sparkling waves in glee.
A poet could not be but gay,
In such a jocund company:
I gazed—and gazed—but little thought
What wealth the show to me had brought:

For oft, when on my couch I lie
In vacant or in pensive mood,
They flash upon that inward eye
Which is the bliss of solitude;
And then my heart with pleasure fills,
And dances with the daffodils.

William Wordsworth

The Apple Rhyme

In my garden grows a tree
Of apple-blossom, where for me
A blackbird perches every day,
Sings his song and flies away.
So since fairies make for birds
Music out of fairy words,
I have learned from it a rhyme
For folk to sing at apple-time,
Which (if you live where apples grow)
You'll find a useful thing to know.

The rhyme to be sung very slowly under an apple-tree
(in August or September).

Apples ripe and apples red,
Grow they high above my head.
Alack-a-day! for I am small
And apple-trees are mostly tall;
Dreary me! But what is sadder,
Nobody can find a ladder.
Call a pixy, green or brown,
And bid him throw the apples down.
Pixy, throw them down as quick
Or quicker than my hands could pick!
One, two, three and now another
Each one bigger than the other.
Pixies green and pixies brown,
Throw the big red apples down.

Madeleine Nightingale

The Tree

Oh, like a tree
Let me grow up to Thee!
And like a tree
Send down my roots to Thee.

Let my leaves stir
In each sigh of the air,
My branches be
Lively and glad in Thee;

Each leaf a prayer,
And green fire everywhere . . .
And all from Thee
The sap within the tree.

And let Thy rain
Fall—or as joy and pain,
So that I be
Yet unforgot of Thee.

Then shall I sing
The new song of Thy Spring,
Every leaf of me
Whispering Love in Thee.

John Freeman

Sowing Seeds

I've dug up all my garden
And got the watering pan,
And packets full of seeds I mean to sow;
I'll have marigolds and pansies,
And Canterbury bells,
And asters all set neatly in a row.
I'll have mignonette and stocks,
And some tall red hollyhocks,
If sun and rain will come to help them grow.

Ursula Cornwall

Flower Chorus

O such a commotion under the ground,
   When March called, "Ho, there! ho!"
Such spreading of rootlets far and wide,
   Such whisperings to and fro!
"Are you ready?" the Snowdrop asked,
   "'Tis time to start, you know."
"Almost, my dear!" the Scilla replied,
   "I'll follow as soon as you go."
Then "Ha! ha! ha!" a chorus came
   Of laughter sweet and slow,
From millions of flowers under the ground,
   Yes, millions beginning to grow.

"I'll promise my blossoms," the Crocus said,
   "When I hear the blackbird sing."
And straight thereafter Narcissus cried,
   "My silver and gold I'll bring."
"And ere they are dulled," another spoke,
   "The Hyacinth bells shall ring."
But the Violet only murmured, "I'm here,"
   And sweet grew the air of Spring.
Then "Ha! ha! ha!" a chorus came
   Of laughter sweet and low,
From millions of flowers under the ground,
   Yes, millions beginning to grow.

O the pretty brave things, thro' the coldest days
   Imprisoned in walls of brown,
They never lost heart tho' the blast shrieked loud,
   And the sleet and the hail came down;
But patiently each wrought her wonderful dress,
   Or fashioned her beautiful crown,
And now they are coming to lighten the world
   Still shadowed by winter's frown.
And well may they cheerily laugh "Ha! ha!"
   In laughter sweet and low,
The millions of flowers under the ground,
   Yes, millions beginning to grow.

Ralph W. Emerson

The Lamp Flower

The campion white
  Above the grass
Her lamps doth light
  Where fairies pass.

Softly they show
  The secret way,
Unflickering glow
  For elf and fay.

My little thought
  Hath donned her shoe,
And all untaught
  Gone dancing too.

Sadly I peer
  Among the grass
And seem to hear
  The fairies pass.

But where they go
  I cannot see,
Too faintly glow
  The lamps for me.

My thought is gone
  With fay and elf,
We mope alone,
  I and myself.

Margaret Cecilia Furse

Bluebells

Throughout the day our sweet bells chime
The hours of the fairy time.
At night with music soft and deep,
We lull a drowsy world to sleep.

P. A. Ropes

Fluttering Leaves

In the the Spring, on the trees
Green leaves flutter in the breeze,
Flutter, flutter, flutter, flutter,
Flutter, flutter in the breeze.

Later on, when they're brown,
Leaves go drifting slowly down,
Flutter, flutter, flutter, flutter,
Flutter, flutter slowly down.

Rodney Bennett

Trees

The Oak is called the King of Trees,
The Aspen quivers in the breeze,
The Poplar grows up straight and tall,
The Pear tree spreads along the wall,
The Sycamore gives pleasant shade,
The Willow droops in watery glade,
The Fir tree useful timber gives,
The Beech amid the forest lives.

S. Coleridge

The Forget-Me-Not

When to the flowers so beautiful
    The Father gave a name,
Back came a little blue-eyed one
    (All timidly it came);
And standing at its Father's feet,
    And gazing in His face,
It said in low and trembling tones,
    "Dear God, the name Thou gavest me,
    Alas! I have forgot."
Then kindly looked the Father down,
    And said, "Forget Me Not."

233

Song of Spring

And O and O,
The daisies blow,
And the primroses are wakened;
And the violets white
Sit in silver light,
And in the green buds are long in the spike end.

J. Keats

Snowdrops

I like to think
That, long ago,
There fell to earth
Some flakes of snow
Which loved this cold,
Grey world of ours
So much, they stayed
As snowdrop flowers.

Mary Vivian

London Trees

These trees that fling their leafy boughs aloft
In city squares
So little know of ocean-scented winds
And country airs—

And yet so green they are,
So deep a shade they swing,
And from their topmost heights
So sweet the blackbirds sing!

Here, in the city's heart,
'Neath smoke-hazed skies,
Green trees do their glad part
To lighten country-weary eyes.

Beryl Netherclift

Violets

Modestly we violets cower,
Each within a little bower,
     Cool and green.
Each contented with the hour,
Welcoming both sun and shower,
     In our leafy home unseen.

P. A. Ropes

I'd Choose to be a Daisy

I'd choose to be a daisy,
     If I might be a flower;
Closing my petals softly
     At twilight's quiet hour;
And waking in the morning,
     When falls the early dew,
To welcome Heaven's bright sunshine,
     And Heaven's bright tear-drops too.

I'd choose to be a skylark,
     If I might be a bird;
My song should be the loudest
     The sun has ever heard;
I'd wander through the cloudland,
     Far, far above the moon,
And reach right up to heaven,
     Where it is always noon.

And yet I think I'd rather
     Be changed into a lamb,
And in the fields spend pleasant days
     A-playing by my dam.
But then, you see, I cannot be
     A flower, or bird or lamb.
And why? Because I'm made to be
     The little child I am!

Heigh Ho!

Heigh ho! daisies and buttercups,
Fair yellow daffodils, stately and tall!
When the wind wakes how they rock in the grasses,
And dance with the cuckoo-buds, slender and small!
Here's two bonny boys, and here's mother's own lasses,
Eager to gather them all.

Heigh ho! daisies and buttercups:
Mother shall thread them a daisy chain;
Sing them a song of the pretty hedge-sparrow,
That loved her brown little ones, loved them full fain;
Sing, "Heart, thou art wide, though the house be but
    narrow"—
Sing once, and sing it again.

Heigh ho! daisies and buttercups,
Sweet wagging cowslips they bend and they bow;
A ship sails afar over warm ocean waters,
And haply one musing doth stand at her prow.
O bonny brown sons, and O sweet little daughters,
Maybe he thinks on you now!

Heigh ho! daisies and buttercups,
Fair yellow daffodils stately and tall;
A sunshiny world full of laughter and leisure,
And fresh hearts unconscious of sorrow and thrall;
Send down on their pleasure smiles passing its measure—
God, that is over us all.

Jean Ingelow

Pimpernel

I'm the pert little pimpernel,
Who ever so cleverly weather foretells;
If I open my eye,
There's a cloudless sky;
If I shut it again,
Then it's sure to rain.

Charlotte Druitt Cole

236

Shady Woods

When the sun is shining overhead
'Tis nice to make a leafy bed
   Deep in the shady wood;
To lie and gaze towards the sky
Peeping through the leaves on high,
   Above the shady wood.

E. M. Adams

Tall Trees

With their feet in the earth
   And their heads in the sky
The tall trees watch
   The clouds go by.

When the dusk sends quickly
   The birds to rest,
The tall trees shelter them
   Safe in a nest.

And then in the night
   With the tall trees peeping,
The moon shines down
   On a world that's sleeping.

Eileen Mathias

The Five-Fingered Maple

"Green leaves, what are you doing
Up there on the tree so high?"
"We are shaking hands with the breezes,
As they go singing by."

"What, green leaves! Have you fingers?"
Then the Maple laughed with glee:
"Yes, just as many as you have;
Count us, and you will see!"

Kate Louise Brown

237

Violets

I know, blue modest violets
  Gleaming with dew at morn—
I know the place you come from
  And the way that you are born!

When God cut holes in heaven—
  The holes the stars look through—
He let the scraps fall down to earth;
  The little scraps are you!

The Field Daisy

I'm a pretty little thing,
Always coming with the Spring;
In the meadows green I'm found,
Peeping just above the ground;
And my stalk is covered flat
With a white and yellow hat.

Little Mary, when you pass
Lightly o'er the tender grass,
Skip about, but do not tread
On my bright but lowly head;
For I always seem to say,
"Surely Winter's gone away."

Jane Taylor

Foxgloves

The foxglove bells, with lolling tongue,
Will not reveal what peals were rung
In Faery, in Faery,
A thousand ages gone.
All the golden clappers hang
As if but now the changes rang;
Only from the mottled throat
Never any echoes float.
Quite forgotten, in the wood,
Pale, crowded steeples rise;

All the time that they have stood
None has heard their melodies,
Deep, deep in wizardry
All the foxglove belfries stand.
Should they startle over the land,
None would know what bells they be.
Never any wind can ring them,
Nor the great black bees that swing them—
Every crimson bell, down-slanted,
Is so utterly enchanted.

Mary Webb

The Thief

Autumn wind came stealing
    Through the woods one day,
And, creeping round the tree, he stole
    Their beauty all away.

He tore their russet dresses,
    Combed off their golden hair;
He blew away the tattered bits—
    And left them brown and bare.

Irene F. Pawsey

Waking Up

Pretty little crocus, in your cosy bed,
Mr. Sun is calling you, won't you show your head?
Mother Earth has sheltered you all the winter through,
Now warm winds are blowing and the skies are blue.

Little baby crocus, in his earthy bed,
With the warm sun drawing him, popped out his tiny head;
Just as he was stirring underneath the ground,
Other little crocuses were looking all around.

Further down the garden, by a running brook,
Two little snowdrops thought they'd have a look;
Saw the sun was shining and the world was gay,
For into the garden Spring had come that day!

239

Poplars

Seven lovely poplars
   Swaying in the breeze,
Seven softly sighing
   Tall and slender trees.

Silver'd by the moonlight,
   Pointing to the sky:
Look! like leafy spears, they
   Hold the stars on high.

Helen Leuty

Snowdrop

Close to the sod
There can be seen
A thought of God
In white and green.
Unmarred, unsoiled,
It cleft the clay;
Serene, unspoiled,
It views the day.

It is so holy
And yet so lowly,
Would you enjoy
Its grace and dower
And not destroy
The living flower?
Then you must, please,
Fall on your knees.

Anna Bunston de Bary

Among the Nuts

A wee little nut lay deep in its nest
Of satin and down, the softest and best;
And slept and grew, while its cradle rocked,
As it hung in the boughs that interlocked.

Now the house was small where the cradle lay,
As it swung in the wind by night and day;
For a thicket of underbush fenced it round,
This little lone cot by the great sun browned.

The little nut grew, and ere long it found
There was work outside on the soft green ground;
It must do its part so the world might know
It had tried one little seed to sow.

And soon the house that had kept it warm
Was tossed about by the winter's storm;
The stem was cracked, the old house fell
And the chestnut burr was an empty shell,

But the little seed, as it waiting lay,
Dreamed a wonderful dream from day to day,
Of how it should break its coat of brown,
And live as a tree to grow up and down.

The Leaves

The leaves had a wonderful frolic,
    They danced to the wind's loud song,
They whirled, and they floated, and scampered,
    They circled and flew along.

The moon saw the little leaves dancing,
    Each looked like a small brown bird.
The man in the moon smiled and listened,
    And this is the song he heard:

The North Wind is calling, is calling,
    And we must whirl round and round,
And then when our dancing is ended
    We'll make a warm quilt for the ground.

Proud Little Spruce Fir

On a cold winter day the snow came down
　　To cover the leafless trees,
Very glad they were of a snow-white gown,
　　To keep out the chilly breeze.

But a little spruce fir, all gaily dressed
　　In tiny sharp leaves of green,
Was drooping beneath the load on its breast,
　　And not a leaf could be seen.

"I'm an evergreen tree," he proudly thought,
　　"And really they ought to know
That I'm looking my best, and care not a jot
　　How bitter the wind may blow."

Jeannie Kirby

The Acorn

In small green cup an acorn grew
　　On tall and stately oak;
The spreading leaves the secret knew,
　　And hid it like a cloak.
The breezes rocked it tenderly,
　　The sunbeams whispered low,
"Some day the smallest acorn here
　　Will make an oak, you know."

The little acorn heard it all,
　　And thought it quite a joke;
How could he dream an acorn small
　　Would ever be an oak?
He laughed so much that presently
　　He tumbled from his cup,
And rolled a long way from the tree,
　　Where no one picked him up.

Close by him was a rabbit hole,
   And when the wind blew high,
Down went the acorn with a roll
   For weeks in gloom to lie.
But, one bright day, a shoot of green
   Broke from his body dry,
And pushed its way with longing keen
   To see the glorious sky.

It grew, and grew, with all its might,
   As weeks and months rolled on:
The sunbeam's words were proving right.
   For, ere a year had gone,
The shoot became a sturdy plant,
   While now the country folk
Can sit beneath the spreading leaves
   Of a mighty forest oak.

Leaves

Myriads and myriads plumed their glittering wings,
As fine as any bird that soars and sings,
As bright as fireflies or the dragon-flies
Or birds of paradise.

Myriads and myriads waved their sheeny fans,
Soft as the dove's breast, or the pelican's;
And some were gold, and some were green, and some
Pink-lipped, like apple-bloom.

A low wind tossed the plumage all one way,
Rippled the gold feathers, and green and gray—
A low wind that in moving sang one song
All day and all night long.

Some trees hung lanterns out, and some had stars
Silver as Hesper, and rose-red as Mars;
A low wind flung the lanterns low and high—
A low wind like a sigh.

Katharine Tynan

Apple Harvest

O down in the orchard
　'Tis harvesting time,
And up the tall ladders
　The fruit pickers climb.

Among the green branches
　That sway overhead
The apples are hanging
　All rosy and red.

Just ripe for the picking,
　All juicy and sweet!
So pretty to look at
　And lovely to eat!

Helen Leuty

Chestnut Buds

I have a mackintosh shiny brown,
To keep me warm when the rain pours down,
And the baby buds on the chestnut tree
Have shiny brown coverings, just like me.
For they've waited all through the frost and snow
For the Spring to come and the Winter to go;
That's why they've wrapped up so cosily,
Those little brown buds on the chestnut tree.

Evelyn M. Williams

Leaves

Leaves are always beautiful, I think.
At first they part their baby lips to drink
The rain in Spring, then open wider still,
Hungry for sweet winds and the sun, until
They lift their faces to the Summer rain,
Whose heavy drops pit-patter loud and plain.
The Autumn comes upon them and they change,
Decked out in glorious colours, rich and strange.
Then in the Winter they come flying down
Light as a breath, and crisp, and brown.
They fly before the wind like little elves,
And oh, I know they must enjoy themselves.

J. M. Westrup

244

The Lavender Bush

At her doorway Mrs. Mayle
Grows a bush of lavender.
Large, and round, and silver-pale,
Where the blooms, a misty blur,
Lift their purple spikes on high,
Loved of butterflies and moths,
And on these, to bleach and dry,
Mrs. Mayle spreads little cloths.

Tray cloths, mats of cobweb-weave,
All of them too fairy-fine
For a careful soul to leave
Dangling on a washing-line,
Mrs. Mayle lays softly there
Till she brings them in once more,
Sweet with blossom-scented air,
From the bush beside the door.

Elizabeth Fleming

The Secret Joy

Face to face with the sunflower,
Cheek to cheek with the rose,
We follow a secret highway
Hardly a traveller knows.
The gold that lies in the folded bloom
Is all our wealth;
We eat of the heart of the forest
With innocent stealth.
We know the ancient roads
In the leaf of a nettle,
And bathe in the blue profound
Of a speedwell petal.

Mary Webb

Out and About

is good to be out on the road, and going one knows not where

Leisure

What is this life if, full of care,
We have no time to stand and stare?

No time to stand beneath the boughs
And stare as long as sheep or cows.

No time to see, when woods we pass,
Where squirrels hide their nuts in grass.

No time to see, in broad daylight,
Streams full of stars, like skies at night.

No time to turn at Beauty's glance,
And watch her feet, how they can dance.

No time to wait till her mouth can
Enrich that smile her eyes began.

A poor life this if, full of care,
We have no time to stand and stare.

W. H. Davies

The Song of a Traveller

I will make you brooches and toys for your delight
Of bird-song at morning and star-shine at night.
I will make a palace fit for you and me
Of green days in forests and blue days at sea.

I will make my kitchen, and you shall keep your room,
Where white flows the river and bright blows the broom,
And you shall wash your linen and keep your body white
In rainfall at morning and dewfall at night.

And this shall be for music when no one else is near,
The fine song for singing, the rare song to hear!
That only I remember, that only you admire,
Of the broad road that stretches and the roadside fire.

Robert Louis Stevenson

Puppy and I

I met a Man as I went walking;
We got talking,
Man and I.
"Where are you going to, Man?" I said
   (I said to the Man as he went by).
"Down to the village, to get some bread.
   Will you come with me?" "No, not I."

I met a Horse as I went walking;
We got talking,
Horse and I.
"Where are you going to, Horse, to-day?"
   (I said to the Horse as he went by).
"Down to the village to get some hay.
   Will you come with me?" "No, not I."

I met a Woman, as I went walking;
We got talking,
Woman and I.
"Where are you going to, Woman, so early?"
   (I said to the Woman as she went by).
"Down to the village to get some barley.
   Will you come with me?" "No, not I."

I met some Rabbits as I went walking;
We got talking,
Rabbits and I.
"Where are you going in your brown fur coats?"
   (I said to the Rabbits as they went by).
"Down to the village to get some oats.
   Will you come with us?" "No, not I."

I met a Puppy as I went walking;
We got talking,
Puppy and I.
"Where are you going this nice fine day?"
   (I said to the Puppy as he went by).
"Up in the hills to roll and play."
   "I'll come with you, Puppy," said I.

A. A. Milne

When Mary Goes Walking

When Mary goes walking
 The autumn winds blow,
The poplars they curtsey,
 The larches bend low;
The oaks and the beeches
 Their gold they fling down,
To make her a carpet,
 To make her a crown.

Patrick R. Chalmers

Tewkesbury Road

It is good to be out on the road, and going one knows not
 where,
 Going through meadow and village, one knows not
 whither nor why;
Through the grey light drift of the dust, in the keen cool
 rush of the air.
 Under the flying white clouds, and the broad blue lift of
 the sky.

And to halt at the chattering brook, in the tall green fern
 at the brink
 Where the harebell grows, and the gorse, and the
 foxgloves purple and white;
Where the shy-eyed delicate deer come down in a troop
 to drink
 When the stars are mellow and large at the coming on
 of the night.

O, to feel the beat of the rain, and the homely smell of the
 earth,
 Is a tune for the blood to jig to, a joy past power of
 words;
And the blessed green comely meadows are all a-ripple
 with mirth
 At the noise of the lambs at play and the dear wild cry
 of the birds.

John Masefield

Pedlar Jim

A dusty road is mine to tread,
From grey of dawn to sunset red,
    And slow my pace because, alack!
    I've all my wealth upon my back.

'Tis honest toil for homely fare,
A penny here, a sixpence there,
    Or maybe, on my lucky days,
    A seat beside the good wife's blaze.

With fairy tales and legends gay
I cheer the lasses when I may,
    And oft the little children cry,
    "Be sure to call as you pass by."

Florence Hoare

Weathers

This is the weather the cuckoo likes,
    And so do I:
When showers betumble the chestnut spikes,
    And nestlings fly;
And the little brown nightingale bills his best,
And they sit outside at "The Travellers' Rest,"
And maids come forth sprig-muslin drest,
And citizens dream of the south and west,
    And so do I.

This is the weather the shepherd shuns,
    And so do I;
When beeches drip in browns and duns,
    And thresh, and ply;
And hill-hid tides throb, throe on throe,
And meadows rivulets overflow,
And drops on gate-bars hang in a row,
And rooks in families homeward go,
    And so do I.

Thomas Hardy

The Night

In a scented wood
    An owl is calling;
O'er the resting land
    The night is falling;
The air is sweet
    With the scent of may;
The birds are asleep,
    They are waiting for day.

In the purple night
    No light is showing;
O'er the silent land
    A breeze is blowing,
It rustles the leaves
    With a soft little sigh;
The owl is so still,
    Then gives, softly, a cry.

Helen Leuty

The Road to Town

The road to town goes up and down,
    The road to the sea is winding,
With a follow me Jack, and a follow me Jill,
And jiggetty, joggetty over the hill,
    And a follow me over the down, O!

The road to town is easily found,
    The other takes some finding,
With a follow me Jack, and a follow me Jill,
And jiggetty, joggetty over the hill,
    And a follow me over the down, O!

The road to town is broad and fair,
    The road to the sea is shady,
With a follow me Jack, and a follow me Jill,
And jiggetty, joggetty over the hill,
    And a follow me over the down, O!

H. M. Sarson

Sunset

The summer sun is sinking low;
  Only the tree-tops redden and glow;
Only the weather-cock on the spire
Of the village church is a flame of fire;
  All is in shadow below.

H. W. Longfellow

Evening

She sweeps with many-coloured brooms,
And leaves the shreds behind;
Oh, housewife in the evening west,
Come back, and dust the pond!

You dropped a purple ravelling in,
You dropped an amber thread;
And now you've littered all the East
With duds of emerald!

And still she plies her spotted brooms,
And still the aprons fly,
Till brooms fade softly into stars—
And then I come away.

Emily Dickinson

The Silver Road

Last night I saw a Silver Road
  Go straight across the Sea;
And quick as I raced along the Shore,
  That quick Road followed me.

It followed me all round the Bay,
  Where small Waves danced in tune;
And at the end of the Silver Road
  There hung a Silver Moon.

A large round Moon on a pale green Sky,
  With a Pathway bright and broad;
Some night I shall bring that Silver Moon
  Across that Silver Road!

Hamish Hendry

253

The Early Morning

The moon on the one hand, the dawn on the other:
The moon is my sister, the dawn is my brother.
The moon on my left and the dawn on my right.
My brother, good morning: my sister, good night.

H. Belloc

To Senaca Lake

On thy fair bosom, silver lake,
   The wild swan spreads his snowy sail,
And round his breast the ripples break,
   As down he bears before the gale.

On thy fair bosom, waveless stream,
   The dippling paddle echoes far,
And flashes in the moonlight gleam,
   And bright reflects the polar star.

The waves along thy pebble shore,
   As blows the north-wind, heave their foam,
And curl around the dashing oar,
   As late the boatman hies him home.

How sweet, at set of sun, to view
   Thy golden mirror spreading wide,
And see the mist of mantling blue
   Float round the distant mountain's side.

At midnight hour, as shines the moon,
   A sheet of silver spreads below,
And swift she cuts, at highest noon,
   Light clouds, like wreaths of purest snow.

On thy fair bosom, silver lake!
   O, I could ever sweep the oar,
When early birds at morning wake,
   And evening tells us toil is o'er.

J. G. Percival

Night

The sun descending in the west,
　The evening star does shine,
The birds are silent in their nest,
　And I must seek for mine.
　　The moon, like a flower,
　　In heaven's high bower,
　　With silent delight
　　Sits and smiles on the night.

William Blake

The Moon

The moon was but a chin of gold
　A night or two ago,
And now she turns her perfect face
　Upon the world below.

Her forehead is of amplest blond;
　Her cheek like beryl stone;
Her eye unto the summer dew
　The likest I have known.

Her lips of amber never part;
　But what must be the smile
Upon her friend she could bestow
　Were such her silver will!

And what a privilege to be
　But the remotest star!
For certainly her way might pass
　Beside your twinkling door.

Her bonnet is the firmament,
　The universe her shoe,
The stars the trinkets at her belt,
　Her dimities of blue.

Emily Dickinson

Travellers

Come, let us go a-roaming!
  The world is all our own,
And half its paths are still untrod,
  And half its joys unknown.

The way that leads to winter
  Will lead to summer too,
For all roads end in other roads
  Where we may start anew.

Arthur St. John Adcock

The Traveller's Return

Sweet to the morning traveller
  The song amid the sky,
Where, twinkling in the dewy light,
  The skylark soars on high.

And cheering to the traveller
  The gales that round him play,
When faint and heavily he drags
  Along his noontide way.

And when beneath the unclouded sun
  Full wearily toils he,
The flowing water makes to him
  A soothing melody.

And when the evening light decays.
  And all is calm around,
There is sweet music to the ear
  In the distant sheep-bell's sound.

But, oh! of all delightful sounds
  Of evening or of morn,
The sweetest is the voice of Love
  That welcomes his return.

Sweet Surprises

A dance of blue-bells in the shady places;
  A crimson flush of sunset in the west;
The cobwebs, delicate as fairy laces:
  The sudden finding of a wood-bird's nest.

S. Doudney

Roadways

One road leads to London,
  One road runs to Wales,
My road leads me seawards
  To the white dipping sails.

One road leads to the river,
  As it goes singing slow;
My road leads to shipping,
  Where the bronzed sailors go.

Leads me, lures me, calls me
  To salt, green, tossing sea;
A road without earth's road-dust
  Is the right road for me.

A wet road, heaving, shining,
  And wild with seagulls' cries,
A mad salt sea-wind blowing
  The salt spray in my eyes.

My road calls me, lures me
  West, east, south, and north;
Most roads lead men homewards,
  My road leads me forth.

To add more miles to the tally
  Of grey miles left behind,
In quest of that one beauty
  God put me here to find.

John Masefield

The Fountain

Into the sunshine, full of light,
Leaping and flashing from morn till night;
Into the moonlight, whiter than snow,
Waving so flower-like when the winds blow.
Into the starlight, rushing in spray,
Happy at midnight, happy by day;
Ever in motion, blithesome and cheery,
Still climbing heavenwards, never aweary.
Glad of all weathers, still seeming best,
Upward or downward motion thy rest;
Ceaseless aspiring, ceaseless content,
Darkness or sunshine thy element;
Full of nature nothing can tame,
Changed every moment, ever the same:
Glorious fountain! let my heart be
Fresh, changeful, constant, upward, like thee!

James Russell Lowell

The Rain

I hear leaves drinking Rain;
    I hear rich leaves on top
Giving the poor beneath
    Drop after drop;
'Tis a sweet noise to hear
These green leaves drinking near.

And when the Sun comes out,
    After this Rain shall stop,
A wondrous Light will fill
    Each dark, round drop;
I hope the Sun shines bright:
'Twill be a lovely sight.

W. H. Davies

There—

If I could climb the garden wall
I'd see an elm tree green and tall.
If I could climb the green elm tree,
A grand and grassy hill I'd see.
If I could climb the grassy hill,
I'd see a mountain larger still.
If I could climb the mountain steep,
I'd see the ocean broad and deep
With great ships sailing from the bay
To foreign countries far away.

Rodney Bennett

And Back

Then, when I'd seen them leave the bay
For those strange countries far away,
If on the sea I turned my back
And faced the dizzy mountain track,
I'd see a rather little hill,
And then an elm tree smaller still,
And last, and furthest off of all,
A tiny speck—the garden wall.

Rodney Bennett

It Is a Pleasant Day

Everything is laughing, singing,
All the pretty flowers are springing;
See the kitten, full of fun,
Sporting in the brilliant sun;
Children too may sport and play.
For it is a pleasant day.

Bring the hoop, and bring the ball,
Come with happy faces all;
Let us make a merry ring,
Talk and laugh and dance and sing.
Quickly, quickly, come away,
For it is a pleasant day.

The Wood of Flowers

I went to the Wood of Flowers,
    (No one was with me)
I was there alone for hours;
    I was as happy as could be
In the Wood of Flowers.

There was grass on the ground,
    There were buds on the tree,
And the wind had a sound
    Of such gaiety,
That I was as happy,
    As happy could be,
In the Wood of Flowers.

James Stephens

Day and Night

When the bright eyes of the day
    Open on the dusk, to see
Mist and shadow fade away
    And the sun shine merrily,
Then I leave my bed and run
Out to frolic in the sun.

Through the sunny hours I play
    Where the stream is wandering,
Plucking daisies by the way;
    And I laugh and dance and sing,
While the birds fly here and there
Singing on the sunny air.

When the night comes, cold and slow,
    And the sad moon walks the sky;
When the whispering wind says "Boh,
    Little boy!" and makes me cry,
By my mother I am led
Home again and put to bed.

James Stephens

The Upper Skies

The upper skies are palest blue,
    Mottled with pearl and fretted snow:
With tattered fleece of inky hue
    Close overhead the storm-clouds go.

Their shadows fly along the hill
    And o'er the crest mount one by one,
The whitened planking of the mill
    Is now in shade and now in sun.

Robert Bridges

The Pedlar's Caravan

I wish I lived in a caravan,
With a horse to drive, like a pedlar-man!
Where he comes from nobody knows,
Nor where he goes to, but on he goes.

His caravan has windows two,
With a chimney of tin that the smoke comes through,
He has a wife, and a baby brown,
And they go riding from town to town.

Chairs to mend and delf to sell—
He clashes the basins like a bell.
Tea-trays, baskets, ranged in order,
Plates, with the alphabet round the border.

The roads are brown, and the sea is green,
But his house is just like a bathing-machine.
The world is round, but he can ride,
Rumble, and splash to the other side.

With the pedlar-man I should like to roam,
And write a book when I come home.
All the people would read my book,
Just like the Travels of Captain Cook.

W. B. Rands
261

Go Out

Go out
When the wind's about;
Let him buffet you
Inside out.

Go out
In a rainy drizzle;
Never sit by the fire
To sizzle.

Go out
When the snowflakes play;
Toss them about
On the white highway.

Go out
And stay till night;
When the sun is shedding
Its golden light.

Eileen Mathias

Pine Music

Last night, within my dreaming,
  There somehow came to me
The faint and fairy music
  Of the far-off, singing sea.

This morning, 'neath the pine tree,
  I heard that song once more;
And I seemed to see the billows,
  As they broke against the shore.

O wandering summer breezes!
  The pine harps touch again
For the child who loves the ocean,
  And longs for it in vain.

Kate Louise Brown

Madrigal

Sister, awake, close not your eyes,
    The day her light discloses;
And the bright morning doth arise
    Out of her bed of roses.

See, the dear sun, the world's bright eye
    In at our windows peeping;
Lo! how he blushes to espy
    Us idle wenches, sleeping.

Therefore awake, make haste, I say,
    And let us without staying,
All in our gowns of green so gay,
    Into the park a-maying.

Lady Moon

Lady Moon, Lady Moon, where are you roving?
    Over the sea.
Lady Moon, Lady Moon, whom are you loving?
    All that love me.

Are you not tired with rolling, and never
    Resting to sleep?
Why look so pale and sad, as forever
    Wishing to weep?

Ask me not this, little child, if you love me:
    You are too bold;
I must obey my dear Father above me,
    And do as I'm told.

Lady Moon, Lady Moon, where are you roving?
    Over the sea.
Lady Moon, Lady Moon, whom are you loving?
    All that love me.

Lord Houghton

Half Holiday

What shall I do this afternoon?
Shall I go down to the river soon?
Or to the field where kingcups grow?
Or sail my kite if the breezes blow?

What shall I do that's best of all?
And shall I take my ship or ball?
For there are plenty of things to do,
The sunbeams dance and skies are blue.

P'r'aps I might hear the cuckoo sing,
Or find a new-grown fairy ring,
I saw a squirrel once over the hill,
P'r'aps he'd come out if I sat still.

What shall I do? Where shall I go?
See how the yellow gorse is a-glow,
All things are lovely that I see,
I'll follow this happy bumble-bee.

Olive Enoch

Up, Up! Ye Dames and Lasses Gay

Up, up! ye dames and lasses gay!
To the meadows trip away.
'Tis you must tend the flocks this morn,
And scare the small birds from the corn,
  Not a soul at home must stay:
  For the shepherds must go
  With lance and bow
To hunt the wolf in the woods to-day.

Leave the hearth and leave the house
To the cricket and the mouse;
Find grannam out a sunny seat,
With babe and lambkin at her feet.
  Not a soul at home may stay:
  For the shepherds must go
  With lance and bow
To hunt the wolf in the woods to-day.

Samuel Taylor Coleridge

I Must Away

I know the hedge in Briar Lane
Is white with hawthorn snow again,
And scented in the summer rain.

I know that at this very hour
The lovely lilac is in flower;
Laburnum, too, a golden shower.

The Days pass—each a precious link
In summer's chain; and oh, to think
Of orchards dressed in white and pink.

The little lambs are out to play,
The countryside keeps holiday,
The birds have never been so gay.

Because the town is smoked and grey—
Good-bye! I cannot stay.

May Sarson

The Meadows

We'll go to the meadows, where cowslips do grow,
    And buttercups, looking as yellow as gold;
And daisies and violets beginning to blow;
    For it is a most beautiful sight to behold.

The little bee humming about them is seen,
    The butterfly merrily dances along;
The grasshopper chirps in the hedges so green,
    And the linnet is singing his liveliest song.

The birds and the insects are happy and gay,
    The beasts of the field they are glad and rejoice,
And we will be thankful to God every day,
    And praise His great name in a loftier voice.

He made the green meadows, He planted the flowers.
    He sent His bright sun in the heavens to blaze;
He created these wonderful bodies of ours,
    And as long as we live we will sing of His praise.

Jane and Ann Taylor

265

I Wonder

I wonder why the grass is green,
And why the wind is never seen?

Who taught the birds to build a nest,
And told the trees to take a rest?

O, when the moon is not quite round,
Where can the missing bit be found?

Who lights the stars, when they blow out,
And makes the lightning flash about?

Who paints the rainbow in the sky,
And hangs the fluffy clouds so high?

Why is it now, do you suppose,
That Dad won't tell me, if he knows?

Jeannie Kirby

Such a Blustery Day!

A merry wind danced over the hill,
    A madcap wind,
He shook the daffodil's golden crown,
And ruffled the clover's creamy gown;
Then off he sped, with a laughing shout,
To blow the hurrying clouds about,
And bustling back to earth again
He blew my bonnet all down the lane;

Then he hid behind a tree,
And pounced on me,

He blew me behind,
He blew me before,
He blew me right through the schoolroom door.

Elizabeth Gould

A Sussex Legend

Above the place where children play
A window opens, far away,
For God to hear the happy noise
Made by His little girls and boys.

Charles Dalmon

Madrigal

Come let's begin to revel 't out,
And tread the hills and dales about,
That hills and dales and woods may sound
An echo to this warbling sound:
Fa la la la.

Lads merry be with music sweet,
And Fairies trip it with your feet,
Pan's pipe is dull; a better strain
Doth stretch itself to please your vein:
Fa la la la.

South Wind

Where have you been, South Wind, this May-day morning?
With larks aloft, or skimming with the swallow,
Or with blackbirds in a green sun-glinted thicket?

O, I heard you like a tyrant in the valley,
Your ruffian haste shook the young-blossoming orchards;
You clapped rude hands, hallooing round the chimney
And white your pennons streamed along the river.

You have robbed the bee, South Wind, in your adventure,
Blustering with gentle flowers; but I forgave you
When you stole to me shyly with scent of hawthorn.

Siegfried Sassoon

The Wind In The Grass

The green grass is bowing,
   The morning wind is in it,
'Tis a tune worth thy knowing,
   Though it change every minute.

Ralph W. Emerson

Morning

The little red lark
   Arises with dawn,
And soars to the skies
   From her nest on the lawn.

But the little brown thrush,
   When morning is red,
He flies to our casement,
   And pops in his head.

"Get up, lazy bones!
   Here's your shift! There's your smock!
Get up now. Get up,
   For it's past eight o'clock!"

Ivy O. Eastwick

Come Unto These Yellow Sands

Come unto these yellow sands,
   And then take hands:
Curtsied when you have, and kiss'd,
   The wild waves whist,
Foot it neatly here and there;
   And, sweet sprites, the burthen bear.
     Hark, hark!
     Bow, wow,
   The watch-dogs bark;
     Bow, wow,
   Hark, hark! I hear
The strain of strutting chanticleer
Cry, Cock-a-diddle-dow!

Shakespeare

There Isn't Time

There isn't time, there isn't time
  To do the things I want to do—
With all the mountain tops to climb
  And all the woods to wander through
And all the seas to sail upon,
  And everywhere there is to go,
And all the people, every one,
  Who live upon the earth to know.
There's only time, there's only time
  To know a few, and do a few,
And then sit down and make a rhyme
  About the rest I want to do.

Eleanor Farjeon

In The Woods

Oh where have you been all the day
That you have been so long away?
Oh, I have been a woodland child,
And walked alone in places wild,
Bright eyes peered at me everywhere,
And voices filled the evening air;
All sounds of furred and feathered things,
The footfall soft, the whirr of wings.
Oh, I have seen grey squirrels play
At hide-and-seek the live-long day;
And baby rabbits full of fun
Poked out their noses in the sun,
And, unafraid, played there with me
In that still place of greenery.
A thousand secrets I have heard
From every lovely feathered bird;
The little red and yellow leaves
Danced round me in the autumn breeze,
In merry frolic to and fro,
As if they would not let me go.
How can I stay in this full town,
When those far woods are green and brown?

Dorothy Baker

O Wind, Where Have you Been?

O wind, where have you been,
  That you blow so sweet?
Among the violets
  Which blossom at your feet.

The honeysuckle waits
  For Summer and for heat;
But violets in the chilly Spring
  Make the turf so sweet.

Christina Rossetti

Sun and Moon

The moon shines clear as silver,
  The sun shines bright like gold,
And both are very lovely,
  And very, very old.

God hung them up as lanterns,
  For all beneath the sky;
And nobody can blow them out,
  For they are up too high.

Charlotte Druitt Cole

Laughing Song

When the green woods laugh with the voice of joy,
And the dimpling stream runs laughing by;
When the air does laugh with our merry wit,
And the green hill laughs with the noise of it;

When the meadows laugh with lively green,
And the grasshopper laughs in the merry scene;
When Mary, and Susan, and Emily
With their sweet round mouths sing, "Ha, ha, he!"

When the painted birds laugh in the shade,
When our table with cherries and nuts is spread:
Come live, and be merry, and join with me,
To sing the sweet chorus of "Ha, ha, he!"

William Blake

270

Wild Thyme

On the high hill pastures
　The west wind blows,
And little ones are dancing
　Where wild thyme grows.

Children and fairies
　Have dreams to keep,
Where wild thyme blossoms
　And old folk sleep.

Joyce Sambrook

Pebbles

Pebbles, pebbles, pebbles,
　For miles and miles and miles:
A sloping bank of pebbles
　Round all the British Isles.

Grinding, grinding, grinding,
　Where the heavy billows pound,
Till they are smooth as marbles,
　And often just as round.

White ones, grey ones, brown ones,
　Lime and slate and quartz;
Yellow ones and pink ones,
　Pebbles of all sorts.

Tinkle, tinkle, tinkle,
　How strange it is to think
That after all these ages
　In my tin pail they clink.

Jewels, jewels, jewels
　For every child like me.
Oh, how I love the pebbles,
　Beside the sounding sea.

Edith King

The Sound of the Wind

The wind has such a rainy sound
  Moaning through the town,
The sea has such a windy sound—
  Will the ships go down?

The apples in the orchard
  Tumble from the tree.
Oh, will the ships go down, go down,
  In the windy sea?

Christina Rossetti

The Night Sky

All day long
  The sun shines bright.
The moon and stars
  Come out by night.
From twilight time
  They line the skies
And watch the world
  With quiet eyes.

The Wind

I saw you toss the kites on high
And blow the birds about the sky;
And all around I heard you pass,
Like ladies' skirts across the grass—
  O wind, a-blowing all day long,
  O wind, that sings so loud a song!

I saw the different things you did,
But always you yourself you hid.
I felt you push, I heard you call,
I could not see yourself at all—
  O wind, a-blowing all day long,
  O wind, that sings so loud a song!

O you that are so strong and cold,
O blower, are you young or old?
Are you a beast of field and tree,
Or just a stronger child than me?
  O wind, a-blowing all day long,
  O wind, that sings so loud a song!

Robert Louis Stevenson

Hay Harvest

I met a man mowing
  A meadow of hay;
So smoothly and flowing
  His swathes fell away,
    At break of the day
    Up Hambleden way;
A yellow-eyed collie
  Was guarding his coat—
Loose-limbed and lob-lolly,
  But wise and remote.

The morning came leaping—
  'Twas five o' the clock,
The world was still sleeping
  At Hambleden Lock—
    As sound as a rock
    Slept village and Lock;
"Fine morning!" the man says,
  And I says: "Fine day!"
Then I to my fancies
  And he to his hay!

And lovely and quiet
  And lonely and chill,
Lay river and eyot,
  And meadow and mill;
    I think of them still—
    Mead, river, and mill;
For wasn't it jolly
  With only us three—
The yellow-eyed collie,
  The mower and me?

Patrick R. Chalmers

The Brook

I come from haunts of coot and hern,
   I make a sudden sally,
And sparkle out among the fern,
   To bicker down a valley.

By thirty hills I hurry down,
   Or slip between the ridges,
By twenty thorps, a little town,
   And half a hundred bridges.

I chatter over stony ways,
   In little sharps and trebles,
I bubble into eddying bays,
   I babble on the pebbles.

With many a curve my banks I fret
   By many a field and fallow,
And many a fairy foreland set
   With willow-weed and mallow.

I chatter, chatter, as I flow
   To join the brimming river,
For men may come and men may go,
   But I go on for ever.

I wind about, and in and out,
   With here a blossom sailing,
And here and there a lusty trout,
   And here and there a grayling.

And here and there a foamy flake
   Upon me, as I travel
With many a silvery waterbreak
   Above the golden gravel,

And draw them all along, and flow
   To join the brimming river,
For men may come and men may go,
   But I go on for ever.

I slip, I slide, I gloom, I glance,
   Among my skimming swallows;
I make the netted sunbeam dance
   Against my sandy shallows.

I murmur under moon and stars
   In brambly wildernesses;
I linger by my shingly bars;
   I loiter round my cresses;

And out again I curve and flow
   To join the brimming river,
For men may come and men may go,
   But I go on for ever.

Lord Tennyson

Day

"I am busy," said the sea.
"I am busy. Think of me,
Making continents to be.
I am busy," said the sea.

"I am busy," said the rain.
"When I fall, it's not in vain;
Wait and you will see the grain.
I am busy," said the rain.

"I am busy," said the air.
"Blowing here and blowing there,
Up and down and everywhere.
I am busy," said the air.

"I am busy," said the sun,
"All my planets, every one,
Know my work is never done.
I am busy," said the sun.

Sea and rain and air and sun,
Here's a fellow toiler:—one
Whose task will soon be done.

Sir Cecil Spring-Rice

On a Dark Road

Her eyes the glow-worm lend thee,
The shooting stars attend thee,
    And the elves also,
    Whose little eyes glow
Like the sparks of fire, befriend thee.

No will-o'-the-wisp mislight thee,
Nor snake or slow-worm bite thee;
    But on, on thy way,
    Not making a stay
Since ghost there's none to affright thee.

Let not the dark thee cumber
What though the moon does slumber!
    The stars of the night
    Will lend thee their light
Like tapers clear, without number.

Robert Herrick

Night

The sun that shines all day so bright,
I wonder where he goes at night.
He sinks behind a distant hill
And all the world grows dark and still,
And then I go to bed and sleep
Until the day begins to peep.
And when my eyes unclose, I see
The sun is shining down on me.

While we are fast asleep in bed
The sun must go, I've heard it said,
To other countries far away,
To make them warm and bright and gay.
I do not know—but hope the sun,
When all his nightly work is done,
Will not forget to come again
And wake me through the window-pane.

Pippa's Song

The year's at the spring;
The day's at the morn;
Morning's at seven;
The hill-side's dew-pearled;
The lark's on the wing;
The snail's on the thorn;
God's in His heaven—
All's right with the world!

Robert Browning

The Song of the Grass

Here I come creeping, creeping everywhere;
By the dusty road-side,
On the sunny hill-side,
Close by the noisy brook,
In every shady nook,
I come creeping, creeping everywhere.

Here I come creeping, creeping everywhere;
All around the open door,
Where sit the aged poor,
Here where the children play,
In the bright and merry May,
I come creeping, creeping everywhere.

Here I come creeping, creeping everywhere;
You cannot see me coming,
Nor hear my low, sweet humming;
For in the starry night,
And the glad morning light,
I come quietly creeping everywhere.

Here I come creeping, creeping everywhere;
More welcome than the flowers,
In Summer's pleasant hours;
The gentle cow is glad,
And the merry bird not sad,
To see me creeping, creeping everywhere.

Leigh Hunt

Song

A sunny shaft did I behold,
 From sky to earth it slanted;
And poised therein a bird so bold—
 Sweet bird, thou wert enchanted!

He sank, he rose, he twinkled, he trolled
 Within that shaft of sunny mist;
His eyes of fire, his beak of gold,
 All else of amethyst!

S. T. Coleridge

Rain in Summer

How beautiful is the rain!
After the dust and heat,
In the broad and fiery street,
In the narrow lane,
How beautiful is the rain!

How it clatters along the roofs,
Like the tramp of hoofs!
How it gushes and struggles out
From the throat of the overflowing spout!
Across the window pane
It pours and pours;
And swift and wide,
With a muddy tide,
Like a river down the gutter roars
The rain, the welcome rain!

H. W. Longfellow

The City Child

Dainty little maiden, whither would you wander?
 Whither from this pretty home, the home where mother
  dwells?
"Far and far away," said the dainty little maiden,
 "All among the gardens, auriculas, anemones,
 Roses and lilies and Canterbury-bells."

Dainty little maiden, whither would you wander?
  Whither from this pretty house, this city-house of ours?
"Far and far away," said the dainty little maiden,
  "All among the meadows, the clover and the clematis,
  Daisies and kingcups and honeysuckle-flowers."

Lord Tennyson

The Scarecrow

A scarecrow stood in a field one day,
    Stuffed with straw,
    Stuffed with hay;
He watched the folk on the king's highway,
    But never a word said he.

Much he saw, but naught did heed,
    Knowing not night,
    Knowing not day,
For, having nought, did nothing need,
    And never a word said he.

A little grey mouse had made its nest,
    Oh so wee,
    Oh so grey,
In a sleeve of a coat that was poor Tom's best,
    But the scarecrow naught said he.

His hat was the home of a small jenny wren,
    Ever so sweet,
    Ever so gay,
A squirrel had put by his fear of men,
    And kissed him, but naught heeded he.

Ragged old man, I loved him well,
    Stuffed with straw,
    Stuffed with hay,
Many's the tale that he could tell,
    But never a word says he.

Michael Franklin

The Rivals

I heard a bird at dawn
  Singing sweetly on a tree,
That the dew was on the lawn,
  And the wind was on the lea;
But I didn't listen to him,
  For he didn't sing to me!

I didn't listen to him,
  For he didn't sing to me
That the dew was on the lawn,
  And the wind was on the lea!
I was singing at the time,
  Just as prettily as he!

I was singing all the time,
  Just as prettily as he,
About the dew upon the lawn,
  And the wind upon the lea!
So I didn't listen to him,
  As he sang upon a tree!

James Stephens

Silver

Slowly, silently, now the moon
Walks the night in her silver shoon;
This way, and that, she peers, and sees
Silver fruit upon silver trees;
One by one the casements catch
Her beams beneath the silvery thatch;
Couched in his kennel, like a log,
With paws of silver sleeps the dog;
From their shadowy cote the white breasts peep
Of doves in a silver-feathered sleep;
A harvest mouse goes scampering by,
With silver claws, and silver eye;
And moveless fish in the water gleam,
By silver reeds in a silver stream.

Walter de la Mare

Is the Moon Tired?

Is the moon tired? She looks so pale
Within her misty veil;
She scales the sky from east to west,
And takes no rest.

Before the coming of the night
The moon shows papery white;
Before the dawning of the day,
She fades away.

Christina Rossetti

The Aeroplane

Look at the aeroplane
   Up in the sky,
Seems like a giant lark
   Soaring on high.

See! on its outspread wing
   Flashes the light;
There sits the pilot brave,
   Guiding its flight.

Hark! what a whirring song
   Comes from its throat,
Purr, purr of the engine,
   Its only note.

Now! high and higher yet,
   Upward it goes,
Till but a tiny speck
   'Gainst heaven it shows.

Oh! here it is again,
   Big as before,
Gracefully gliding down
   To earth once more.

Jeannie Kirby

The Little Moon

The night is come, but not too soon,
And sinking silently,
All silently, the little moon
Drops down behind the sky.

H. W. Longfellow

Swinging

Slowly, slowly, swinging low,
Let me see how far I go!
Slowly, slowly, keeping low,
I see where the wild flowers grow!

(Getting quicker):
Quicker, quicker,
Swinging higher,
I can see
A shining spire!
Quicker, quicker,
Swinging higher,
I can see
The sunset's fire!

Faster, faster,
Through the air,
I see almost
Everywhere.
Woods and hills,
And sheep that stare—
And things I never
Knew were there!

(Getting slower):
Slower, slower, now I go,
Swinging, dreaming, getting low;
Slowly, slowly, down I go—
Till I touch the grass below.

Irene Thompson

Under the Greenwood Tree

Under the greenwood tree
Who loves to lie with me,
And tune his merry note
Unto the sweet bird's throat,
Come hither, come hither, come hither;
Here shall he see
No enemy
But Winter and rough weather.

Who doth ambition shun
And loves to live i' the sun,
Seeking the food he eats,
And pleas'd with what he gets,
Come hither, come hither, come hither;
Here shall he see
No enemy
But Winter and rough weather.

Shakespeare

Midsummer Moon

When the woods are green again
With summer suns and gentle rain,
When birds do pipe their sweet refrain
With bees in chorus droning,
When the heat of day is o'er,
And human voice is heard no more,
The evening sounds begin to soar,
An echo sweet intoning.

When upon the hush of night,
There beams a lamp of silver light,
And earth is bathed in radiance bright,
New loveliness revealing;
Then the waking woods resound
With elfin laughter all around,
And from each bush and wooded mound
Is elfin music stealing.

E. M. G. R.

Windy Nights

Whenever the moon and stars are set,
    Whenever the wind is high,
All night long in the dark and wet,
    A man goes riding by.
Late in the night when the fires are out,
Why does he gallop and gallop about?

Whenever the trees are crying aloud,
    And ships are tossed at sea,
By, on the highway, low and loud,
    By at the gallop goes he:
By at the gallop he goes, and then
By he comes back at the gallop again.

Robert Louis Stevenson

The Darkening Garden

Where have all the colours gone?

Red of roses, green of grass,
Brown of tree-trunk, gold of cowslip,
Pink of poppy, blue of cornflower,
Who among you saw them pass?

They have gone to make the sunset

Broidered on the western sky,
All the colours of our garden,
Woven into a lovely curtain,
O'er the bed where Day doth lie.

Wind and the Leaves

"Come, little Leaves," said the Wind one day,
"Come o'er the meadows with me, and play;
Put on your dresses of red and gold;
Summer is gone, and the days grow cold."

Soon as the Leaves heard the Wind's loud call,
Down they came fluttering, one and all;
Over the fields they danced and flew,
Singing the soft little songs they knew.

Dancing and whirling the little Leaves went;
Winter had called them, and they were content.
Soon, fast asleep in their earthy beds,
The snow laid a coverlet over their heads.

A Fine Day

Clear had the day been from the dawn,
    All chequer'd was the sky,
Thin clouds like scarfs of cobweb lawn
    Veiled heaven's most glorious eye.
The Wind had no more strength than this,
    That leisurely it blew,
To make one leaf the next to kiss
    That closely by it grew.

Michael Drayton

The Silver House

There's a silver house in the lovely sky,
    As round as a silver crown;
It takes two weeks to build it up,
    And two to pull it down.
There's a man who lives in the silver house,
    In a lonely sort of way;
But what his name is no one knows,
    Or no one likes to say.

Yet when you go to bed to-night,
    Just draw the window blind,
And peep out at the silver moon,
    This lonely man to find.
But if his house is taken down,
    And all the sky is bare,
Then go to bed, because, of course,
    The poor man won't be there.

John Lea

Chillingham

Through the sunny garden
    The humming bees are still;
The fir climbs the heather,
    The heather climbs the hill.

The low clouds have riven
    The little rift through.
The hill climbs to heaven,
    Far away and blue.

Mary E. Coleridge

A Day at the Farm

Hurrah! for a day with the farmer
    Away in the country so sweet.
Just peep in his beautiful orchard
    And take a nice apple to eat.

Now come to the farmyard so noisy
    And hunt for fresh eggs in the hay,
We'll see the fat turkeys and chickens
    All crackling so loudly to-day.

We'll peep at the pigs and the horses,
    Then off to the meadow we'll run
To play in the grass in the sunshine
    And tumble and roll, Oh! what fun!

Oh, look at kind Betty the milkmaid,
    She's off to the cowshed, I see.
She will take the new milk to the dairy:
    I think there's a glassful for me.

How lovely and sweet is the country!
    How happy the farmer must be!
We all love to pay him a visit,
    His wonderful farmyard to see.

L. J.

The Far-Farers

The broad sun,
  The bright day,
White sails
  On the blue bay:
The far-farers
  Draw away.

Light the fires
  And close the door.
To the old homes,
  To the loved shore,
The far-farers
  Return no more.

Robert Louis Stevenson

Farewell to the Farm

The coach is at the door at last;
The eager children, mounting fast
And kissing hands, in chorus sing:
"Good-bye, good-bye, to everything!

"To house and garden, field and lawn,
The meadow-gates we swang upon,
To pump and stable, tree and swing,
Good-bye, good-bye, to everything!

"And fare you well for evermore,
O ladder at the hayloft door,
O hayloft where the cobwebs cling,
Good-bye, good-bye, to everything!"

Crack goes the whip, and off we go;
The trees and houses smaller grow;
Last, round the woody turn we swing:
"Good-bye, good-bye, to everything!"

Robert Louis Stevenson

Gipsy Jane

She had cornflowers in her ear,
    As she came up the lane;
"What may be your name, my dear?"
    "Oh, sir, Gipsy Jane."

"You are berry-brown, my dear" —
    "That, sir, well may be;
For I live, more than half the year,
    Under tent or tree."

Shine, Sun, blow, Wind!
    Fall gently, Rain!
The year's declined; be soft and kind,
    Kind to Gipsy Jane.

                                W. B. Rands

The Fiddle

When I was young, I had no sense,
I bought a fiddle for eighteenpence,
And the only tune that I could play
Was "Over the Hills and Far Away."

To learn another I had no care,
For oh, it was a wondrous air,
And all the wee things of the glen
Came out and gathered round me then.

The furry folk that dwelt in wood
Quitted their hushed green solitude,
Sat round about me, unafraid,
And skipped to the music that I made.

Birds of the moor, birds of the tree,
Took up the tune with fiddle and me,
Happy were we on that summer day
With "Over the Hills and Far Away."

                                Neil Munro

Joys

We may shut our eyes,
But we cannot help knowing
That skies are clear
And grass is growing;
The breeze comes whispering in our ear,
That dandelions are blossoming near,
That corn has sprouted,
That streams are flowing,
That the river is bluer than the sky,
That the robin is plastering his home hard by.

J. R. Lowell

Foreign Lands

Up into the cherry tree
Who should climb but little me?
I held the trunk with both my hands
And looked abroad on foreign lands.

I saw the next-door garden lie,
Adorned with flowers, before my eye,
And many pleasant places more
That I had never seen before.

I saw the dimpling river pass
And be the sun's blue looking-glass;
The dusty roads go up and down
With people tramping into town.

If I could find a higher tree,
Farther and farther I should see,
To where the grown-up river slips
Into the sun among the ships.

To where the roads on either hand
Lead onward into fairy-land,
Where all the children dine at five,
And all the playthings come alive.

Robert Louis Stevenson

Mr. Scarecrow

There's a ragged old man in the garden to-day,
And Gardener, laughing, says there he can stay;
His coat is in tatters, he wears an old hat,
And the birds do not like him, I'm quite sure of that.

They chatter, chit-chatter up there in the tree,
And aren't half as friendly as they used to be;
But Gardener says: "That's a good job, indeed!
If it weren't for that old man, they'd have all my seed!"

Sheila Braine

The Bells of Youth

The Bells of Youth are ringing in the gateways of the South;
   The bannerets of green are now unfurled;
Spring has risen with a laugh, a wild-rose in her mouth,
   And is singing, singing, singing thro' the world.

The Bells of Youth are ringing in the silent places,
   The primrose and the celandine are out:
Children run a-laughing with joy upon their faces,
   The west wind follows after with a shout.

The Bells of Youth are ringing from the forests to the moun-
     tains,
   From the meadows to the moorlands, hark their ringing!
Ten thousand thousand splashing rills and fern-dappled
     fountains
   Are flinging wide the Song of Youth, and onward flowing
     singing.

The Bells of Youth are ringing in the gateways of the South;
   The bannerets of green are now unfurled;
Spring has risen with a laugh, a wild-rose in her mouth,
   And is singing, singing, singing thro' the world.

"Fiona Macleod" (William Sharp)

The Cliff-Top

The cliff-top has a carpet
  Of lilac, gold and green:
The blue sky bounds the ocean,
  The white clouds scud between.

A flock of gulls are wheeling
  And wailing round my seat;
Above my head the heaven,
  The sea beneath my feet.

Robert Bridges

The Boy's Song

Where the pools are bright and deep,
Where the grey trout lies asleep,
Up the river and o'er the lea—
That's the way for Billy and me.

Where the blackbird sings the latest,
Where the hawthorn blooms the sweetest,
Where the nestlings chirp and flee—
That's the way for Billy and me.

Where the mowers mow the cleanest,
Where the hay lies thick and greenest,
There to trace the homeward bee—
That's the way for Billy and me.

Where the hazel bank is steepest,
Where the shadow falls the deepest,
Where the clustering nuts fall free—
That's the way for Billy and me.

There let us walk, there let us play,
Through the meadows, among the hay,
Up the water, and o'er the lea—
That's the way for Billy and me.

James Hogg

291

Frolic

The children were shouting together
  And racing along the sands,
A glimmer of dancing shadows,
  A dove-like flutter of hands.

The stars were shouting in heaven,
  The sun was chasing the moon,
The game was the same as the children's,
  They danced to the self-same tune.

The whole of the world was merry,
  One joy from the vale to the height,
Where the blue woods of twilight encircled
  The lovely lawns of the light.

A. E.

The Day Before April

The day before April
  Alone, alone,
I walked in the woods
  And I sat on a stone.

I sat on a broad stone
  And sang to the birds,
The tune was God's making,
  But I made the words.

May Carolyn Davies

Rainy Nights

I like the town on rainy nights
  When everything is wet—
When all the town has magic lights
  And streets of shining jet!

When all the rain about the town
  Is like a looking-glass,
And all the lights are upside down
  Below me as I pass.

In all the pools are velvet skies,
  And down the dazzling street
A fairy city gleams and lies
  In beauty at my feet.

Irene Thompson

Glow-Worms

With a yellow lantern
  I take the road at night,
And chase the flying shadows
  By its cheerful light.

From the banks and hedgerows
  Other lanterns shine,
Tiny elfin glimmers,
  Not so bright as mine.

Those are glow-worm lanterns,
  Coloured green and blue,
Orange, red and purple,
  Gaily winking through.

See the glow-worms hurry!
  See them climb and crawl!
They go to light the dancers
  At the fairy ball.

P. A. Ropes

Dawn

A thrush is tapping a stone
  With a snail-shell in its beak;
A small bird hangs from a cherry
  Until the stem shall break:
No waking song has begun,
And yet birds chatter and hurry
And throng in the elm's gloom,
Because an owl goes home.

Gordon Bottomley

Cobwebs

Between me and the rising sun,
This way and that the cobwebs run;
Their myriad wavering lines of light
Dance up the hill and out of sight.

There is no land possesses half
So many lines of telegraph
As those the spider-elves have spun
Between me and the rising sun.

E. L. M. King

The Piper

A piper in the streets to-day
Set up and tuned, and started to play,
And away, away, away on the tide
Of his music we started; on every side
Doors and windows were opened wide,
And men left their work and came,
And women with petticoats coloured like flame,
And little bare feet that were blue with cold,
Went dancing back to the age of gold,
And all the world went gay, went gay,
For half an hour in the street to-day.

Seumas O'Sullivan

Hie Away!

Hie away! hie away!
Over bank and over brae,
Where the copsewood is the greenest,
Where the fountains glisten sheenest,
Where the lady-fern grows strongest,
Where the morning dew lies longest,
Where the black-cock sweetest sips it,
Where the fairy latest trips it;
Hie to haunts right seldom seen,
Lovely, lonesome, cool and green:
Over bank and over brae
Hie away! hie away!

Sir Walter Scott

Castles in the Sand

I've built a castle in the sand
   In less than half an hour,
With grim portcullis, and a moat,
   And battlements and tower.

The seaweed banners wave, and when
   I let the drawbridge down,
The knights come riding two by two
   In armour rusty brown.

And ladies lean from turrets high,
   And watch them as they pass,
And wave their floating silken scarves,
   As light and green as grass.

But see! across the shining sand,
   That enemy the sea
Creeps slowly to my castle walls,
   Advancing stealthily.

No bugles sound a wild alarm,
   No warders close the gate;
The knights and ladies disappear,
   And all alone I wait.

For where my fairy fortress stood
   And glistened in the sun,
There lies a heap of ruins now,
   My work is all undone.

Dorothy Baker

The Wind

What way does the Wind come? What way does he go?
He rides over the water, and over the snow,
Through wood and through vale: and o'er rocky height
Which goat cannot climb, takes his sounding flight.
He tosses about in every bare tree,
As, if you look up, you plainly may see;
But how he will come, and whither he goes,
There's never a scholar in England knows.

Dorothy Wordsworth

The Caravan

If I could be a gipsy-boy
    And have a caravan
I'd travel all the world, I would,
    Before I was a man;
We'd drive beyond the far blue hills—
    We two, my horse and me—
And on and on and on and on
    Until we reached the sea.

And there I'd wash his legs quite clean
    And bid him come inside,
Whilst I would stand upon the roof
    And scan the flowing tide,
And he and I would sail away
    And scour the Spanish main,
And when we'd swept the Spaniards out
    We'd p'raps sail home again.

Or if my horse was very tired
    Of ships and being good,
And wanted most to stretch his legs
    (As many horses would),
We'd call a whale to tow us
    To a desert island beach,
And there we'd search for coconuts
    And have a whole one each.

If I could be a gipsy-boy
    I wouldn't bring a load
Of pots and pans and chairs and things
    And sell them in the road.
Oh, if I was a gipsy-boy
    And had a caravan,
I'd see the whole wide world, I would,
    Before I was a man.

Madeline Nightingale

Freedom

Out in the garden, sunny and still,
  Nothing to do till tea,
Let's go up to the top of the hill!
  Come along, puppy, with me.

Up on the hill-top, sunny and tall,
  Nothing to do till tea,
Let's go down to the old stone wall!
  Come along, puppy, with me.

Down by the old wall, sunny and grey,
  Nothing do to till tea,
Let's go out to the meadow to play!
  Come along, puppy, with me!

Out in the meadow, sunny and wide,
  Come along, puppy, with me.
Let's go right to the other side!
  And then go home to tea.

Joan Agnew

Afternoon on a Hill

I will be the gladdest thing
  Under the sun!
I will touch a hundred flowers
  And not pick one.

I will look at cliffs and clouds
  With quiet eyes,
Watch the wind bow down the grass
  And the grass rise.

And when the lights begin to show
  Up from the town,
I will mark which must be mine,
  And then start down!

Edna St. Vincent Millay

297

The Swing

Now so high,
Now so low,
Up in the air,
Then down I go.
Up to the sky,
Down to the grass,
I watch birds fly,
I see worms pass.

With feet in front,
And hair behind,
I race the birds,
I race the wind,
Over the world,
Under the tree,
Nobody knows
What things I see.
Wonderful lands
Where children play
From early morn
All thro' the day.

Mary I. Osborn

The Night

The night was creeping on the ground;
She crept and did not make a sound
Until she reached the tree, and then
She covered it, and stole again
Along the grass beside the wall.

I heard the rustle of her shawl
As she threw blackness everywhere
Upon the sky and ground and air,
And in the room where I was hid:
But no matter what she did
To everything that was without,
She could not put my candle out.

So I stared at the night, and she
Stared back solemnly at me.

James Stephens

The Lighthouse

Burning upon some hidden shore
  Across the sea one night
("A little reef," the Captain said),
  We saw a shining light.

He said there was a lighthouse there
  Where, lonely in the sea,
Men lived to guard that moving light,
  And trim the lamp for me.

For me, for him, for every ship
  That passes by that way.
I thought it must be strange and quiet
  To be there every day.

They have no shops, no fields, no streets;
  No whispering sound of trees,
But always shouting at their feet
  The great voice of the seas.

And when we sleep at night they wake,
  And over every wave
They send that straight strong arm of light
  Stretched like a rope to save.

Marjorie Wilson

Daybreak in a Garden

I heard the farm cocks crowing loud, and faint, and thin,
When hooded night was going and one clear planet winked;
I heard shrill notes begin down the spired wood distant
When cloudy shoals were chinked and gilt with fires of day.
White-misted was the weald; the lawns were silver-grey;
The lark his lonely field for heaven had forsaken;
And the wind upon the way whispered the boughs of may
And touched the nodding peony-flowers to bid them waken.

Siegfried Sassoon

299

The Playhouse Key

This is the key to the playhouse,
   In the woods by the pebbly shore,
It's winter now; I wonder if
   There's snow about the door?

I wonder if the fir trees tap
   Green fingers on the pane,
If sea gulls cry and the roof is wet
   And tinkle-y with rain?

I wonder if the flower-sprigged cups
   And plates sit on their shelf,
And if my little painted chair
   Is rocking by itself?

Rachel Field

The Lady Moon

The Lady Moon is sailing,
High up in heaven she rides;
I see her shining silver car,
Attended by full many a star,
   Keeping the tides.

Oh, Lady Moon! so shining,
Your face is sweet and mild;
I long with you, dear moon, to be
Afloat upon that silver sea,
   A happy child.

Oh, Lady Moon! still sailing,
A constant watch you keep;
From east to west you steer your car;
I feel your smile, dear moon, afar,
   Guarding my sleep.

Kate Louise Brown

Colour

Colour is a lovely thing.
Given to soothe our sight,
Blue for sky, green for grass,
And brown for roads where wee folks pass;
Golden sun that shines o'er head,
Silver for moon, for sunset red,
Soft cool black for night!

Flying

I saw the moon,
One windy night,
Flying so fast—
All silvery white—
Over the sky
Like a toy balloon
Loose from its string—
A runaway moon.
The frosty stars
Went racing past,
Chasing her on
Ever so fast.
Then everyone said,
"It's the clouds that fly,
And the stars and moon
Stand still in the sky."
But I don't mind—
I saw the moon
Sailing away
Like a toy
Balloon.

J. M. Westrup

From a Walking Song

Here we go a-walking, so softly, so softly,
   Down the world, round the world, back to London town,
To see the waters and the whales, the emus and the mandarins,
   To see the Chinese mandarins, each in a silken gown.

Here we go a-walking, so softly, so softly,
   Through the vast Atlantic waves, back to London town,
To see the ships made whole again that sank below the tempest,
   The Trojan and Phoenician ships that long ago went down.
And there are sailors keeping watch on many a Roman galley,
   And silver bars and golden bars and mighty treasure hid,
And splendid Spanish gentlemen majestically walking
   And waiting on their Admiral as once in far Madrid.

Here we go a-walking, so softly, so softly,
   Down and under to New York, back to London town,
To see the face of Liberty that smiles upon all children,
   But when too soon they come of age she answers with a
     frown.

Here we go a-walking, so softly, so softly,
   O'er the wide Tibetan plains, back to London town,
To see the Youthful Emperor among his seventy princes,
   Who bears the magic sceptre, who wears the magic crown.

Here we go a-walking, so softly, so softly,
   Through the jungles African, back to London town,
To see the shining rivers and the drinking place by moonlight,
   And the lions and hyenas and the zebras coming down:
To see bright birds and butterflies, the monstrous hippopotami,
   The silent secret crocodiles that keep their ancient guile,
The white road of the caravans that stretches o'er Sahara,
   And the Pharaoh in his litter at the fording of the Nile.

Here we go a-walking, so softly, so softly,
   Up the hills of Hampstead, back to London town,
And the garden gate stands open and the house door swings
     before us,
   And the candles twinkle happily as we lie down.

For here the noble lady is who meets us from our wanderings,
    Here are all the sensible and very needful things,
Here are blankets, here is milk, here are rest and slumber,
    And the courteous prince of angels with the fire about his
        wings.

Charles Williams

The Echoing Green

The Sun doth arise,
And make happy the skies;
The merry bells ring
To welcome the Spring;
The skylark and thrush,
The birds of the bush
Sing louder around
To the bells' cheerful sound,
While our sports shall be seen
On the Echoing Green.

Old John, with white hair,
Does laugh away care,
Sitting under the oak,
Among the old folk;
They laugh at our play,
And soon they all say:
"Such, such were the joys
When we all, girls and boys,
In our youth time were seen
On the Echoing Green."

Till the little ones, weary,
No more can be merry;
The sun does descend,
And our sports have an end.
Round the laps of their mothers
Many sisters and brothers,
Like birds in their nest,
Are ready for rest,
And sport no more seen
On the darkening Green.

William Blake
303

The King's Wood

The King is out a-hunting,
A-hunting in the King's Wood;
Hang the house with bunting,
    The King is riding by.

With him the Queen is riding,
A-riding to the King's Wood;
Oh, who'd be idly biding,
    When the King and Queen go by?

Come lords and ladies prancing,
A-prancing to the King's Wood;
And eager eyes are glancing,
    As stately they go by.

With morn they're quickly pacing,
A-pacing to the King's Wood;
The tall red deer a-chasing,
    They let the day go by.

Then home they come returning,
Returning to the King's Wood;
And gallant hearts are burning
    As beauty passes by.

C. S. Holder

The Sea

Take your bucket, and take your spade,
    And come to the sea with me,
Building castles upon the sand
    Is the game for you and me!
Races run with the tumbling waves,
Then rest awhile in the cool, dark caves.
Oh, the greatest joy in the summer time
    Is the sea, the sparkling sea!

E. M. Adams

The Tree in the Garden

There's a tree out in our garden which is very nice to climb,
And I often go and climb it when it's fine in summer time,
And when I've climbed right up it I pretend it's not a tree
But a ship in which I'm sailing, far away across the sea.

Its branches are the rigging and the grass so far below
I make believe's the ocean over which my ship must go;
And when the wind is blowing then I really seem to be
A-sailing, sailing, sailing, far away across the sea.

Then I hunt for desert islands and I very often find
A chest stuffed full of treasure which some pirate's left
    behind—
My good ship's hold is filled with gold—it all belongs to me—
For I've found it when I'm sailing far away across the sea.

It's a lovely game to play at—though the tree trunk's rather
    green,
Still, when I'm in my bath at night I always come quite clean.
And so through all the summer, in my good ship Treasure-
    Tree,
I shall often go a-sailing far away across the sea.

Christine Chaundler

Youth

Oh, the wild joy of living; the leaping from rock to rock,
The strong rending of boughs from the fir-trees, the cool
    silver shock
Of the plunge in the pool's living water, the hunt of the bear,
And the sultriness showing the lion is couch'd in his lair.
And the meal, the rich dates yellow'd over with gold-dust
    divine,
And the locust fresh steeped in the pitcher, the full draught of
    wine,
And the sleep in the dried river-channel where bulrushes tell
That the water was wont to go warbling so softly and well.
How good is man's life, the mere living! how fit to employ
All the heart and the soul and the senses for ever in joy!

Robert Browning

A Rune of Riches

I have a golden ball,
  A big, bright shining one,
Pure gold; and it is all
  Mine. It is the sun.

I have a silver ball,
  A white and glistering stone
That other people call
  The moon—my very own!

The jewel things that prick
  My cushion's soft blue cover
Are mine—my stars, thick, thick,
  Scattered the sky over.

And everything that's mine
  Is yours, and yours, and yours—
The shimmer and the shine!—
  Let's lock our wealth out-doors!

Florence Converse

Where Lies the Land?

Where lies the land to which the ship would go?
Far, far ahead is all her seamen know.
And where the land she travels from? Away,
Far, far behind, is all that they can say.

On sunny noons upon the deck's smooth face,
Linked arm in arm, how pleasant here to pace!
Or, o'er the stern reclining, watch below
The foaming wake far-widening as we go.

On stormy nights when wild north-westerns rave,
How proud a thing to fight with wind and wave!
The dripping sailor on the reeling mast
Exults to bear, and scorns to wish it past.

Where lies the land to which the ship would go?
Far, far ahead is all her seamen know.
And where the land she travels from? Away,
Far, far behind is all that they can say.

Arthur Hugh Clough

Daybreak

A wind came up out of the sea,
And said, "O mists, make room for me."

It hailed the ships, and cried, "Sail on,
Ye mariners, the night is gone."

And hurried landward far away,
Crying, "Awake! it is the day."

It said unto the forest, "Shout!
Hang all your leafy banners out!"

It touched the wood-bird's folded wing,
And said, "O bird, awake and sing."

And o'er the farms, "O chanticleer,
Your clarion blow; the day is near."

It whispered to the fields of corn,
"Bow down, and hail the coming morn."

It shouted through the belfry tower,
"Awake, O bell! proclaim the hour."

It crossed the churchyard with a sigh,
And said, "Not yet! in quiet lie."

H. W. Longfellow

The Lights

I know the ships that pass by day:
I guess their business, grave or gay,
   And spy their flags, and learn their names,
      And whence they come and where they go—
      But in the night I only know
   Some little starry flames.

And yet I think these jewelled lights
Have meanings full as noonday sights:
   For every emerald signs to me
      That ship and souls are harbour near,
      And every ruby rich and clear
   Proclaims them bound for sea.

And all the yellow diamonds set
On mast and deck and hull in jet
   Have meanings real as day can show:
      They tell of care, of watchful eyes,
      Of labour, slumber, hopes, and sighs—
   Of human joy and woe.

O ships that come and go by night,
God's blessing be on every light!

J. J. Bell

Sherwood

Sherwood in the twilight, is Robin Hood awake?
Grey and ghostly shadows are gliding through the brake;
Shadows of the dappled deer, dreaming of the morn,
Dreaming of a shadowy man that winds a shadowy horn.

Robin Hood is here again; all his merry thieves
Hear a ghostly bugle-note, shivering through the leaves,
Calling as he used to call, faint and far away,
In Sherwood, in Sherwood, about the break of day.

Merry, merry England has kissed the lips of June;
All the wings of fairyland are here beneath the moon;
Like a flight of rose-leaves fluttering in a mist
Of opal and ruby and pearl and amethyst.

Merry, merry England is waking as of old,
With eyes of blither hazel and hair of brighter gold:
For Robin Hood is here again beneath the bursting spray
In Sherwood, in Sherwood, about the break of day.

Love is in the greenwood building him a house
Of wild rose and hawthorn and honeysuckle boughs;
Love is in the greenwood: dawn is in the skies;
And Marian is waiting with a glory in her eyes.

Hark! the dazzled laverock climbs the golden steep:
Marian is waiting: is Robin Hood asleep?
Round the fairy grass-rings frolic elf and fay,
In Sherwood, in Sherwood, about the break of day.

Oberon, Oberon, rake away the gold,
Rake away the red leaves, roll away the mould,
Rake away the gold leaves, roll away the red,
And wake Will Scarlett from his leafy forest bed.

Friar Tuck and Little John are riding down together
With quarter-staff and drinking-can and grey goose-feather
The dead are coming back again; the years are rolled away
In Sherwood, in Sherwood, about the break of day.

Softly over Sherwood the South wind blows;
All the heart of England hid in every rose
Hears across the greenwood the sunny whisper leap,
Sherwood in the red dawn, is Robin Hood asleep?

Hark, the voice of England wakes him as of old
And, shattering the silence with a cry of brighter gold,
Bugles in the greenwood echo from the steep,
Sherwood in the red dawn, is Robin Hood asleep?

Where the deer are gliding down the shadowy glen
All across the glades of fern he calls his merry men;
Doublets of the Lincoln green glancing through the May
In Sherwood, in Sherwood, about the break of day;

Call them and they answer; from aisles of oak and ash
Rings the *Follow! Follow!* and the boughs begin to crash;
The ferns begin to flutter and the flowers begin to fly;
And through the crimson dawning the robber band goes by.

Robin! Robin! Robin! all his merry thieves
Answer as the bugle-note shivers through the leaves;
Calling as he used to call, faint and far away,
In Sherwood, in Sherwood, about the break of day.

A. Noyes

The Windmill

If you should bid me make a choice
    'Twixt wind- and water-mill,
In spite of all the mill-pond's charms
I'd take those gleaming, sweeping arms
    High on a windy hill.

The miller stands before his door
    And whistles for a breeze;
And, when it comes, his sails go round
With such a mighty rushing sound
    You think of heavy seas.

And if the wind declines to blow
    The miller takes a nap
(Although he'd better spend an hour
In brushing at the dust and flour
    That line his coat and cap).

Now, if a water-mill were his,
    Such rest he'd never know,
For round and round his crashing wheel,
His dashing, splashing, plashing wheel,
    Unceasingly would go.

So, if you'd bid me take a choice
    'Twixt wind- and water-mill,
In spite of all a mill-pond's charms,
I'd take those gleaming, sweeping arms
    High on a windy hill.

E. V. Lucas

White Horses

Far out at sea
    There are horses to ride,
Little white horses
    That race with the tide.

Their tossing manes
    Are the white sea-foam,
And the lashing winds
    Are driving them home—

To shadowy stables
    Fast they must flee,
To the great green caverns
    Down under the sea.

Irene F. Pawsey

The Gallant Ship

Upon the gale she stooped her side,
And bounded o'er the swelling tide,
    As she were dancing home;
The merry seamen laughed to see
Their gallant ship so lustily
    Furrow the sea-green foam.

Sir Walter Scott

All Creatures Great and Small

Little children, never give
Pain to things that feel and live

The Browny Hen

A browny hen sat on her nest
    With a hey-ho for the springtime!
Seven brown eggs 'neath her downy breast,
    With a hey-ho for the springtime!

A brown hen clucks all day from dawn,
    With a hey-ho for the springtime!
She's seven wee chicks as yellow as corn,
    With a hey-ho for the springtime!

Irene F. Fawsey

Duck's Ditty

All along the backwater,
    Through the rushes tall,
Ducks are a-dabbling,
    Up tails all!

Duck's tails, drakes' tails,
    Yellow feet a-quiver,
Yellow bills all out of sight
    Busy in the river!

Slushy green undergrowth
    Where the roach swim,
Here we keep our larder
    Cool and full and dim!

Every one for what he likes!
    We like to be
Heads down, tails up,
    Dabbling free!

High in the blue above
    Swifts whirl and call—
We are down a-dabbling,
    Up tails all!

Kenneth Grahame,

314

Michael's Song

Because I set no snare
 But leave them flying free,
All the birds of the air
 Belong to me.

From the blue-tit on the sloe
 To the eagle on the height,
Uncaged they come and go
 For my delight.

And so the sunward way
 I soar on the eagle's wings,
And in my heart all day
 The blue-tit sings.

Wilfrid Gibson

The Grasshopper and the Cricket

The poetry of earth is never dead:
When all the birds are faint with the hot sun,
And hide in cooling trees, a voice will run
From hedge to hedge about the new-mown mead:
This is the grasshopper's—he takes the lead
In summer luxury—he has never done
With his delights, for when tired out with fun,
He rests at ease beneath some pleasant weed.
The poetry of earth is ceasing never:
On a lone winter evening, when the frost
Has wrought a silence, from the stove there shrills,
The Cricket's song, in warmth increasing ever,
And seems to one in drowsiness half lost,
The grasshopper's among the grassy hills.

J. Keats

The Eagle

He clasps the crag with crooked hands;
Close to the sun in lonely lands,
Ringed with the azure world, he stands.

The wrinkled sea beneath him crawls;
He watches from his mountain walls,
And like a thunderbolt he falls.

Lord Tennyson

Gay Robin is seen no More

Gay Robin is seen no more:
   He is gone with the snow,
   For winter is o'er
   And Robin will go.
In need he was fed, and now he is fled
   Away to his secret nest.
   No more will he stand
   Begging for crumbs,
   No longer he comes
   Beseeching our hand
   And showing his breast
   At window and door:—
Gay Robin is seen no more.

Blithe Robin is heard no more:
   He gave us his song
   When summer was o'er
   And winter was long:
   Beseeching our hand
He sang for his bread, and now he is fled
   Away to his secret nest,
   And there in the green
   Early and late
   Alone to his mate
   He pipeth unseen
   And swelleth his breast;
   For us it is o'er:—
Blithe Robin is heard no more.

Robert Bridges

L'Oiseau Bleu

(The Blue Bird)

The lake blue below the hill.
  O'er it, as I looked, there flew
Across the waters, cold and still,
  A bird whose wings were palest blue.

The sky above was blue at last,
  The sky beneath me blue in blue.
A moment, ere the bird had passed,
  It caught his image as he flew.

Mary E. Coleridge

The Birds on the School Windowsill

Robin: I'm hungry, oh so hungry!
         I'd love a piece of bread!
Sparrow: I've looked for nice cold water,
         But found hard ice instead.
Birds: Please, please, do give us food and drink!
         You boys and girls are kind, I think.

Alec: Here's piece of crust.
Betty: Here's another, too.
Charles: Don't be frightened, pretty birds,
         We love you, yes, we do.
Dorothy: Here's a drink of water
         In a little dish:
         Help yourselves, poor thirsty birds;
         There's still more if you wish.

Children: Come again, Cock Sparrow;
         Robin Redbreast, too,
         Please come every morning—
         There's always food for you.
Birds: Thank you, thank you, children,
         And now we'll fly away
         To bring our hungry friends to share
         The feast we've found to-day.

Evelyn Dainty

317

The Tadpole

Underneath the water-weeds
    Small and black, I wriggle,
And life is most surprising!
    Wiggle! waggle! wiggle!
There's every now and then a most
    Exciting change in me,
I wonder, wiggle! waggle!
    What I *shall* turn out to be!

E. E. Gould

The Brown Thrush

There's a merry brown thrush sitting up in the tree,
"He's singing to me! He's singing to me!"
And what does he say, little girl, little boy?
"Oh, the world's running over with joy!
Don't you hear? don't you see?
Hush! Look! In my tree
I'm as happy as happy can be!"

And the brown thrush keeps singing, "A nest do you see,
And five eggs, hid by me in the juniper-tree?
Don't meddle! don't touch! little girl, little boy,
Or the world will lose some of its joy!
Now I'm glad! now I'm free!
And I always shall be,
If you never bring sorrow to me."

So the merry brown thrush sings away in the tree,
To you and to me, to you and to me;
And he sings all the day, little girl, little boy,
"Oh, the world's running over with joy!
But long it won't be,
Don't you know? don't you see?
Unless we are as good as can be!"

Lucy Larcom

The Curliest Thing

The squirrel is the curliest thing
    I think I ever saw;
He curls his back, he curls his tail,
    He curls each little paw,
He curls his little vest so white,
    His little coat so grey—
He is the most curled-up wee soul
    Out in the woods at play!

Zoo Manners

Be careful what
    You say or do
When you visit the animals
    At the Zoo.

Don't make fun
    Of the Camel's hump
He's very proud
    Of his noble bump.

Don't laugh too much
    At the Chimpanzee
He thinks he's as wise
    As you or me.

And the Penguins
    Strutting round the lake
Can understand
    Remarks you make.

Treat them as well
    As they do you,
And you'll always be welcome
    At the Zoo.

Eileen Mathias.

319

The Poor Snail

The snail says, "Alas!"
And the snail says, "Alack!
Why must I carry
My house on my back?
You have a home
To go in and out,
Why must mine always be
Carried about?
Not any tables,
Not any chairs,
Not any windows,
Not any stairs,
Pity my misery,
Pity my wail—
For I must always be
Just a poor snail."
But he's terribly slow,
So perhaps it's as well
That his shell is his home,
And his home is his shell.

J. M. Westrup

The Fifteen Acres

I cling and swing
On a branch, or sing
Through the cool, clear hush of Morning, O!
Or fling my wing
On the air, and bring
To sleepier birds a warning, O!
That the night's in flight,
And the sun's in sight,
And the dew is the grass adorning, O!
And the green leaves swing

As I sing, sing, sing,
Up by the river,
Down the dell,
To the little wee nest,
Where the big tree fell,
So early in the morning, O!

I flit and twit
 In the sun for a bit
When his light so bright is shining, O!
 Or sit and fit
 My plumes, or knit
Straw plaits for the nest's nice lining, O!
 And she with glee
 Shows unto me
Underneath her wings reclining, O!
 And I sing that Peg
 Has an egg, egg, egg,
  Up by the oat-field
   Round the mill,
  Past the meadow,
   Down by the hill,
So early in the morning, O!

I stoop and swoop
 On the air, or loop
Through the trees, and then go soaring, O!
 To group with a troop
 On the gusty poop
While the wind behind is roaring, O!
 I skim and swim
 By a cloud's red rim
And up to the azure flooring, O!
 And my wide wings drip
 As I slip, slip, slip
  Down through the rain-drops,
   Back where Peg
  Broods in the nest
   On the little white egg,
So early in the morning, O!

James Stephens

The Elephant

When people call this beast to mind,
 They marvel more and more
At such a little tail behind
 So *large* a trunk before.

Hilaire Belloc

321

Lambs at Play

On the grassy banks
Lambkins at their pranks;
Woolly sisters, woolly brothers,
Jumping off their feet
While their woolly mothers
Watch by them and bleat.

Christina Rossetti

Michael Met a Duck

Michael met a white duck
Walking on the green.
"How are you?" said Michael.
"How fine the weather's been!
Blue sky and sunshine,
All thro'out the day;
Not a single raindrop
Came to spoil our play."

But the sad white duck said,
"I myself want rain.
I'd like to see the brooklets
And the streams fill up again.
Now I can't go swimming,
It really makes me cry
To see the little duckponds
Look so very dry."

But behold, next morning,
The clouds are looking black:
Down the rain came pouncing,
Said the duck, "Quack, quack.
Ponds are full of water,
Ducks are full of joy."
But someone else is not pleased,
And that's the little boy.

J. Dupuy

The Duck

If I were in a fairy tale,
   And it were my good luck
To have to wish, I'd choose to be
   A lovely snow-white duck.

When she puts off into the pond
   And leaves me on the brink,
She wags her stumpy tail at me,
   And gives a saucy wink

Which says as plain as words could say,
   I'm safe as safe can be,
Stay there, or you will drown yourself,
   This pond was made for me.

She goes a-sailing to and fro,
   Just like a fishing-boat,
And steers and paddles all herself,
   And never wets her coat.

Then in the water, upside down,
   I've often see her stand,
More neatly than the little boys
   Who do it on the land.

And best of all, her children are
   The ducklings, bright as gold,
Who swim about the pond with her
   And do as they are told.

Edith King

The Brown Frog

To-day as I went out to play
I saw a brown frog in the way,
I know that frogs are smooth and green,
But this was brown—what could it mean?
I asked a lady in the road;
She said it was a spotted toad!

Mary K. Robinson

Milk for the Cat

When the tea is brought at five o'clock,
And all the neat curtains are drawn with care,
The little black cat with bright green eyes
Is suddenly purring there.

At first she pretends, having nothing to do,
She has come in merely to blink by the grate;
But, though tea may be late or the milk may be sour,
She is never late.

And presently her agate eyes
Take a soft large milky haze,
And her independent casual glance
Becomes a stiff hard gaze.

Then she stamps her claws or lifts her ears,
Or twists her tail and begins to stir,
Till suddenly all her lithe body becomes
One breathing trembling purr.

The children eat and wriggle and laugh;
The two old ladies stroke their silk:
But the cat is grown small and thin with desire,
Transformed to a creeping lust for milk.

The white saucer like some full moon descends
At last from the clouds of the table above;
She sighs and dreams and thrills and glows,
Transfigured with love.

She nestles over the shining rim,
Buries her chin in the creamy sea;
Her tail hangs loose; each drowsy paw
Is doubled under each bending knee.

A long dim ecstasy holds her life;
Her world is an infinite shapeless white,
Till her tongue has curled the last holy drop,
Then she sinks back into the night.

Draws and dips her body to heap
Her sleepy nerves in the great arm-chair,
Lies defeated and buried deep
Three or four hours unconscious there.

Harold Monro

Prayer for Gentleness to all Creatures

To all the humble beasts there be,
To all the birds on land and sea,
Great Spirit, sweet protection give
That free and happy they may live!

And to our hearts the rapture bring
Of love for every living thing;
Make us all one kin, and bless
Our ways with Christ's own gentleness!

John Galsworthy

The Woodman's Dog

Shaggy, and lean, and shrewd, with pointed ears,
And tail cropp'd short, half lurcher and half cur—
His dog attends him. Close behind his heel
Now creeps he slow; and now, with many a frisk
Wide-scampering, snatches up the drifted snow
With ivory teeth, or ploughs it with his snout;
Then shakes his powder'd coat, and barks for joy.

William Cowper

325

The Mouse

I heard a mouse
Bitterly complaining
In a crack of moonlight
Aslant on the floor.

"Little I ask
And that little is not granted.
There are very few crumbs
In the world any more.

"The bread box is tin
And I cannot get in.

"The jam's in a jar
My teeth cannot mar.

"The cheese sits by itself
On the pantry shelf.

"All night I run
Searching and seeking,
All night I run
About on the floor.

"Moonlight is there
And a bare place for dancing,
But no little feast
Is spread any more."

Elizabeth Coatsworth

The Autumn Robin

Sweet little bird in russet coat,
    The livery of the closing year,
I love thy lonely plaintive note
    And tiny whispering song to hear,
While on the stile or garden seat
    I sit to watch the falling leaves,
The song thy little joys repeat
    My loneliness relieves.

John Clare

Browny Bee

Little Mr. Browny Bee,
Gather honey for my tea;
Come into my garden, do,
I've every kind of flower for you.

There's blossom on my tiny tree,
And daisies in the grass you'll see;
There's lavender, and scented stocks,
And rows of frilly hollyhocks.

I've marigolds, and pansies too,
And Canterbury-bells of blue;
There's rosemary, and scented thyme,
And foxglove heads you'll love to climb.

I've gilly-flowers, and roses red,
All waiting in my garden bed;
Seek honey where my flowers are
To fill my little honey-jar.

Irene F. Pawsey

At Breakfast

When I sit up to bread and milk
I feel a head as soft as silk
Against my knee. And on my sock
A gentle paw. It is my "Jock,"
The dearest doggie ever seen,
My knowing, faithful Aberdeen.
And then two eyes say, "Little Master,
I think these legs would run much faster
And p'raps would grow a little longer,
And certainly would grow much stronger,
If only they were fed more often."
And then, as if my heart to soften,
He wags his tail. And then he begs
Upon his stumpy, short, hind legs.
Of course I give him some. Who would
Refuse to feed him if they could?
And when he looks up in my face
I feel quite sure he's saying Grace.

I. M. Mills

The Caterpillar

Brown and furry
Caterpillar in a hurry,
Take your walk
To the shady leaf, or stalk,
Or what not,
Which may be the chosen spot.
No toad to spy you,
Hovering bird of prey pass by you;
Spin and die,
To live again a butterfly.

Christina Rossetti

The Elephant

Here comes the elephant
Swaying along
With his cargo of children
All singing a song:
To the tinkle of laughter
He goes on his way,
And his cargo of children
Have crowned him with May.
His legs are in leather
And padded his toes;
He can root up an oak
With a whisk of his nose:
With a wave of his trunk
And a turn of his chin
He can pull down a house,
Or pick up a pin.
Beneath his grey forehead
A little eye peers!
Of what is he thinking
Between those wide ears?
Of what does he think?
If he wished to tease,
He could twirl his keeper
Over the trees:

If he were not kind,
He could play cup and ball
With Robert and Helen
And Uncle Paul:
But that grey forehead,
Those crinkled ears,
Have learned to be kind
In a hundred years!
And so with the children
He goes on his way
To the tinkle of laughter
And crowned with the May.

Herbert Asquith

The Field-Mouse

I live among the grasses,
    And watch them growing high,
And as the summer passes
    They seem to touch the sky.

The Spiders are my neighbours,
    Busy people they,
I watch them at their labours,
    Spinning day by day.

The Earwig comes a-calling,
    The Ladybird as well,
And snails go slowly crawling,
    And Slugs, without a shell.

The Bumble, fat and furry,
    A flying visit pays,
And Caterpillars hurry
    Adown the grassy ways.

I am your little brother,
    A Mouse in brown and grey,
So if we meet each other,
    Please let me run away!

Enid Blyton

329

A Friend in the Garden

He is not John, the gardener,
    And yet the whole day long
Employs himself most usefully,
    The flower-beds among.

He is not Tom, the pussy-cat,
    And yet the other day,
With stealthy stride and glistening eye,
    He crept upon his prey.

He is not Dash, the dear old dog,
    And yet, perhaps, if you
Took pains with him and petted him,
    You'd come to love him too.

He's not a Blackbird, though he chirps,
    And though he once was black;
And now he wears a loose grey coat,
    All wrinkled on the back.

He's got a very dirty face,
    And very shining eyes!
He sometimes comes and sits indoors;
    He looks—and p'r'aps is—wise.

But in a sunny flower-bed
    He has his fixed abode;
He eats the things that eat my plants—
    He is a friendly *Toad*.

Juliana Horatia Ewing

Ducks

As I went down the village green,
    Quack-quack! Quack-quack!
Such a sight as never was seen,
    On a fine wet day in the morning.

Three ducks came swimming down the stream,
        Quack-quack! Quack-quack!
    (I was awake: it was no dream)
On a gay grey day in the morning.

    Yet when they saw me standing by,
        Quack-quack! Quack-quack!
    They stood on their heads with their tails to the sky,
On a mild wild day in the morning.

    And when they had done just what I say,
        Quack-quack! Quack-quack!
    They shook their tails and sailed away,
On a fine wet day in the morning.

Norman Ault

What the Thrush Says

        "Come and see! Come and see!"
    The thrush pipes out of the hawthorn tree:
    And I and Dicky on tiptoe go
    To see what treasures he wants to show.
    His call is clear as a call can be—
    And "Come and see!" he says:
            "Come and see!"

        "Come and see! Come and see!"
    His house is there in the hawthorn-tree:
    The neatest house that ever you saw,
    Built all of mosses and twigs and straw:
    The folk who built were his wife and he—
    And "Come and see!" he says:
            "Come and see!"

        "Come and see! Come and see!"
    Within this house there are treasures three:
    So warm and snug in its curve they lie—
    Like three bright bits out of Spring's blue sky.
    We would not hurt them, he knows: not we!
    So "Come and see!" he says:
            "Come and see!"

Queenie Scott-Hopper

Robin's Song

Robins sang in England,
　　Frost or rain or snow,
All the long December days
　　Endless years ago.

Robins sang in England
　　Before the Legions came,
Before our English fields were tilled
　　Or England was a name.

Robins sang in England
　　When forests dark and wild
Stretched across from sea to sea
　　And Jesus was a child.

Listen! in the frosty dawn
　　From his leafless bough
The same brave song he ever sang
　　A robin's singing now.

Rodney Bennett

The Owl

When cats run home and light is come,
　　And dew is cold upon the ground,
And the far-off stream is dumb,
　　And the whirring sail goes round,
　　And the whirring sail goes round;
　　　　Alone and warming his five wits,
　　　　The white owl in the belfry sits.

When merry milkmaids click the latch,
　　And rarely smells the new-mown hay,
And the cock hath sung beneath the thatch
　　Twice or thrice his roundelay,
　　Twice or thrice his roundelay;
　　　　Alone and warming his five wits,
　　　　The white owl in the belfry sits.

Lord Tennyson

Mother Duck

Old Mother Duck has hatched a brood
   Of ducklings, small and callow;
Their little wings are short, their down
   Is mottled, grey and yellow.

There is a quiet little stream
   That runs into the moat,
Where tall green sedges spread their leaves,
   And water-lilies float.

Close by the margin of the brook
   The old duck made her nest,
Of straw, and leaves, and withered grass,
   And down from her own breast.

And there she sat for four long weeks,
   In rainy days and fine,
Until the ducklings all came out—
   Four, five, six, seven, eight, nine.

One peeped out from beneath her wing,
   One scrambled on her back;
"That's very rude," said Old Dame Duck,
   "Get off! quack, quack, quack, quack!"

Aunt Effie's Rhymes

The Blackbird

A slender young Blackbird built in a thorn-tree:
A spruce little fellow as ever could be;
His bill was so yellow, his feathers so black,
So long was his tail, and so glossy his back,
That his good little wife, who sat hatching her eggs,
And only just left them to stretch her poor legs,
And pick for a minute the worm she preferred,
Thought there never was seen such a beautiful bird.

D. M. Mulock

333

The Rabbit

Brown bunny sits inside his burrow
    Till everything is still,
Then out he slips along the furrow,
    Or up the grassy hill.

He nibbles all about the bushes
    Or sits to wash his face,
But at a sound he stamps, and rushes
    At a surprising pace.

You see some little streaks and flashes,
    A last sharp twink of white,
As down his hidey-hole he dashes
    And disappears from sight.

Edith King

The Hedgehog

The hedgehog is a little beast
    Who likes a quiet wood,
Where he can feed his family
    On proper hedgehog food.

He has a funny little snout
    That's rather like a pig's,
With which he smells, like us, of course,
    But also runts and digs.

He wears the queerest prickle coat,
    Instead of hair or fur,
And only has to curl himself
    To bristle like a burr.

He does not need to battle with
    Or run away from foes,
His coat does all the work for him,
    It pricks them on the nose.

Edith King

The Birds

Do you ask what the birds say?
  The sparrow, the dove,
The linnet, and thrush say:
  I love and I love.

In the Winter they're silent,
  The wind is so strong;
What it says I don't know,
  But it sings a loud song.

But green leaves and blossoms,
  And sunny, warm weather,
And singing and loving,
  All come back together.

Then the lark is so brimful
  Of gladness and love,
The green fields below him,
  The blue sky above,

That he sings and he sings,
  And for ever sings he:
I love my love,
  And my love loves me.

S. T. Coleridge

If I were a Pig

If I were a pig and lived under a thatch
With nothing to do but gobble and scratch,
How nice it would be to look out now and then
And see the great winds blowing over the fen.

For pigs, though so greedy and ugly, are wise,
And see quite a lot with their funny slit-eyes—
Little soft breezes that shimmer and shine,
And winds like green oceans, all misty and fine.

Elizabeth Fleming

335

The Bird Bath

There is a bird bath on our grass,
I wait to watch it as I pass,
And see the little sparrow things
Stand on the edge with flapping wings.
They give each eye a merry wink
And stoop to take a little drink,
And then, before I'm fairly gone,
They bath with all their clothing on!

Florence Hoatson

Skippets, the Bad One

High upon the hillside where the shadows play
   Lives gentle Mrs. Rabbit with her family of three,
And Spillikins and Spottikins, it's only right to say,
   Are the dearest little rabbits you can ever hope to see.

       But Skippets is the bad one,
          The mad one,
           The saucy one,
Skippets is the lazy one who won't wash his face.
        Skippets is the naughty one,
          The haughty one,
           The pushing one,
Skippets is the forward one who doesn't know his place.

Spillikins and Spottikins will never stay out late,
   And wander in the gloomy woods as many rabbits do.
Why, even in the summer-time, they're always in by eight —
   In case they catch a cold, you see, by sitting in the dew.

       But Skippets is the frisky one,
          The risky one,
           The roving one,
Skippets is the wilful one whose ways are hard to trace.
        Skippets is the careless one,
          The won't-come-home-at-bedtime one —
Skippets is the wicked one who's always in disgrace!

Christine E. Bradley

Birds' Nests

"Caw," said the rook,
"My nest is here. Look!
At the top of a tree
Is the best place for me."

"Coo," called the dove
From her nest above;
"In the fork of a beech
I am quite out of reach."

"Hark!" carolled a lark,
"I sing until dark,
My nest on the ground
Is not easily found."

"Hush!" sang a thrush,
"In this holly bush
I am safe from all harm
With my blue eggs so warm."

But Robin Redbreast
From her mossy nest
Said never a word,
What a wise little bird!

Millicent Seager

The Song of the Bird

"The rivers rush into the sea,
    By castle and town they go;
The winds behind them merrily
    Their noisy trumpets blow.

"The clouds are passing far and high,
    We little birds in them play;
And everything that can sing and fly
    Goes with us, and far away."

H. W. Longfellow

337

The Robin

Some folk like the Chaffinch,
    Others fancy Tits,
But I prefer the Robin
    That near my window sits.

The Tits they love bright colours;
    Their coats are yellow-green.
That they fancy fine, gay clothing
    Is plainly to be seen.

The Robin dresses simply—
    A brown cap on his head,
Brown coat with soft grey breeches,
    And waistcoat orange-red.

He comes into my kitchen;
    Some crumbs to him I give;
And he shall have my friendship
    As long as he shall live.

O. M. Bent

One Blackbird

The stars must make an awful noise
    In whirling round the sky;
Yet somehow I can't even hear
    Their loudest song or sigh.

So it is wonderful to think
    One blackbird can outsing
The voice of all the swarming stars
    On any day in spring.

Harold Monro

The Crow

Old Crow, upon the tall tree-top
　　I see you sitting at your ease,
You hang upon the highest bough
　　And balance in the breeze.

How many miles you've been to-day
　　Upon your wing so strong and black,
And steered across the dark grey sky
　　Without a guide or track;

Above the city wrapped in smoke,
　　Green fields and rivers flowing clear;
Now tell me, as you passed them o'er,
　　What did you see and hear?

The old crow shakes his sooty wing
　　And answers hoarsely, "Caw, caw, caw,"
And that is all the crow can tell
　　Of what he heard and saw.

Mrs. Alexander

To a Cricket

Voice of summer, keen and shrill,
Chirping round the winter fire,
Of thy song I never tire,
Weary others as they will,
For thy song with summer's filled—
Filled with sunshine, filled with June;
Firelight echo of that noon
Heard in fields when all is still
In the golden light of May,
Bringing scents of new-mown hay,
Bees, and birds, and flowers away,
Prithee, haunt my fireside still,
Voice of summer, keen and shrill.

William Cox Bennett

Grasshopper Green

Grasshopper Green is a comical chap;
    He lives on the best of fare.
Bright little trousers, jacket and cap,
    These are his summer wear.
Out in the meadow he loves to go,
    Playing away in the sun;
It's hopperty, skipperty, high and low—
    Summer's the time for fun.

Grasshopper Green has a quaint little house;
    It's under the hedgerow gay.
Grandmother Spider, as still as a mouse,
    Watches him over the way.
Gladly he's calling the children, I know,
    Out in the beautiful sun;
It's hopperty, skipperty, high and low—
    Summer's the time for fun.

"Four-Paws"

Four-Paws, the kitten from the farm,
    Is come to live with Betsy Jane,
Leaving the stack-yard for the warm
    Flower-compassed cottage in the lane,
To wash his idle face and play
Among chintz cushions all the day.

Under the shadow of her hair
    He lies, who loves him, nor desists
To praise his whiskers and compare
    The tabby bracelets on his wrists—
Omelet at lunch, and milk at tea
Suits Betsy Jane, and so fares he.

Happy beneath her golden hand
    He purrs contentedly, nor hears
His Mother mourning through the land
    The old grey cat with tattered ears
And humble tail and heavy paw
Who brought him up among the straw.

Never by day she ventures nigh,
   But when the dusk grows dim and deep,
And moths flit out of the strange sky
   And Betsy has been long asleep—
Out of the dark she comes and brings
Her dark maternal offerings;

Some field-mouse or throstle caught
   Near netted fruit or in the corn,
Or rat, for this her darling sought
   In the old barn where he was born;
And all lest on his dainty bed
Four-Paws were faint or underfed.

Only between the midnight hours,
   Under the window-panes she walks,
Shrewdly among the scented flowers
   Nor snaps the soft nasturtium stalks,
Uttering still her plaintive cries,
And Four-Paws, from the house, replies,

Leaps from his cushion to the floor,
   Down the brick passage scantly lit,
Waits wailing at the outer door
   Till one arise and open it—
Then, from the swinging lantern's light
Runs to his Mother in the night.

              H. Parry Eden

The Wasp

When the ripe pears droop heavily,
The yellow wasp hums loud and long
His hot and drowsy autumn song.
A yellow flame he seems to be,
When darting suddenly from high
He lights where fallen peaches lie.

Yellow and black—this tiny thing's
A tiger-soul on elfin wings.

              William Sharp
              341

A Green Cornfield

The earth was green, the sky was blue:
   I saw and heard one sunny morn
A skylark hang between the two,
   A singing speck above the corn;

A stage below, in gay accord,
   White butterflies danced on the wing,
And still the singing skylark soared,
   And silent sank and soared to sing.

The cornfield stretched a tender green
   To right and left beside my walks;
I knew he had a nest unseen
   Somewhere among the million stalks.

And as I paused to hear his song
   While swift the sunny moments slid,
Perhaps his mate sat listening long,
   And listened longer than I did.

Christina Rossetti

Bunny Rabbit

Bunny creeps out and caresses his nose,
Combs out his ears with his fluttering toes,
   Blinks at the sun
   And commences to run
   With a skip and a hop
   And a flippety-flop,
Nibbling the clover wherever he goes;
But only when he is quite easy in mind
Does he button his little white tail down behind.

Bunny stops dead and stiffens each hair,
And his eyelids freeze in a terrified stare,
   And he pricks up his ears,
   For the sound that he hears
   Is a low muffled beat
   And a drumming of feet
And an ominous rub-a-dub-dubbing—but where?
He's off like the wind! He's off like the wind!
And his little white tail is unbuttoned behind.

Old Shellover

"Come!" said Old Shellover.
"What?" says Creep.
"The horny old Gardener's fast asleep;
    The fat cock Thrush
    To his nest has gone,
    And the dew shines bright
    In the rising Moon;
Old Sallie Worm from her hole doth peep;
"Come!" says old Shellover.
"Ay!" said Creep.

Walter de la Mare

The Kitten at Play

See the kitten on the wall,
Sporting with the leaves that fall,
Withered leaves, one, two and three,
Falling from the elder-tree;
Through the calm and frosty air
Of the morning bright and fair.

See the kitten, how she starts,
Crouches, stretches, paws and darts;
With a tiger-leap half way
Now she meets her coming prey.
Lets it go as fast as then
Has it in her power again.

Now she works with three and four,
Like an Indian conjurer;
Quick as he in feats of art,
Gracefully she plays her part;
Yet were gazing thousands there,
What would little Tabby care?

William Wordsworth

The City Mouse and the Garden Mouse

The city mouse lives in a house;
    The garden mouse lives in a bower,
He's friendly with the frogs and toads,
    And sees the pretty plants in flower.

The city mouse eats bread and cheese;
    The garden mouse eats what he can;
We will not grudge him seeds and stocks,
    Poor little timid furry man.

Christina Rossetti

Nicholas Nye

Thistle and darnel and dock grew there,
    And a bush, in the corner, of may,
On the orchard wall I used to sprawl
    In the blazing heat of the day;
Half asleep and half awake,
    While the birds went twittering by,
And nobody there my lone to share
    But Nicholas Nye.

Nicholas Nye was lean and grey,
    Lame of a leg and old,
More than a score of donkey's years
    He had seen since he was foaled;
He munched the thistles, purple and spiked,
    Would sometimes stoop and sigh,
And turn to his head, as if he said,
    "Poor Nicholas Nye!"

Alone with his shadow he'd drowse in the meadow,
    Lazily swinging his tail,
At break of day he used to bray—
    Not much too hearty and hale;
But a wonderful gumption was under his skin,
    And a clean calm light in his eye,
And once in a while, he'd smile—
    Would Nicholas Nye.

Seem to be smiling at me, he would,
 From his bush, in the corner, of may—
Bony and ownerless, widowed and worn,
 Knobble-kneed, lonely and grey;
And over the grass would seem to pass
 'Neath the deep dark blue of the sky,
Something much better than words between me
 And Nicholas Nye.

But dusk would come in the apple boughs,
 The green of the glow-worm shine,
The birds in nest would crouch to rest,
 And home I'd trudge to mine;
And there, in the moonlight, dark with dew,
 Asking not wherefore nor why,
Would brood like a ghost, and still as a post,
 Old Nicholas Nye.

                                        W. de la Mare

Grey Brother

The grey goat grazed on the hill,
 The grey hare grazed by his side,
And never a word they said
 From morning till eventide,
And never a word they said,
 Though each understood the other,
For the wind that played on the hill
 Whispered, "My dear grey brother."

The grey goat went home at dusk,
 Down to the cottage door,
The grey hare scuttled away
 To his burrow across the moor.
And never a word they said,
 Though each understood the other,
For the wind that slept on the hill
 Murmured, "Good night, grey brother."

                                        U. M. Montgomery

Birds' Nests

The skylark's nest among the grass
  And waving corn is found;
The robin's on a shady bank,
  With oak leaves strewn around.

The wren builds in an ivied thorn,
  Or old and ruined wall;
The mossy nest, so covered in,
  You scarce can see at all.

The martins build their nests of clay,
  In rows beneath the eaves;
While silvery lichens, moss and hair,
  The chaffinch interweaves.

The cuckoo makes no nest at all,
  But through the wood she strays
Until she finds one snug and warm,
  And there her egg she lays.

The sparrow has a nest of hay,
  With feathers warmly lined;
The ring-dove's careless nest of sticks
  On lofty trees we find.

Rooks build together in a wood,
  And often disagree;
The owl will build inside a barn
  Or in a hollow tree.

The blackbird's nest of grass and mud
  In brush and bank is found;
The lapwing's darkly spotted eggs
  Are laid upon the ground.

The magpie's nest is girt with thorns
  In leafless trees or hedge;
The wild duck and the water-hen
  Build by the water's edge.

Birds build their nests from year to year,
　　According to their kind,
Some very neat and beautiful,
　　Some easily designed.

The habits of each little bird,
　　And all its patient skill,
Are surely taught by God Himself
　　And ordered by His will.

The Pig's Tail

A furry coat has the bear to wear,
　　The tortoise a coat of mail,
The yak has more than his share of hair,
　　But—the pig has the curly tail.

The elephant's tusks are sold for gold,
　　The slug leaves a silver trail,
The parrot is never too old to scold,
　　But—the pig has the curly tail.

The lion can either roar or snore,
　　The cow gives milk in a pail,
The dog can guard a door, and more,
　　But—the pig has the curly tail.

The monkey makes you smile a while,
　　The tiger makes you quail,
The fox has many a wile of guile,
　　But—the pig has the curly tail.

For the rest of the beasts that prey or play,
　　From tiny mouse to the whale,
There's much that I could say to-day,
　　But—the pig has the curly tail.

Norman Ault

347

Secret Places

Nests well hidden,
  Secret treasure—
Bird's black eyes are
  Bright with pleasure.

Woods have many
  Secret spaces;
Violet-scented,
  Silent places.

Buds are cradles;
  Leaves and flowers
Wake when called
  By sun and showers.

Bees know where
  The blossoms keep
Their sweetest secrets
  Hidden deep.

After flying,
  After roaming,
Swallows know
  The way back—homing!

Irene Thompson

The Blackbird

In the far corner,
close by the swings,
every morning
a blackbird sings.

His bill's so yellow,
his coat's so black,
that he makes a fellow
whistle back.

Ann, my daughter,
thinks that he
sings for us two
especially.

Humbert Wolfe

348

Hark! Hark! The Lark

Hark! hark! the lark at heaven's gate sings,
   And Phoebus 'gins arise,
His steeds to water at those springs
   On chalic'd flowers that lies;
And winking Mary-buds begin
   To ope their golden eyes:
With everything that pretty bin,
   My lady sweet, arise!

Shakespeare

Vespers

O Blackbird, what a boy you are!
How do you go it!
Blowing your bugle to that one sweet star—
How do you blow it!
And does she hear you, blackbird boy, so far?
Or is it wasted breath?
"Good Lord. She is so bright
To-night!"
The Blackbird saith.

T. E. Brown

The Bells of Heaven

'Twould ring the bells of Heaven
   The wildest peal for years,
If Parson lost his senses
   And people came to theirs,
And he and they together
   Knelt down with angry prayers
For tamed and shabby tigers,
   And dancing dogs and bears,
And wretched, blind pit-ponies,
   And little hunted hares.

Ralph Hodgson
349

The Silent Snake

The birds go fluttering in the air,
   The rabbits run and skip,
Brown squirrels race along the bough,
   The May-flies rise and dip;
But, whilst these creatures play and leap,
The silent snake goes creepy-creep!

The birdies sing and whistle loud,
   The busy insects hum,
The squirrels chat, the frogs say "croak!"
   But the snake is always dumb.
With not a sound through grasses deep
The silent snake goes creepy-creep!

The Snail

To grass, or leaf, or fruit, or wall,
The Snail sticks close, nor fears to fall,
As if he grew there, house and all
               Together.

Within that house secure he hides,
When danger imminent betides
Of storms, or other harm besides,
               Of weather.

Give but his horns the slightest touch,
His self-collecting power is such,
He shrinks into his house with much
               Displeasure.

Where'er he dwells, he dwells alone,
Except himself has chattels none,
Well satisfied to be his own
               Whole treasure.

Thus hermit-like, his life he leads,
Nor partner of his Banquet needs,
And if he meets one, only feeds
                    The faster.

Who seeks him must be worse than blind
(He and his house are so combined)
If, finding it, he fails to find
                    Its master.

William Cowper

My Dog, Spot

I have a white dog
  Whose name is Spot,
And he's sometimes white
  And he's sometimes not.
But whether he's white
  Or whether he's not,
There's a patch on his ear
  That makes him Spot.

He has a tongue
  That is long and pink,
And he lolls it out
  When he wants to think,
He seems to think most
  When the weather is hot.
He's a wise sort of dog,
  Is my dog, Spot.

He likes a bone
  And he likes a ball,
But he doesn't care
  For a cat at all.
He waggles his tail
  And he knows what's what,
So I'm glad that he's my dog,
  My dog, Spot.

Rodney Bennett

351

The Secret

Jenny Wren's got a house
    Very cosy and round,
In a nook of green boughs
    Not too far from the ground.
And she sits very still
    In case people should know
Of the little warm eggs
    She is hiding, below.

Jenny Wren's little nest
    Has a secret to-day;
It's one that I guessed
    When I passed by that way.
For small Jenny Wren
    Was so busy about
I knew in a moment
    Her eggs had hatched out!

Elizabeth Fleming

The Greedy Little Pig

A little pig lived in a sty,
    He fed on meals three times a day,
He drank sweet milk from a shining trough
    And slept at night on a bed of hay.

This little pig once left his sty
    And roam'd three fields or more away,
He found the slope where the oak trees grew
    And where the plump brown acorns lay.
      And he ate, and he ate,
        As little pigs do;
      He ate and he ate,
        The whole day through.
Then he came back home to his bed of hay,
Grunt-grunt-grunting all the way.

Irene F. Pawsey

Sheep and Lambs

All in the April evening,
    April airs were abroad;
The sheep with their little lambs
    Pass'd me by on the road.

The sheep with their little lambs
    Pass'd me by on the road;
All in the April evening
    I thought on the Lamb of God.

Up in the blue, blue mountains
    Dewy pastures are sweet:
Rest for the little bodies,
    Rest for the little feet.

All in the April evening,
    April airs were abroad;
I saw the sheep with their lambs,
    And thought on the Lamb of God.

Katharine Tynan

Mr Squirrel

I saw a brown squirrel to-day in the wood,
He ran here and there just as fast as he could;
I think he was looking for nuts for his store,
He'd found quite a lot, but he still wanted more.

He can't find much food once the winter is here,
He hides all his nuts in a hole somewhere near,
Then settles himself for a long winter sleep,
Coming out now and then for a nut and a peep.

His long bushy tail keeps him cosy and warm,
His nest's far away from the wind and the storm.
But when Springtime comes back, I think that, maybe,
He'll be waiting again in the woodland for me.

V. M. Julian

The Snare

I hear a sudden cry of pain!
   There is a rabbit in a snare;
Now I hear the cry again,
   But I cannot tell from where.

But I cannot tell from where
   He is calling out for aid;
Crying on the frightened air,
   Making everything afraid.

Making everything afraid,
   Wrinkling up his little face,
As he cries again for aid;
   And I cannot find the place!

And I cannot find the place
   Where his paw is in the snare;
Little one! Oh, little one!
   I am searching everywhere.

James Stephens

Whale

Wouldn't you like to be a whale
And sail serenely by—
An eighty-foot whale from the tip of your tail
And a tiny, briny eye?
Wouldn't you like to wallow
Where nobody says "Come out!"?
Wouldn't you *love* to swallow
And blow all the brine about?
Wouldn't you like to be always clean
But never to have to wash, I mean,
And wouldn't you love to spout—
   O yes, just think—
A feather of spray as you sail away,
And rise and sink and rise and sink,
And blow all the brine about?

Geoffrey Dearmer

The Old Brown Horse

The old brown horse looks over the fence
   In a weary sort of way;
He seems to be saying to all who pass:
   "Well, folks, I've had my day—
I'm simply watching the world go by,
   And nobody seems to mind,
As they're dashing past in their motor-cars,
   A horse who is lame and half-blind."

The old brown horse has a shaggy coat,
   But once he was young and trim,
And he used to trot through the woods and lanes
   With the man who was fond of him.
But his master rides in a motor-car,
   And it makes him feel quite sad
When he thinks of the days that used to be,
   And of all the times they had.

Sometimes a friendly soul will stop
   Near the fence, where the tired old head
Rests wearily on the topmost bar,
   And a friendly word is said.
Then the old brown horse gives a little sigh
   As he feels the kindly touch
Of a hand on his mane or his shaggy coat,
   And he doesn't mind so much.

So if you pass by the field one day,
   Just stop for a word or two
With the old brown horse who was once as young
   And as full of life as you.
He'll love the touch of your soft young hand,
   And I know he'll seem to say—
"Oh, thank you, friend, for the kindly thought
   For a horse who has had his day."

W. F. Holmes

Just Jumbo

A big grey elephant
  Lives in the Zoo,
And what does that big
  Grey elephant do?

He spends all day long
  Going back and fore,
Carrying children
  By the score.

Little Richard
  And Robin and Claude,
Angela Jane
  And her sister Maude.

Big grey elephant—
  He never tires,
In the hottest sunshine
  He never perspires.

Patient and quiet
  He walks to-day
And waves his trunk
  With a gentle sway.

Eileen Mathias

From Ducks

Yes, ducks are valiant things
On nests of twigs and straws,
And ducks are soothy things
And lovely on the lake
When that the sunlight draws
Thereon their pictures dim
In colours cool.
And when beneath the pool
They dabble, and when they swim
And make their rippling rings,
O ducks are beautiful things!

But ducks are comical things—
As comical as you.
Quack!
They waddle round, they do.
They eat all sorts of things,
And then they quack.
By barn and stable and stack
They wander at their will,
But if you go too near
They look at you through black
Small topaz-glinted eyes
And wish you ill.
Triangular and clear
They leave their curious track
In mud at the water's edge,
And there amid the sedge
And slime they gobble and peer
Saying "Quack! quack!"

F. W. Harvey

The Girl and her Fawn

With sweetest milk and sugar first
I it at my own fingers nursed;
And as it grew, so every day
It wax'd more white and sweet than they—
It had so sweet a breath! and oft
I blush'd to see its foot more soft
And white—shall I say?—than my hand,
Nay, any lady's of the land!

It is a wondrous thing how fleet
'Twas on those little silver feet:
With what a pretty skipping grace
It oft would challenge me the race:—
And when't had left me far away
'Twould stay, and run again, and stay:
For it was nimbler much than hinds,
And trod as if on the four winds.

A. Marvell

357

The Thrush's Nest

Within a thick and spreading hawthorn bush
   That overhung a molehill large and round,
I heard from morn to morn a merry thrush
   Sing hymns to sunrise, and I drank the sound
With joy; and often, an intruding guest,
   I watched her secret toil from day to day.
How true she warped the moss, to form a nest,
   And modelled it within with wood and clay;
And by and by, like heath bells gilt with dew,
   There lay her shining eggs, as bright as flowers,
Ink-spotted over shells of greeny blue;
   And there I witnessed in the sunny hours
A brood of Nature's minstrels chirp and fly,
Glad as the sunshine and the laughing sky.

John Clare

The Cow and the Ass

Beside a green meadow a stream used to flow,
So clear, you might see the white pebbles below;
To this cooling brook, the warm cattle would stray,
To stand in the shade on a hot summer's day.

A cow quite oppressed by the heat of the sun,
Came here to refresh as she often had done;
And, standing quite still, stooping over the stream
Was musing, perhaps—or perhaps she might dream.

But soon a brown ass of respectable look
Came trotting up also to taste of the brook,
And to nibble a few of the daisies and grass.
"How d'ye do?" said the cow. "How d'ye do?" said the
    ass.

"Take a seat!" said the cow, gently waving her hand.
"By no means, dear madam," said he, "while you stand!"
Then, stooping to drink, with a very low bow,
"Ma'am, your health!" said the ass.
"Thank you, sir," said the cow.

Ann and Jane Taylor

Hiawatha's Childhood

At the door on summer evenings
Sat the little Hiawatha;
Heard the whispering of the pine-trees,
Heard the lapping of the water,
Sounds of music, words of wonder;
"Minne-wawa!" said the pine-trees,
"Mudway-aushka!" said the water.
        Saw the fire-fly, Wah-wah-taysee,
Flitting through the dusk of evening,
With the twinkle of its candle
Lighting up the brakes and bushes,
And he sang the song of children,
Sang the song Nokomis taught him:
        "Wah-wah-taysee, little firefly,
Little, flitting, white-fire insect,
Little, dancing, white-fire creature,
Light me with your little candle,
Ere upon my bed I lay me,
Ere in sleep I close my eyelids!"

Henry Wadsworth Longfellow

Hiawatha's Brothers

Then the little Hiawatha
Learned of every bird its language,
Learned their names and all their secrets,
How they built their nest in summer,
Where they hid themselves in winter,
Talked with them whene'er he met them,
Called them "Hiawatha's chickens."
Of all beasts he learned the language,
Learned their names and all their secrets,
How the beavers built their lodges,
Where the squirrels hid their acorns,
How the reindeer ran so swiftly,
Why the rabbit was so timid,
Talked with them whene'er he met them,
Called them "Hiawatha's brothers."

Henry Wadsworth Longfellow

Pensioners

My pensioners who daily
   Come here to beg their fare,
For all their need dress gaily,
   And have a jaunty air.
With "Tira-lira-lira—
   Now of your charity,
Pray help the little brethern
   Of noble poverty."

One shines in glossy sable,
   One wears a russet coat,
And one who seeks a table
   Has red about his throat.
With "Tira-lira-lira"—
   Gay waistcoat, speckled vest,
Black cap and fine blue bonnet,
   They come so bravely dressed.

To all I gladly scatter
   In this their time of need,
Heap bread upon their platter
   And ask not for my meed,
But in their jocund spring-time
   Their songs give back to me
A thousandfold, my brethern,
   Of noble poverty.

W. M. Letts

The Hedgehog and His Coat

The owls have feathers lined with down
   To keep them nice and warm;
The rats have top-coats soft and brown
   To wrap in from the storm;
And nearly every bird and beast
   Has cosy suits to wear,
But Mr Hedgehog has the least
   Of any for his share.

His back is stuck with prickly pins
    That breezes whistle through,
And when the winter-time begins
    The only thing to do
Is just to find a leafy spot,
    And curl up from the rain,
Until the Spring comes, bright and hot,
    To waken him again.

The owls and rats and all their folk
    Are soft and smooth to touch,
But hedgehogs are not nice to stroke,
    Their prickles hurt so much.
So, though it looks a little queer,
    His coat is best of all;
For nobody could interfere
    With such a bristly ball!

                                        Elizabeth Fleming

The Lamb

        Little lamb, who made thee?
        Dost thou know who made thee,
    Gave thee life, and bade thee feed
    By the stream and o'er the mead.
    Gave thee clothing of delight,
    Softest clothing, woolly, bright;
    Gave thee such a tender voice,
    Making all the vales rejoice?
        Little lamb, who made thee?
        Dost thou know who made thee?

        Little lamb, I'll tell thee;
        Little lamb, I'll tell thee:
    He is called by thy name,
    For He calls Himself a Lamb;
    He is meek, and He is mild,
    He became a little child.
    I a child, and thou a lamb,
    We are called by His name.
        Little lamb, God bless thee!
        Little lamb, God bless thee!

                                        William Blake

361

The Tyger

Tyger! Tyger! burning bright
In the forests of the night,
What immortal hand or eye
Could frame thy fearful symmetry?

In what distant deeps or skies
Burnt the fire of thine eyes?
On what wings dare he aspire?
What the hand dare seize the fire?

And what shoulder, and what art,
Could twist the sinews of thy heart?
And when thy heart began to beat,
What dread hand? and what dread feet?

What the hammer? what the chain?
In what furnace was thy brain?
What the anvil? what dread grasp
Dare its deadly terrors clasp?

When the stars threw down their spears,
And watered Heaven with their tears,
Did he smile his work to see?
Did He who made the Lamb make thee?

Tyger! Tyger! burning bright
In the forests of the night,
What immortal hand or eye,
Dare frame thy fearful symmetry?

William Blake

Fan, the Filly

Bumpety, bumpety, bump.
The horses run down the green hill.
There's Fan the wild filly again at her tricks!
She rears at the fence and she knocks down the sticks
To get at the hay at the base of the ricks.
Bumpety, bumpety, bump.

362

Bumpety, bumpety, bump.
The horses run down the green hill.
They're all of them wanting a share of the hay,
The Roan and the Dapple, the Black and the Bay;
They follow the filly and gallop away.
Bumpety, bumpety, bump.

Bumpety, bumpety, bump.
The horses run up the green hill.
For old Farmer Brown has come out with his man
To halter the mischievous filly called Fan,
And sell her for gold at the Fair if he can.
Bumpety, bumpety, bump.

Bumpety, bumpety, bump.
The horses run up the green hill,
But where there were five there are now only four,
For Fan the wild filly will gallop no more;
She stands in the shafts at a gentleman's door.
Bumpety, bumpety, bump.

Wilfred Thorley

The Badgers

Brocks snuffle from their holt within
A writhen root of black-thorn old,
And moonlight streaks the gashes bold
Of lemon fur from ear to chin.
They stretch and snort and snuff the air,
Then sit, to plan the night's affair.

The neighbours, fox and owl, they heed
And many whispering scents and sounds
Familiar on their secret rounds,
Then silently make sudden speed,
Paddling away in single file
Adown the eagle fern's dim aisle.

Eden Philpotts

The Nightingale

The speckled bird sings in the tree
  When all the stars are silver-pale.
Come, children, walk the night with me,
  And we shall hear the nightingale.

The nightingale is a shy bird,
  He flits before you through the night.
And now the sleepy vale is stirred
  Through all its green and gold and white.

The moon leans from her place to hear,
  The stars shed golden star-dust down,
For now comes in the sweet o' the year,
  The country's gotten the greenest gown.

The blackbird turns upon his bed,
  The thrush has oped a sleeping eye,
Quiet each downy sleepy-head;
  But who goes singing up the sky?

It is, it is the nightingale,
  In the tall tree upon the hill.
To moonlight and the dewy vale
  The nightingale will sing his fill.

He's but a homely, speckled bird,
  But he has gotten a golden flute,
And when his wondrous song is heard,
  Blackbird and thrush and lark are mute.

Troop, children dear, out to the night,
  Clad in the moonlight silver-pale,
And in the world of green and white
  'Tis you shall hear the nightingale.

Katharine Tynan

The Squirrel

The pretty red Squirrel lives up in a tree,
A little blithe creature as ever can be;
He dwells in the boughs where the stock-dove broods,
Far in the shades of the green summer woods,
His food is the young juicy cones of the pine,
And the milky beech-nut is his bread and his wine.
In the joy of his nature he frisks with a bound
To the topmost twigs, and then down to the ground,
Then up again like a wingèd thing,
And from tree to tree with a vaulting spring;
Then he sits up aloft, and looks waggish and queer,
As if he would say, "Ay, follow me here!"
And then he grows pettish, and stamps his foot;
And then independently cracks his nut!
And thus he lives the long summer through.
Without a care or a thought of sorrow,
But, small as he is, he knows he may want
In the bleak winter weather, when food is scant:
So he finds a hole in an old tree's core,
And there makes his nest and lays up his store;
Then when cold winter comes and the trees are bare,
When the white snow is falling and keen is the air,
He heeds it not, as he sits by himself
In his warm little nest, with his nuts on his shelf.
O wise little squirrel! no wonder that he,
In the green summer woods, is as blithe as can be!

Mary Howitt

Valentine's Day

Oh! I wish I were a tiny brown bird from out the south,
 Settled among the alder holts, and twittering by the stream;
I would put my tiny tail down, and put up my tiny mouth,
 And sing my tiny life away in one melodious dream.

I would sing about the blossoms, and the sunshine and the sky
 And the tiny wife I mean to have in such a cosy nest;
And if someone came and shot me dead, why then I could but
 die,
 With my tiny life and tiny song just ended at their best.

Charles Kingsley

The Sea-Gull

Oh, the white Sea-gull, the wild Sea-gull,
   A joyful bird is he,
As he lies like a cradled thing at rest
   In the arms of a sunny sea!
The little waves rock to and fro,
   And the white Gull lies asleep,
As the fisher's bark, with breeze and tide,
   Goes merrily over the deep.
The ship, with her fair sails set, goes by,
   And her people stand to note
How the Sea-gull sits on the rocking waves,
   As if in an anchored boat.

The sea is fresh, the sea is fair,
   And the sky calm overhead,
And the Sea-gull lies on the deep, deep sea,
   Like a king in his royal bed!
Oh, the white Sea-gull, the bold Sea-gull,
   A joyful bird is he,
Throned like a king, in calm repose
   On the breast of the heaving sea!

The waves leap up, the wild wind blows,
   And the Gulls together crowd,
And wheel about, and madly scream
   To the deep sea roaring loud.
And let the sea roar ever so loud,
   And the wind pipe ever so high,
With a wilder joy the bold Sea-gull
   Sends forth a wilder cry.

For the Sea-gull, he is a daring bird,
   And he loves with the storm to sail;
To ride in the strength of the billowy sea,
   And to breast the driving gale!
The little boat, she is tossed about,
   Like a sea-weed, to and fro;
The tall ship reels like a drunken man,
   As the gusty tempests blow.

But the Sea-gull laughs at the fear of man,
    And sails in a wild delight
On the torn-up breast of the night-black sea,
    Like a foam cloud, calm and white.
The waves may rage and the winds may roar,
    But he fears not wreck nor need;
For he rides the sea, in its stormy strength,
    As a strong man rides his steed.

Oh, the white Sea-gull, the bold Sea-gull!
    He makes on the shore his nest,
And he tries what the inland fields may be;
    But he loveth the sea the best!
And away from land a thousand leagues,
    He goes 'mid surging foam;
What matter to him is land or shore,
    For the sea is his truest home!

Mary Howitt

Kindness to Animals

Little children, never give
Pain to things that feel and live:
Let the gentle robin come
For the crumbs you save at home, —
As his meat you throw along
He'll repay you with a song;
Never hurt the timid hare
Peeping from her green grass lair,
Let her come and sport and play
On the lawn at close of day;
The little lark goes soaring high
To the bright windows of the sky,
Singing as if 'twere always spring,
And fluttering on an untired wing, —
Oh! let him sing his happy song,
Nor do these gentle creatures wrong.

The Plaint of the Camel

Canary-birds feed on sugar and seed,
    Parrots have crackers to crunch;
And as for the poodles, they tell me the noodles
    Have chicken and cream for their lunch.
But there's never a question
About MY digestion,
    ANYTHING does for me.

Cats, you're aware, can repose in a chair,
    Chickens can roost upon rails;
Puppies are able to sleep in a stable,
    And oysters can slumber in pails.
But no one supposes
A poor Camel dozes.
    ANY PLACE does for me.

Lambs are enclosed where it's never exposed,
    Coops are constructed for hens;
Kittens are treated to houses well heated,
    And pigs are protected by pens.
But a Camel comes handy
Wherever it's sandy,
    ANYWHERE does for me.

People would laugh if you rode a giraffe,
    Or mounted the back of an ox;
It's nobody's habit to ride on a rabbit,
    Or try to bestraddle a fox.
But as for a Camel, he's
Ridden by families—
    ANY LOAD does for me.

A snake is as round as a hole in the ground;
    Weasels are wavy and sleek;
And no alligator could ever be straighter
    Than lizards that live in a creek.
But a camel's all lumpy,
And bumpy, and humpy,
    ANY SHAPE does for me.

Charles Edward Carryl

The Elephant

The Elephant is like a wall,
He is broad and very tall.
Upon his back we have a ride,
And swing and sway from side to side.

E. J. Falconer

The Bird at Dawn

What I saw was just one eye
In the dawn as I was going:
A bird can carry all the sky
In that little button glowing.

Never in my life I went
So deep into a firmament.

He was standing on a tree,
All in blossom overflowing;
And purposely looked hard at me,
At first, as if to question merrily:
"Where are you going?"
But next some far more serious thing to say:
I could not answer, could not look away.

Oh, that hard, round, and so distracting eye:
Little mirror of all sky!—
And then the after-song another tree
Held, and sent radiating back on me.

If no man had invented human word,
And a bird-song had been
The only way to utter what we mean,
What would we men have heard,
What understood, what seen,
Between the trills and pauses, in between
The singing and the silence of a bird?

Harold Monro

369

Familiar Friends

The horses, the pigs,
And the chickens,
The turkeys, the ducks,
And the sheep!
I can see all my friends
From my window
As soon as I waken
From sleep.

The cat on the fence
Is out walking.
The geese have gone down
For a swim.
The pony comes trotting
Right up to the gate;
He knows I have candy
For him.

The cows in the pasture
Are switching
Their long tails
To keep off the flies.
And old mother dog
Has come out in the yard
With five pups, to give me
A surprise.

James S. Tippett

To the Cuckoo

O blithe new-comer, I have heard,
  I hear thee, and rejoice:
O Cuckoo! shall I call thee bird
  Or but a wandering voice?

While I am lying on the grass,
  The two-fold shout I hear;
From hill to hill it seems to pass,
  At once far off and near.

Though babbling only to the vale
    Of sunshine and of flowers,
Thou bringest unto me a tale
    Of visionary hours.

Thrice, welcome, darling of the Spring!
    Even yet thou art to me
No bird, but an invisible thing,
    A voice, a mystery.

W. Wordsworth

The Sheep

Lazy sheep, pray tell me why
In the grassy fields you lie,
Eating grass and daisies white,
From the morning till the night?
Everything can something do,
But what kind of use are you?

Nay, my little master, nay,
Do not serve me so, I pray;
Don't you see the wool that grows
On my back to make you clothes?
Cold, and very cold you'd get,
If I did not give you it.

Sure it seems a pleasant thing
To nip the daisies in the spring,
But many chilly nights I pass
On the cold and dewy grass,
Or pick a scanty dinner where
All the common's brown and bare.

Then the farmer comes at last,
When the merry spring is past,
And cuts my woolly coat away
To warm you in the winter's day;
Little master, this is why
In the grassy fields I lie.

Ann Taylor

371

A Number of Things

I love all beauteous things,
I seek and adore them

Mrs. MacQueen
(OR The Lollie-Shop)

With glass like a bull's eye,
   And shutters of green,
Down on the cobbles
   Lives Mrs. MacQueen.

At six she rises;
   At nine you see
Her candle shine out
   In the linden tree;

And at half-past nine
   Not a sound is nigh,
But the bright moon's creeping
   Across the sky;

Or a far dog baying;
   Or a twittering bird
In its drowsy nest,
   In the darkness stirred;

Or like the roar
   Of a distant sea
A long-drawn S-s-sh!
   In the linden tree.

Walter de la Mare

The Lace Pedlar

Who'll buy my laces? I've laces to sell!
Long laces, strong laces, short laces as well.
Laces of cotton, of silk and mohair,
Laces of leather, a penny a pair;
A lace for your body, a lace for your shoe;
Black laces, white laces, scarlet and blue,
Here is leather for schoolboys, and silk for a girl;
But a queen must have silver with taggles of pearl.

Catherine A. Morin

Everyday Things

Millionaires, presidents—even kings
Can't get along without everyday things.

Were you president, king or millionaire,
You'd use a comb to comb your hair.

If you wished to be clean—and you would, I hope—
You'd take a bath with water and soap.

And you'd have to eat—if you wanted to eat—
Bread and vegetables, fish and meat;

While your drink for breakfast would probably be
Milk or chocolate, coffee or tea.

You'd have to wear—you could hardly refuse—
Under clothes, outer clothes, stockings and shoes.

If you wished to make a reminding note,
You'd take a pencil out of your coat;

And you couldn't sign a letter, I think,
With anything better than pen and ink.

If you wanted to read, you'd be sure to look
At newspaper, magazine, or book;

And if it happened that you were ill,
You'd down some oil or choke on a pill.

If you had a cold I can only suppose
You'd use a handkerchief for your nose.

When you wanted to rest your weary head,
Like other folks, you'd hop into bed.

Millionaires, presidents—even kings
Can't get along without everyday things.

Jean Ayer

In the Train

As we rush, as we rush in the train,
　The trees and the houses go wheeling back,
But the starry heavens above the plain
　Come flying on our track.

All the beautiful stars of the sky,
　The silver doves of the forest of night,
Over the dull earth swarm and fly,
　Companions of our flight.

We will rush ever on without fear;
　Let the goal be far, the flight be fleet!
For we carry the heavens with us, dear,
　While the earth slips from under our feet!

James Thomson ("B.V.")

The Balloon Man

He always comes on market days,
　And holds balloons—a lovely bunch—
And in the market square he stays,
　And never seems to think of lunch.

They're red and purple, blue and green,
　And when it is a sunny day
Tho' carts and people get between
　You see them shining far away.

And some are big and some are small,
　All tied together with a string,
And if there is a wind at all
　They tug and tug like anything.

Some day perhaps he'll let them go
　And we shall see them sailing high,
And stand and watch them from below—
　They *would* look pretty in the sky!

Rose Fyleman

I Love All Beauteous Things

I love all beauteous things,
    I seek and adore them;
God hath no better praise,
And man in his hasty days
    Is honoured for them.

I too will something make
    And joy in the making;
Although tomorrow it seem
Like the empty words of a dream
    Remembered on waking.

Robert Bridges

Snow In Town

Nothing is quite so quiet and clean
    As snow that falls in the night;
And isn't it jolly to jump from bed
    And find the whole world white?

It lies on the window ledges,
    It lies on the boughs of the trees,
While sparrows crowd at the kitchen door,
    With a pitiful "If you please?"

It lies on the arm of the lamp-post,
    Where the lighter's ladder goes
And the policeman under it beats his arms,
    And stamps to feel his toes;

No sound there is in the snowy road
    From the horse's cautious feet,
And all is hushed but the postman's knocks
    Rat-tatting down the street.

Till men come round with shovels
    To clear the snow away,—
What a pity it is that when it falls
    They never let it stay!

Rickman Mark

My Playmate

I often wonder how it is
 That on a rainy day,
A little boy, just like myself,
 Comes out with me to play.

And we step in all the puddles
 When walking into town,
But though I stand the right way up,
 He's always upside down.

I have to tread upon his feet,
 Which is a sorry sight,
With my right foot on his left foot,
 My left foot on his right.

I really wish he'd talk to me,
 He seems so very kind
For when I look and smile at him
 He does the same, I find.

But I never hear him speaking,
 So surely he must be
In some strange land the other side,
 Just opposite to me.

Mary I. Osborn

Street Scene

In the placid summer midnight,
 Under the drowsy sky,
I seem to hear in the stillness
 The moths go glimmering by.

One by one from the windows
 The lights have all been sped,
Never a blind looks conscious—
 The street is asleep in bed!

W. E. Henley

Postman's Knock

Rattat! Rattat!
  There's the postman at the door,
He always knocks like that,
  No matter who it's for.
It may be a letter
  And it might be a box,
So I'm always very glad
  When the postman knocks.

Rattat! Rattat!
  Shall I run along to see
If he is on the mat
  With something meant for me?
It may be just a postcard,
  But it might be a box,
So I always run to look
  When the postman knocks.

Rodney Bennett

Mr Coggs

A watch will tell the time of day,
Or tell it nearly, any way,
Excepting when it's overwound,
Or when you drop it on the ground.

If any of our watches stop,
We haste to Mr Cogg's shop,
For though to scold he pretends
He's quite among our special friends.

He fits a dice-box in his eye,
And takes a long and thoughtful spy,
And prods the wheels, and says, "Dear, dear!
More carelessness I greatly fear!"

And then he lays his dice-box down
And frowns a most prodigious frown;
But if we ask him what's the time,
He'll make his gold repeater chime.

E. V. Lucas

Blacksmith

All the night
And all day long
I hark to the sound
Of the blacksmith's song.

Red his fire—
The bright sparks fly
To dance with stars
In the joyous sky.

B. K. Pyke

The Engine Driver

Onward flies the rushing train,
Now in sunshine, now in rain;
Now through pleasant banks we ride,
Now o'er fenland stretching wide.

Now it is a forest nook.
Now a village by a brook,
Now a tunnel, black as night,
Shutting all things from the sight.

Now through meadows green we sweep,
Now below a wooded steep,
Now by smoky hives of men,
Now through quiet fields again.

Still the fiery steeds obey,
Still we rattle on our way;
Now beneath the placid moon,
Silvering the woods of June.

Now beneath a wilder sky,
Where the moon rides fast and high;
Now through snowflakes on the blast,
To the lights of home at last.

Who is he that drives the train,
In the sunshine and the rain;
Weather-beaten, bluff and strong,
Hero worthy of a song?

Who more earnest, brave and true,
In the work he has to do?
First in danger, first in blame,
No man earns a nobler name.

G.S.O.

The Journey

We are going on a journey,
    We are going all the way,
A-riding in a wagon
    On soft sweet-scented hay:
The Wagoner is waiting
    (A jolly coachman he)
To take us on our journey
    To a farm-house by the sea.
Our great big friends the horses
    Are joining in the fun,
A knowing look they're wearing
    While waiting in the sun;
It's such a jolly farm-house
    In the valley by the sea,
And the farmer's just as jolly
    As any man could be.
There isn't any hurry,
    The ride is spendid sport,
A wood, a windy common,
    Then a little sleepy port.
The farmer's wife is waiting,
    With strawberries for tea,
And cream and smiles of welcome,
    In the farm-house by the sea.
And when the day is over,
    All tired with sheer delight,
We'll climb up to our bedroom
    To sleep away the night
Where linen smells of lavender;
    Then waking full of glee,
We'll hear the farmer calling,
    And murmur of the sea.

Aidan Clarke

A Bit of Colour

Grey was the morn, all things were grey,
  'Twas winter more than spring;
A bleak east wind swept o'er the land,
  And sobered everything.

Grey was the sky, the fields were grey,
  The hills, the woods, the trees—
Distance and foreground—all the scene
  Was grey in the grey breeze.

Grey cushions, and a grey skin rug,
  A dark grey wicker trap,
Grey were the ladies' hats and cloaks,
  And grey my coat and cap.

A narrow, lonely, grey old lane;
  And lo, on a grey gate,
Just by the side of a grey wood,
  A sooty sweep there sat!

With grimy chin 'twixt grimy hands
  He sat and whistled shrill;
And in his sooty cap he wore
  A yellow daffodil.

And often when the days are dull,
  I seem to see him still—
The jaunty air, the sooty face—
  And the yellow daffodil.

Horace Smith

Gypsies

Last night the gypsies came—
  Nobody knows from where.
Where they've gone to nobody knows,
  And nobody seems to care!

Between the trees on the old swamp road
  I saw them round their fire:
Tattered children and dogs that barked
  As the flames leaped high and higher;
There were black-eyed girls in scarlet shawls,
  Old folk wrinkled with years,
Men with handkerchiefs round their throats
  And silver loops in their ears.
Ragged and red like maple leaves
  When frost comes in the fall,
The gypsies stayed but a single night;
  In the morning gone were all—
Never a shaggy gypsy dog,
  Never a gypsy child;
Only a burnt-out gypsy fire
  Where danced that band so wild.

All gone and away,
  Who knows where?
Only the wind that sweeps
  Maple branches bare.

Rachel Field

The Idlers

The gipsies lit their fires by the chalk-pit anew,
And the hoppled horses supped in the further dusk and dew;
The gnats flocked round the smoke like idlers as they were
And through the grass and bushes the owls began to churr.

An ell above the woods the last of sunset glowed
With a dusky gold that filled the pond beside the road;
The cricketers had done, the leas all silent lay,
And the carrier's clattering wheels went past and died away.

The gipsies lolled and gossipped, and ate their stolen swedes,
Made merry with mouth-organs, worked toys with piths of
    reeds:
The old wives puffed their pipes, nigh as black as their hair,
And not one of them all seemed to know the name of care.

Edmund Blunden

The Deserted House

There's no smoke in the chimney,
   And the rain beats on the floor;
There's no glass in the window,
   There's no wood in the door;
The heather grows behind the house,
   And the sand lies before.

No hand hath trained the ivy,
   The walls are grey and bare;
The boats upon the sea sail by,
   Nor never tarry there.
No beast of the field comes nigh,
   Nor any bird of the air.

Mary E. Coleridge

In Days Gone By

I feel that in the days gone by
   I did not live with walls and roofs.
Long years ago in deserts dry
I lived beneath the open sky
   And heard the roar of thudding hoofs,
     And I was racing madly,
     My head bent to the wind,
     And fifty thousand horsemen
      Galloping behind!

I feel that in that long ago
   I must have been a Nomad child
Feeling the desert sun's fierce glow,
And then, in saddle, head bent low,
   Heading a horde of Bedouins wild.
     I shut my eyes an instant
     And see them in my mind,
     These fifty thousand horsemen
      Galloping, galloping,
     Fifty thousand horsemen
      Galloping behind!

Ida M. Mills

The Watchmaker's Shop

A street in our town
   Has a queer little shop
With tumble-down walls
   And a thatch on the top;
And all the wee windows
   With crookedy panes
Are shining and winking
   With watches and chains.

(All sorts and all sizes
   In silver and gold,
And brass ones and tin ones
   And the new ones and old;
And clocks for the kitchen
   And clocks for the hall,
High ones and low ones
   And wag-at-the-wall.)

The watchmaker sits
   On a long-leggèd seat
And bids you the time
   Of the day when you meet;
And round and about him
   There's ticketty-tock
From the tiniest watch
   To the grandfather clock.

I wonder he doesn't
   Get tired of the chime
And all the clocks ticking
   And telling the time;
But there he goes winding
   Lest any should stop,
This queer little man
   In the watchmaker's shop.

Caravans

I've seen caravans
Going to the fair!
   Come along,
   Come along,
Let's go there!

Hurrah! roundabouts
Lovely little swings,
   Coconuts,
   Coconuts,
Heaps of things!

See all the animals
Waiting for the show;
   Elephants,
   Elephants,
Let's all go!

Look! There's a tiger
Watching baby bears;
   Come away,
   Come away,
How he stares!

Hark! how the music plays
Ready for the fun!
   Come along,
   Come along,
Let's all run.

Irene Thompson

A Kayak Song

Over the dark water
  See the kayak steal;
Father's going searching
  For the fish and seal.

Will he have good hunting
Out beyond the floe?
He may see a bear there
'Mid the ice and snow.

If he gets a walrus,
There will be for me
Thongs and reins for sledges,
Whips of ivory.

Over the dark water
See the kayak steal
Softly— lest it frighten
Hidden fish and seal.

Lucy Diamond

Through the Porthole

(At Night)

When I went to bed at night,
Then my porthole was a frame:
If I watched a little while,
I would find that pictures came.

Once I saw the mast-head light
Of a far-off passing ship:
On the rolling, splashing sea
I could see it rise and dip.

In the great dark sky above
Stars were scattered everywhere,
Ships, I thought, were just like stars
As I lay and watched them there.

For a world is every star
In a heaven of its own:
Every ship a little world
Out upon the sea alone.

Marjorie Wilson

The Train

A green eye—and a red—in the dark,
Thunder—smoke—and a spark.

It is there—it is here—flashed by.
Whither will the wild thing fly?

It is rushing, tearing through the night,
Rending her gloom in its flight.

It shatters her silence with shrieks.
What is it the wild thing seeks?

Alas! for it hurries away
Them that are fain to stay.

Hurrah! for it carries home
Lovers and friends that roam.

Mary E. Coleridge

The Window Cleaner

A window cleaner's life is grand!
  Hurrying up his ladder-stair,
He sets himself with mop in hand
  To let in sunshine everywhere;
It makes me feel I'd like to be
  A window cleaner too, like him,
Taking my ladder round with me
  To get at windows dark and dim.

Having my polisher and mop
  On every dull and grimy pane,
I'd rub, and rub, and never stop
  Until I made them bright again;
I'd do the same by high and low,
  Making their glass so shiny-clean
That all who looked through it would know
  At once—the window-man had been!

Elizabeth Fleming

Fires

The kitchen fire that wakes so soon
   And has to work so hard,
Would rather be the fire that burns
   Behind the nursery guard.

The nursery fire that burns all day,
   And keeps alive so late,
Would rather be the pretty fire
   Within the parlour grate.

The parlour fire, so swept and fine,
   Would rather be, I know,
The gipsy fire that sparks away
   With all the winds that blow.

The gipsy fire burns out-of-doors
   In places wild and free;
I'd rather be a gipsy fire
   Than any fire, says she!

Elizabeth Fleming

The Flower-Seller

The Flower-seller's fat, and she wears a big shawl!
She sits on the kerb with her basket and all;
The wares that she sells us are not very dear
And are always the loveliest things of the year.
     Daffodils in April,
      Purple flags in May,
     Sweet peas like butterflies
      Upon a summer day,
     Brown leaves in autumn,
      Green leaves in spring,
     And berries in the winter
      When the carol-singers sing.
The Flower-seller sits with her hands in her lap,
When she's not crying Roses, she's taking a nap;
Her bonnet is queer, and she calls you My dear,
And sells you the loveliest things of the year.

Eleanor Farjeon

The Upside-Down World

I know a place that holds the Sky
A place where little white clouds lie;

The edge is all green as Grass,
The middle is as smooth as Glass;

And there the round sun makes his Bed;
And there a Tree stands on its Head;

Sometimes a Bird sits on that Tree;
Sometimes it sings a Song to me;

And always in that shining place
I see a little smiling Face;

She nods and smiles; but all the same
The Girl down there won't tell her name!

Hamish Hendry

The Scissor-Man

Sing a song of Scissor-men,
    "Mend a broken plate,
Bring your knives and garden shears,
    I'll do them while you wait.
Buzz-a-wuzz! Buzz-a-wuzz!
    Fast the wheel or slow,
Ticker Tacker! Ticker Tack!
    Rivets in a row."

Sing a song of Scissor-men,
    Sitting in the sun,
Sing it when the day begins,
    Sing it when it's done.
Be it hard or be it soft,
    Here's a jolly plan;
Sing to make the work go well,
    Like the Scissor-man.

Madeleine Nightingale

Shining Things

I love all shining things—
                  the lovely moon,
The silver stars at night,
                  gold sun at noon.
A glowing rainbow in
                  a stormy sky,
Or bright clouds hurrying
                  when wind goes by.

I love the glow-worm's elf-light
                  in the lane,
And leaves a-shine with glistening
                  drops of rain,
The glinting wings of bees,
                  and butterflies,
My purring pussy's green
                  and shining eyes.

I love the street-lamps shining
                  through the gloom,
Tall candles lighted in
                  a shadowy room,
New-tumbled chestnuts from
                  the chestnut tree,
And gleaming fairy bubbles
                  blown by me.

I love the shining buttons
                  on my coat,
I love the bright beads round
                  my mother's throat.
I love the coppery flames
                  of red and gold,
That cheer and comfort me,
                  when I'm a-cold.

The beauty of all shining things
                  is yours and mine,
It was a *lovely* thought of God
                  to make things shine.

Elizabeth Gould

391

The Shepherd Boy

The shepherd boy a kingdom rules,
　An emerald hill his throne;
Crown'd with golden sunshine,
　He reigneth there alone.

His goats, court-players are;
　Each wears a tinkling bell,
And the bird's sweet pipings,
　A royal concert tell.

And the piping and the bells,
　With the brook's soft rhymes,
Lull the drowsy king to sleep,
　While gently nod the pines.

Heinrich Heine

Topsy-Turvy Land

The people walk upon their heads,
　The sea is made of sand,
The children go to school by night,
　In Topsy-Turvy Land.

The front-door step is at the back,
　You're walking when you stand,
You wear your hat upon your feet,
　In Topsy-Turvy Land.

And 'buses on the sea you'll meet,
　While pleasure boats are planned
To travel up and down the streets
　Of Topsy-Turvy Land.

You pay for what you never get,
　I think it must be grand,
For when you go you're coming back,
　In Topsy-Turvy Land.

H. E. Wilkinson

The Ships

For many a year I've watched the ships a-sailing to and fro,
The mighty ships, the little ships, the speedy and the slow;
And many a time I've told myself that some day I would go
    Around the world that is so full of wonders.

The swift and stately liners, how they run without a rest!
The great three-masters, they have touched the East and told
    the West!
The monster burden-bearers—oh, they all have plunged and
    pressed
    Around the world that is so full of wonders!

The cruiser and the battleship that loom as dark as doubt,
The devilish destroyer and the hateful, hideous scout—
These deathly things may also rush, with roar and snarl and
    shout,
    Around the world that is so full of wonders!

The shabby tramp that like a wedge is hammered through the
    seas,
The little brown sailed brigantine that traps the lightest
    breeze—
Oh, I'd be well content to fare aboard the least of these
    Around the world that is so full of wonders.

The things I've heard, the things I've read, the things I've
    dreamed might be,
The boyish tales, the old men's yarns—they will not pass
    from me.
I've heard, I've read, I've dreamed—but all the time I've
    longed to *see*
    Around the world that is so full of wonders.

So year by year I watch the ships a-sailing to and fro,
The ships that come as strangers and the ships I've learned to
    know—
Folk smile to hear an old man say that *some* day he will go
    Around the world that is so full of wonders.

J. J. Bell

Dream Pedlary

If there were dreams to sell,
    What would you buy?
Some cost a passing bell;
    Some a light sigh,
That shakes from Life's fresh crown
Only a rose-leaf down.
If there were dreams to sell,
Merry and sad to tell,
And the crier rang the bell,
    What would you buy?

A cottage lone and still,
    With bowers nigh,
Shadowy, my woes to still,
    Until I die.
Such pearl from Life's fresh crown
Fain would I shake me down,
Were dreams to have at will,
This would best heal my ill,
    This would I buy.

                    Thomas Lovell Beddoes

The Old Kitchen Clock

Listen to the Kitchen Clock,
To itself it ever talks,
From its place it never walks;
"Tick-tock—tick-tock,"
Tell me what it says.

"I'm a very patient clock,
Never moved by hope or fear,
Though I've stood for many a year;
Tick-tock—tick-tock,"
That is what it says.

"I'm a very truthful clock;
People say, about the place,
Truth is written on my face;
Tick-tock—tick-tock,"
That is what it says.

"I'm a very active clock,
For I go while you're asleep.
Though you never take a peep.
Tick-tock—tick-tock,"
That is what it says.

"I'm a most obliging clock;
If you wish to hear me strike,
You may do it when you like;
Tick-tock—tick-tock,"
That is what it says.

What a talkative old clock!
Let us see what it will do
When the pointer reaches two.
"Ding-ding—tick-tock."
That is what it says.

Ann Hawkshawe

My Hut

I built a hut in a little wood;
Nobody came there—nobody could;
Only a bird and a rabbit perhaps—
Only the wind with three small taps.

You'll never find my hut in the wood;
If I can't find it, nobody could.
For the wind one day, crazy with play,
Carried my little hut away.

He didn't come with three small taps,
He banged on the door with thunderous raps,
Then he carried my lonely house away,
And I've searched for it now for a year and a day.

E. Mathias

New Sights

I like to see a thing I know
   Has not been seen before,
That's why I cut my apple through
   To look into the core.

It's nice to think, though many an eye
   Has seen the ruddy skin,
Mine is the very first to spy
   The five brown pips within.

Old Morgan

Old Morgan had a lovely harp,
   But he was no musician.
One day a man called at his door
   Upon a curious mission.

"I'm very hungry," said the man,
   "Just hear my tummy rumble."
"Come in," said Morgan, "take a seat,
   I'm not the man to grumble."

"I've eaten nothing," said the man,
   "I'm as empty as a drum."
"Sit down," said Morgan, "rest yourself,
   And please don't suck your thumb.

"Here's bread and cheese and butter,
   And the kettle singing sweetly.
We'll make a cup of tea," said he,
   As he spread the cloth on neatly.

And so the stranger ate his fill,
   And Morgan he ate with him,
"Play me a tune," said the stranger,
   And Morgan groaned within him.

Then sitting down beside his harp
   He made his sad confession.
"I love my lovely harp," he said,
   "But I am no musician.

"My music isn't fit to hear,
　　The noise I make's outrageous,
My fingers won't do what I want,
　　My thumbs are most rampageous."

"What is your dearest wish, sir?"
　　Said the stranger most benignly.
"To play my harp," said Morgan,
　　"I'd like to play divinely."

"I must be off," said the stranger,
　　"I really cannot linger.
You've been most kind to me," said he,
　　And he touched the harp with his finger.

And then the stranger vanished quite,
　　He vanished in a twinkling.
Old Morgan rubbed his wond'ring eyes,
　　And then he fell a-thinking.

But when his fingers touched the strings
　　The liquid notes came dancing,
And all the neighbours crowded in—
　　The music was entrancing.

G. D. Roberts

Shell Secrets

Tell me your secrets, pretty shell,
I will promise not to tell!

Humming, humming, soft and low—
All about the sea, I know.

You are murmuring, I think,
Of the sea-weeds, green and pink,

Of the tiny baby shells
Where the mother mermaid dwells.

Pretty shell, I'm waiting here,
Come, and whisper in my ear.

Pictures

I can see a picture.
   Tell me what you see—
Blue-bells in a beech wood.
   And green leaves on a tree.

I can see a picture.
   Tell me what you see—
A fleet, a fleet of fishing boats
   And sunshine on the sea.

I can see a picture.
   Tell me what you see—
Apples on the bending bough,
   As rosy as can be.

I can see a picture.
   Tell me what you see—
A choir of children carolling
   Around a Christmas Tree.

F. Ann Elliott

The Balloon Seller

I'd like to peddle toy balloons;
With globes like jolly suns and moons
Bobbing and bouncing there, I'd stay
Holding them high the live-long day.

I'd make them dance like anything,
All fastened to a bit of string,
Their golds and greens, and blues and reds
Glimmering over people's heads.

And all the folks would turn and stare,
And long to free them on the air.

Elizabeth Fleming

Playgrounds

In summer I am very glad
  We children are so small,
For we can see a thousand things
  That men can't see at all.

They don't know much about the moss
  And all the stones they pass:
They never lie and play among
  The forests in the grass:

They walk about a long way off:
  And, when we're at the sea,
Let father stoop as best he can
  He can't find things like me.

But, when the snow is on the ground
  And all the puddles freeze,
I wish that I were very tall,
  High up above the trees.

L. Alma Tadema

The Clothes-Line

Hand in hand they dance in a row,
Hither and thither, and to and fro,
Flip! Flap! Flop! and away they go—
Flutt'ring creatures as white as snow,
Like restive horses they caper and prance;
Like fairy-tale witches they wildly dance;
Rounded in front, but hollow behind,
They shiver and skip in the merry March wind.
One I saw dancing excitedly,
Struggling so wildly till she was free,
Then, leaving pegs and clothes-line behind her,
She flew like a bird, and no one can find her.
I saw her gleam, like a sail, in the sun,
Flipping and flapping and flopping for fun.
Nobody knows where she now can be,
Hid in a ditch, or drowned in the sea.
She was my handkerchief not long ago,
But she'll never come back to my pocket, I know.

Charlotte Druitt Cole

399

The Children's Bells

Where are your Oranges?
   Where are your Lemons?
What, are you silent now,
   Bells of St. Clement's?
You, of all bells that rang
   Once in old London,
You, of all bells that sang,
   Utterly undone?
You whom all children know
   Ere they know letters,
Making Big Ben himself
   Call you his betters?
Where are your lovely tones
   Fruitful and mellow,
Full-flavoured orange-gold,
   Clear lemon-yellow?
Ring again, sing again,
   Bells of St. Clement's!
Call as you swing again,
   "Oranges! Lemons!"
Fatherless children
   Are listening near you—
Sing for the children,
   The fathers will hear you.

Eleanor Farjeon

Tall Nettles

Tall nettles cover up, as they have done
   These many springs, the rusty harrow, the plough
Long worn out, and the roller made of stone;
   Only the elm butt tops the nettles now.

This corner of the farmyard I like most:
   As well as any bloom upon a flower
I like the dust on the nettles, never lost
   Except to prove the sweetness of a shower.

Edward Thomas

The Merry Heart

Jog on, jog on, the footpath way,
And merrily hent the stile-a;
A merry heart goes all the day,
Your sad tires in a mile-a.

Shakespeare

Beautiful Meals

How nice it is to eat!
All creatures love it so,
That they who first did spread,
Ere breaking bread,
A cloth like level snow,
Were right, I know.

And they were wise and sweet
Who, glad that meats taste good,
Used speech in an arch style,
And oft would smile
To raise the cheerful mood,
While at their food.

And those who first, so neat,
Placed fork and knife quite straight,
The glass on the right hand;
And all, as planned,
Each day set round the plate,—
Be their praise great!

For then, their hearts being light,
They plucked hedge-posies bright—
Flowers who, their scent being sweet,
Give nose and eye a treat:
'Twas they, my heart can tell,
Not eating fast but well,
Who wove the spell
Which finds me every day,
And makes each meal-time gay;
I know 'twas they.

T. Sturge Moore

Bread

"Farmer, is the harvest ready
  For we must have bread?"
"Go and look at all my fields,"
  Is what the farmer said.

So we ran and saw the wheat
  Standing straight and tall.
"There's your bread," the farmer said,
  "Have no fear at all."

"Miller, is the flour ready
  For we must have bread?"
"Go and look in all my sacks,"
  Is what the miller said.

So we ran and saw the flour,
  Soft and white as snow.
"There's your flour," the miller said,
  As we turned to go.

"Mother, is the oven ready
  For we must have bread?"
"Go and open wide the door,"
  Is what our mother said.

So we ran and saw the loaves
  Crisp and brown to see.
"There's your bread," our mother said,
  "Ready for your tea."

H. E. Wilkinson

Wireless

By the wireless I can hear
Voices sounding loud and clear,
Some alone and some in choirs,
Coming over with no wires,
Floating out upon the air,
From one small room to everywhere.

Rodney Bennett

Amy Elizabeth Ermyntrude Annie

Amy Elizabeth Ermyntrude Annie
Went to the country to visit her Grannie;

Learnt to churn butter and learnt to make cheese,
Learnt to milk cows and take honey from bees;

Learnt to spice roseleaves and learnt to cure ham,
Learnt to make cider and black-currant jam.

When she came home she could not settle down,
Said there was nothing to do in the town.

Nothing to do there and nothing to see:
Life was all shopping and afternoon tea!

Amy Elizabeth Ermyntrude Annie
Ran away back to the country and Grannie!

Queenie Scott-Hopper

The Little Things That Happen

The Little Things That Happen
  Are tucked into your mind,
And come again to greet you
  (Or most of them, you'll find).

Through many little doorways,
  Of which you keep the keys,
They crowd into your thinking—
  We call them Memories.

But some of them are rovers
  And wander off and get
So lost, the keys grow rusty,
  And that means—you forget.

But some stay ever near you;
  You'll find they never rove—
The keys are always shining—
Those are the things you love.

Marjorie Wilson

403

The Town Child

I live in the town
   In a street;
It is crowded with traffic
   And feet;
There are buses and motors
   And trams;
I wish there were meadows
   And lambs.

The houses all wait
   In a row,
There is smoke everywhere
   That I go.
I don't like the noises
   I hear—
I wish there were woods
   Very near.

There is only one thing
   That I love,
And that is the sky
   Far above,
There is plenty of room
   In the blue
For castles of clouds
   And me, too!

Irene Thompson

The Country Child

My home is a house
   Near a wood
(I'd live in a street
   If I could!).
The lanes are so quiet,
   Oh, dear!
I do wish that someone
   Lived near.

There is no one to play with
        At all,
The trees are so high
        And so tall;
And I should be lonely
        For hours,
Were it not for the birds
        And the flowers.

I wish that I lived
        In a town —
To see all the trams
        Going down
A twinkling street
        That is bright
With wonderful colours,
        At night!

Irene Thompson

From a Railway Carriage

Faster than fairies, faster than witches,
Bridges and houses, hedges and ditches;
And charging along like troops in a battle,
All through the meadows the horses and cattle;
All of the sights of the hill and the plain
Fly as thick as driving rain;
And ever again, in the wink of an eye,
Painted stations whistle by.

Here is a child who clambers and scrambles,
All by himself and gathering brambles;
Here is a tramp who stands and gazes;
And there is the green for stringing the daisies!
Here is a cart run away in the road
Lumping along with man and load;
And here is a mill, and there is a river:
Each a glimpse and gone for ever!

Robert Louis Stevenson

The Last Gate

I know a garden with three strange gates
    Of silver, of gold, and glass,
At every gate, in a deep, soft voice,
    A sentinel murmurs, "Pass."

At night I passed through the silver gate,
    An ivory moon rode high;
I heard the song of the silver stars
    That swung in the silver sky.

I walked at dawn through the gate of gold,
    And came to a golden sea,
Seven mermaids rose from the golden waves
    And fluttered white hands to me.

At last I came to the other gate,
    The sentinel murmured, "Pass!"
I never will tell what lovely things
    I saw through that gate of glass.

Stella Mead

Meg Merrilees

Old Meg she was a gipsy,
    And lived upon the moors;
Her bed it was the brown heath turf,
    And her house was out of doors,
Her apples were swart blackberries,
    Her currants, pods o' broom;
Her wine was dew of the wild white rose,
    Her book a churchyard tomb.

Her brothers were the craggy hills,
    Her sisters larchen trees;
Alone with her great family
    She lived as she did please.
No breakfast had she many a morn,
    No dinner many a noon,
And, 'stead of supper, she would stare
    Full hard against the moon.

But every morn, of woodbine fresh,
    She made her garlanding,
And, every night, the dark glen yew
    She wove, and she would sing.
And with her fingers, old and brown,
    She plaited mats of rushes,
And gave them to the cottagers
    She met among the bushes.

Old Meg was brave as Margaret Queen,
    And tall as Amazon;
An old red blanket cloak she wore,
    A chip-hat had she on:
God rest her aged bones somewhere!
    She died full long agone!

J. Keats

Danny Murphy

He was as old as old could be,
His little eye could scarcely see,
His mouth was sunken in between
His nose and chin, and he was lean
And twisted up and withered quite,
So that he couldn't walk aright.

His pipe was always going out,
And then he'd have to search about
In all his pockets, and he'd mow—
O deary me! and, musha now!
And then he'd light his pipe, and then
He'd let it go clean out again.

He couldn't dance or jump or run,
Or ever have a bit of fun
Like me and Susan, when we shout
And jump and throw ourselves about—
But when he laughed, then you could see
He was as young as young could be!

James Stephens

407

"Sooeep!"

Black as a chimney is his face,
    And ivory white his teeth,
And in his brass-bound cart he rides,
    The chestnut blooms beneath.

"Sooeep, Sooeep!" he cries, and brightly peers
    This way and that to see
With his two light-blue shining eyes
    What custom there may be.

And once inside the house, he'll squat,
    And drive his rods on high,
Till twirls his sudden sooty brush
    Against the morning sky.

Then 'mid his bulging bags of soot,
    With half the world asleep,
His small cart wheels him off again,
    Still hoarsely bawling, "Sooeep!"
                        Walter de la Mare

Street Lanterns

Country roads are yellow and brown.
We mend the roads in London town.

Never a hansom dare come nigh,
Never a cart goes rolling by.

An unwonted silence steals
In between the turning wheels.

Quickly ends the autumn day,
And the workman goes his way.

Leaving, midst the traffic rude,
One small isle of solitude.

Lit, throughout the lengthy night,
By the little lantern's light.

Jewels of the dark have we,
Brighter than the rustic's be.

Over the dull earth are thrown
Topaz, and the ruby stone.

Mary E. Coleridge

An Eskimo Baby

If you were an Eskimo baby
You'd live in a bag all day.
    Right up from your toes
    To the tip of your nose,
All in thick cosy furs tucked away.

And if you went out for an airing
In mother's warm hood you would go,
    Tied close to her back,
    Like a soft, furry pack,
You could laugh at the cold and the snow.

But if they brought water at bedtime—
As people at home always do—
    You'd cough and you'd sneeze,
    And perhaps you would freeze,
You would certainly turn very blue!

An Eskimo mummy would rub you
With oil from your heels to your head.
    And then you'd be rolled
    (For it's terribly cold)
In warm furs, and put safely to bed.

No nice creamy milk for your supper,
But bits of raw blubber and fat!
    Would you like to go
    To the land of the snow,
Where they have such a bedtime as that?

Lucy Diamond

Foreign Children

Little Indian, Sioux, or Crow,
Little frosty Eskimo,
Little Turk or Japanee,
O! don't you wish that you were me?

You have seen the scarlet trees,
And the lions overseas;
You have eaten ostrich eggs,
And turned the turtles off their legs.

Such a life is very fine,
But it's not so nice as mine;
You must often, as you trod,
Have wearied not to be abroad.

You have curious things to eat,
I am fed on proper meat;
You must dwell beyond the foam,
But I am safe and live at home.

Little Indian, Sioux, or Crow,
Little frosty Eskimo,
Little Turk or Japanee,
O! don't you wish that you were me?

Robert Louis Stevenson

No Thoroughfare

In a dear little home of tarpaulin and boards,
  Where the wood-blocks are "up" in our street,
Lives a little old man dressed in sacking and cords,
  Crouching snug on a low wooden seat.

There's a brazier of charcoal that flickers and glows
  Where the wigwam's front door ought to be;
As the little old man toasts his fingers and nose
  How I wish he had room there for me!

I could hang out the lanterns on trestles and poles,
  Like big rubies all shining and red,
And to guard a wide street full of wood-blocks and holes
  Is far nicer than going to bed.

I could stay all night long by the little old man
  Keeping watch o'er each pickaxe and spade,
Frying sausages too, in a battered old pan,
  For the dark would not make me afraid.

And the little old man might drop off in a doze
  Till the sky turned to orange and pink,
But the street would be safe from all brigands and foes
  For *I* should not have slumbered a wink.

Ruth Holmes

The Shiny Little House

I wish, how I wish that I had a little house,
With a mat for the cat and a hole for a mouse,
And a clock going "tock" in a corner of the room,
And a kettle, and a cupboard, and a big birch broom.

To school in the morning the children off would run,
And I'd give them a kiss and a penny and a bun,
But directly they had gone from this little house of mine,
I'd clap my hands and snatch a cloth, and shine, shine, shine.

I'd shine all the knives, all the windows, and the floors,
All the grates, all the plates, all the handles on the doors,
Every fork, every spoon, every lid, and every tin,
Till everything was shining like a new bright pin.

At night, by the fire, when the children were in bed,
I'd sit and I'd knit, with a cap upon my head,
And the kettles and the saucepans they would shine, shine,
    shine,
In this tweeny little, cosy little house of mine!

Nancy M. Hayes

411

Sea Shell

Sea Shell, Sea Shell,
    Sing me a song, O please!
A song of ships, and sailor men,
    And parrots, and tropical trees,
Of islands lost in the Spanish Main
Which no man ever may find again,
Of fishes and corals under the waves,
And sea-horses stabled in great green caves.
Sea Shell, Sea Shell,
Sing of the things you know so well.

Amy Lowell

The Shell

See what a lovely shell,
Small and pure as a pearl,
Lying close to my foot,
Frail, but a work divine,
Made so fairly well
With delicate spire and whorl,
How exquisitely minute,
A miracle of design!

What is it? a learnèd man
Could give it a clumsy name.
Let him name it who can,
The beauty would be the same.

The tiny cell is forlorn,
Void of the little living will
That made it stir on the shore.
Did he stand at the diamond door
Of his house in a rainbow frill?
Did he push, when he was uncurl'd,
A golden foot or fairy horn
Thro' his dim water-world?

Slight, to be crush'd with a tap
Of my finger-nail on the sand;
Small, but a work divine,
Frail, but of force to withstand,
Year upon year, the shock
Of cataract seas that snap
The three-decker's oaken spine
Athwart the ledges of rock,
Here on the Breton strand!

Lord Tennyson

The Shell

And then I pressed the shell
   Close to my ear
And listened well,
And straightway like a bell
   Came low and clear
The slow, sad murmur of far distant seas,
Whipped by an icy breeze
Upon a shore
Wind-swept and desolate.
It was a sunless strand that never bore
The footprint of a man,
Nor felt the weight
Since time began
Of any human quality or stir
Save what the dreary winds and waves incur.
And in the hush of waters was the sound
Of pebbles rolling round,
For ever rolling with a hollow sound.
And bubbling sea-weeds as the waters go
Swish to and fro
Their long, cold tentacles of shiny grey.
There was no day,
Nor ever came a night
Setting the stars alight
To wonder at the moon:
Was twilight only and the frightened croon,
Smitten to whimpers, of the dreary wind
And waves that journeyed blind—
And then I loosed my ear—O, it was sweet
To hear a cart go jolting down the street.

James Stephens

A Widow Bird

A widow bird sate mourning for her love
    Upon a wintry bough;
The frozen wind crept on above,
    The freezing stream below.

There was no leaf upon the forest bare,
    No flower upon the ground,
And little motion in the air
    Except the mill-wheel's sound.

P. Bysshe Shelley

Wishing

Ring-ting! I wish I were a primrose,
A bright yellow primrose blowing in the spring!
    The stooping boughs above me,
    The wandering bee to love me,
The fern and moss to creep across,
    And the elm-tree for our king!

Nay, stay! I wish I were an elm-tree,
A great lofty elm-tree, with green leaves gay!
    The winds would set them dancing,
    The sun and moonshine glance in,
And birds would house among the boughs,
    And sweetly sing!

Oh—no! I wish I were a robin,
A robin or a little wren, everywhere to go;
    Through forest, field or garden,
    And ask no leave or pardon,
Till winter comes with icy thumbs
    To ruffle up our wing.

Well—tell! Where should I fly to,
Where go to sleep in the dark wood or dell?
    Before a day was over,
    Home comes the rover,
For mother's kiss—sweeter this
    Than any other thing!

W. Allingham

Dust

The grey dust runs on the ground like a mouse,
Over the doorstep and into the house,
Under the bedsteads and tables and chairs,
Up to the rooms at the top of the stairs,
Down to the cellar, across the brick floor—
There! It is off again by the back door!
Never a mousetrap can catch the grey mouse
Who keeps the brooms busy all over the house!

P. A. Ropes

On the Banisters

Sliding down the banisters,
    The day it rained all day,
We played at flying fairies
    Coming down a rainbow ray.
I slit my frock a little bit,
    And Billy tore the mat—
But fairies aren't particular
    About such things as that.

Sliding down the banisters
    The day it rained all day,
We played at sailing aeroplanes
    To countries miles away.
I hurt my hand a little bit,
    And Billy bumped his nose,
But airmen take no notice,
    Of such little things as those.

Sliding down the banisters
    The day it rained all day,
We played at swings and switchbacks
    Like they have Olympia way.
Then folks came in, all wet and cross,
    And made us stop our play.
But oh, we did enjoy ourselves
    The day it rained all day.

Margaret E. Gibbs

Gold

Evening is tawny on the old
   Deep-windowed farm,
And the great elm-trees fold on fold
   Are golden-warm.

And a fountain-basin drips its gold
   'Mid gleaming lawns
Where mellow statue-bases hold
   Their gilded fawns.

Martin Armstrong

Overheard on a Saltmarsh

Nymph, nymph, what are your beads?
Green glass, goblin. Why do you stare at them?
Give them me.
        No.
Give them me. Give them me.
               No.
Then I will howl all night in the reeds,
Lie in the mud and howl for them.

Goblin, why do you love them so?

They are better than stars or water,
Better than voices of winds that sing,
Better than any man's fair daughter,
Your green glass beads on a silver ring.

Hush, I stole them out of the moon.

Give me your beads, I want them.
           No.

I will howl in a deep lagoon
For your green glass beads, I love them so.
Give them me. Give them me.
        No.

Harold Monro

The Shepherd

How sweet is the shepherd's sweet lot!
  From the morn to the evening he strays;
He shall follow his sheep all the day,
  And his tongue shall be filled with praise.

For he hears the lambs' innocent call,
  And he hears the ewes' tender reply;
He is watchful while they are in peace,
  For they know when their shepherd is nigh.

William Blake

The Little Herd-Boy's Song

Where the buttercups so sweet
Dust with gold my naked feet,
Where the grass grows green and long,
Sit I here and sing my song,
And the brown bird cries "Cuckoo!"
Under skies for ever blue!

Now and then, while I sing loud,
Flits a little fleecy cloud,
And uplooking I behold
How it turns to rain of gold,
Falling lightly, while around
Comes the stir of its soft sound!

Bright above and dim below
Is the many colour'd Bow;
'Tis the only light I mark,
Till the mountain tops grow dark,
And uplooking I espy
Shining glow-worms in the sky.

Then I hear the runlet's call,
And the voice of the waterfall
Growing louder, and 'tis cold
As I guide my flocks to fold;
But no City, great or small,
Have I ever seen at all.

Robert Buchanan

417

Little Things

From a little seed
 A flower grows.
From a little flower
 A fragrance blows—
A little fragrance
 That's wafted to me
As I lie in the shade
 Of the chestnut tree.

Eileen Mathias

A Rhyme Sheet of Other Lands

The Japanese have funny things
 For dinner, so they say;
The tails of fish and dragon's wings
 Are eaten every day.

Of all the men who search for gold,
 Some find as much of it
As both their restless hands can hold,
 And others ne'er a bit.

I think this picture here shall be
 The famous river Nile
And, lying near the bank, you see
 The curious crocodile.

The Greeks of old were wise and skilled,
 What wonders they could do!
What towns and temples they could build,
 And stately houses, too!

Now every child in China knows
 The way to spell and write with speed;
From right to left the writing goes—
 It must be very hard indeed!

I'd love to go to Switzerland,
 Although the air is colder:
There's little doubt that it's a land
 I'll go to when I'm older.

Hugh Chesterman

Chimes

Brief, on a flying night,
   From the shaken tower,
A flock of bells take flight,
   And go with the hour.

Like birds from the cote to the gales,
   Abrupt--O hark!
A fleet of bells sets sails,
   And go to the dark.

Sudden the cold airs swing,
   Alone, aloud,
A verse of bells takes wing
   And flies with the cloud.

Alice Meynell

"Littles"

From "A Ternarie of Littles"

A little Saint best fits a little Shrine,
A little Prop best fits a little Vine,
As my small Cruse best fits my little Wine.

A little Seed best fits a little Soil,
A little Trade best fits a little Toil,
As my small Jar best fits my little Oil.

A little Bin best fits a little Bread,
A little Garland fits a little Head,
As my small Stuff best fits my little Shed.

A little Hearth best fits a little Fire,
A little Chapel fits a little Choir,
As my small Bell best fits my little Spire.

A little Stream best fits a little Boat,
A little Lead best fits a little Float,
As my small Pipe best fits my little Note.

Robert Herrick

The World

Great, wide, beautiful, wonderful world,
With the wonderful water round you curled,
And the wonderful grass upon your breast—
World, you are beautifully drest.

The wonderful air is over me,
And the wonderful wind is shaking the tree,
It walks on the water, and whirls the mills,
And talks to itself on the tops of the hills.

You friendly Earth! how far you go,
With wheat-fields that nod, and the rivers that flow,
With cities and gardens, and cliffs and isles,
And people upon you for thousands of miles!

Ah! you are so great, and I am so small,
I tremble to think of you, World, at all;
And yet, when I said my prayers to-day,
A whisper inside me seemed to say,
"You are more than the Earth, though you are such a dot:
You can love and think, and the Earth cannot!"

W. B. Rands

A Town Window

Beyond my window in the night
   Is but a drab inglorious street,
Yet there the frost and clean starlight
   As over Warwick woods are sweet.

Under the grey drift of the town
   The crocus works among the mould
As eagerly as those that crown
   The Warwick spring in flame and gold.

420

And when the tramway down the hill
  Across the cobbles moans and rings,
There is about my window-sill
  The tumult of a thousand wings.

John Drinkwater

The Hurdy-Gurdy Man

There's lots of things I'd like to be,
A sailor sailing on the sea;
A soldier standing stiff and straight
Beside King George's palace gate;
A baker kneading mounds of dough;
The man who shovels up the snow;
The pilot of an aeroplane;
The engine driver on a train;
A gipsy in a caravan,
Or else a hurdy-gurdy man.

There are so many things to choose—
A blacksmith making horses' shoes;
The man who works a windmill sails;
A writer writing fairy-tales;
The man with toy balloons to sell;
The muffin man who rings a bell;
The Lord Mayor in the Lord Mayor's Show—
I'd like to be them all, but oh!
I'm going to manage, if I can,
To be a hurdy-gurdy man!

A hurdy-gurdy is so gay,
I'd like to go with one all day,
And turn the handle round and round
And listen to the jolly sound;
I'd see the people peering out,
And watch the children crowd about,
And tap their feet in time and sing—
Oh, what a lot of fun I'd bring
If I could carry out my plan,
And be a hurdy-gurdy man!

Elizabeth Fleming

Song for a Little House

I'm glad our house is a little house,
  Not too tall nor too wide;
I'm glad the hovering butterflies
  Feel free to come inside.

Our little house is a friendly house,
  It is not shy or vain;
It gossips with the talking trees
  And makes friends with the rain.

And quick leaves cast a shimmer of green
  Against our whited walls,
And in the phlox, the courteous bees
  Are paying duty calls.

Christopher Morley

The Song of the Bath

Bring the biggest bath you've seen,
Water hot and towels clean,
Bring the soap that smells so sweetly;
Bring the nighties, folded neatly—
Bath time! Bath time! Hip hooray!
Jolliest time of all the day!

Bring the funny rubber toys,
Bring the little girls and boys;
Sticky fingers, grubby knees,
Rub them, scrub them, if you please.
Bath time! Bath time! Work away—
Busiest time of all the day.

Bring the grumbles and complainings,
Bring the little aches and painings,
All the frowns and all the tears,
Drown them in the bath, my dears.
Bath time! Bath time! Kiss, and say,
Happiest time of all the day!

Margaret Gibbs

Marching Song

Bring the comb and play upon it!
   Marching, here we come!
Willie cocks his Highland bonnet,
   Johnnie beats the drum.

Mary Jane commands the party,
   Peter leads the rear;
Feet in time, alert and hearty,
   Each a Grenadier!

All in the most martial manner
   Marching double-quick;
While the napkin like a banner
   Waves upon the stick!

Here's enough of fame and pillage,
   Great commander Jane!
Now that we've been round the village
   Let's go home again.

Robert Louis Stevenson

The Saint Wears a Halo

The saint wears a halo;
   The king wears a crown;
The milkmaid a bonnet
   To match her white gown;
The toadstool a hat
   And the foxgloves a hood;
A canopy covers
   The trees in the wood.

The elf has a cap
   That fits close to his head;
The witch stole a steeple
   (The storybook said).
But when I go running,
   I leave my head bare
To feel the warm sun
   And the wind in my hair!

"Peter"

423

Someone

Someone came knocking
  At my wee, small door;
Someone came knocking,
  I'm sure—sure—sure;
I listened, I opened,
  I looked to left and right,
But nought there was a-stirring
  In the still dark night.
Only the busy beetle
  Tap-tapping in the wall,
Only from the forest
  The screech-owl's call.
Only the cricket whistling
  While the dewdrops fall,
So I know not who came knocking,
  At all, at all, at all.

Walter de la Mare

The Scarf

Old Mrs. Tressider
Over at Winches
Is knitting a scarf
Of many gay inches,
An inch of scarlet,
Another of blue,
An inch of green
(The apple'y hue),
Another, bright
As a sunlit meadow,
And yet a third
Like a tree in shadow;
Crimson like sunset,
Rosy like dawn,
Purple like twilight
Over a lawn;
Noonday blue
And rain-cloud grey,
And an inch of white
As flowers-o'-May.

So she purls
And plains them together—
All the moods
Of the world and weather—
Into a scarf
Of many gay inches—
Old Mrs. Tressider
Over at Winches.

Ivy O. Eastwick

My Early Home

Here sparrows build upon the trees,
    And stockdove hides her nest;
The leaves are winnowed by the breeze
    Into a calmer rest;
The blackcap's song was very sweet,
    That used the rose to kiss;
It made the Paradise complete:
    My early home was this.

The red-breast from the sweet briar bush
    Drop't down to pick the worm;
On the horse-chestnut sang the thrush,
    O'er the house where I was born;
The moonlight, like a shower of pearls,
    Fell o'er this "bower of bliss,"
And on the bench sat boys and girls:
    My early home was this.

The old house stooped just like a cave,
    Thatched o'er with mosses green;
Winter around the walls would rave,
    But all was calm within;
The trees are here all green agen,
    Here bees the flowers still kiss,
But flowers and trees seemed sweeter then:
    My early home was this.

John Clare

The Trains

A Child's Fancy

Every morning at break of day
I can hear (so far away,
They sound like voices in a dream!)
The trains in the station whistle and scream.

Every morning in the week
I can hear them whistle and shriek,
But who are the people that go away
Into the country at break of day?

Seumas O'Sullivan

The Old Woman of the Roads

O, to have a little house!
    To own the hearth and stool and all!
The heaped-up sods upon the fire,
    The pile of turf against the wall!

To have a clock with weights and chains
    And pendulum swinging up and down!
A dresser filled with shining delph,
    Speckled and white and blue and brown!

I could be busy all the day
    Clearing and sweeping hearth and floor,
And fixing on their shelf again
    My white and blue and speckled store!

I could be quiet there at night,
    Beside the fire and by myself,
Sure of a bed; and loth to leave
    The ticking clock and the shining delph!

Oh! but I'm weary of mist and dark,
    And roads where there's never a house or bush,
And tired I am of the bog, and the road,
    And the crying wind and the lonesome hush!

And I am praying to God on high,
   And I am praying Him night and day,
For a little house—a house of my own—
   Out of the wind's and the rain's way.

Padraic Column

Who's In?

"The door is shut fast
   And everyone's out."
But people don't know
   What they're talking about!
Say the fly on the wall,
And the flame on the coals,
And the dog on his rug,
And the mice in their holes,
And the kitten curled up,
And the spiders that spin—
"What, everyone out?
   Why, everyone's in!"

Elizabeth Fleming

The Little Dancers

A London Vision

Lonely, save for a few faint stars, the sky
Dreams; and lonely, below, the little street
Into its gloom retires, secluded and shy.
Scarcely the dumb roar enters this soft retreat;
And all is dark, save where come flooding rays
From a tavern window: there to the brisk measure
Of an organ that down in an alley merrily plays,
Two children, all alone and no one by,
Holding their tatter'd frocks, through an airy maze
Of motion, lightly threaded with nimble feet,
Dance sedately; face to face they gaze,
Their eyes shining, grave with a perfect pleasure.

Laurence Binyon

Vacation Time

Good-bye, little desk at school, good-bye,
We're off to the fields and the open sky.
The bells of the brooks and the woodland bells
Are ringing us out to the vales and dells,
To meadow-ways fair, and to hilltops cool,
Good-bye, little desk at school.

Good-bye, little desk at school, good-bye,
We've other brave lessons and tasks to try;
But we shall come back in the fall, you know,
And as gay to come as we are to go,
With ever a laugh and never a sigh—
Good-bye, little desk, good-bye!

Frank Hutt

Chimney-Tops

Ah! the morning is grey;
And what kind of day
Is it likely to be?
You must look up and see
What the chimney-tops say.

If the smoke from the mouth
Of the chimney goes south,
'Tis the north wind that blows
From the country of snows;
Look out for rough weather.
The cold and the north wind
Are always together.

If the smoke pouring forth
From the chimney goes north,
A mild day it will be,
A warm time we shall see;
The south wind is blowing
From lands where the orange
And fig trees are growing.

428

Every Day

There are so many things to do to-day
   In city, field and street,
And people are going everywhere,
   With quickly hurrying feet.

Some are ploughing and sowing the seed,
   And some are reaping the grain;
And some, who worked the whole night through,
   Are coming home again.

Over the hills the shepherd goes,
   While in the busy town
People and carts and motor cars
   Are running up and down;

And everywhere they come and go
   In sun and rain and sleet,
That we may have warm clothes to wear,
   And food enough to eat.

Mary Osborn

The Speed Track

The Hour-hand and the Minute-hand upon a polished dial
A meeting planned at twelve o'clock to walk and talk awhile.
The Hour-hand with the Minute-hand could never keep
   apace.
"The speed at which you move," he said, "is really a dis-
   grace!"

Then laughed the Minute-hand and sang, "The way that I
   must go
Is marked with milestones all along, and there are twelve,
   you know.
And I must call at each of these before my journey's done,
While you are creeping like a snail from twelve o'clock to
   one.
So now, farewell! But we shall meet again, good sir,"
   said he,
"The road that we are following is circular, you see!"

"Peter"

429

Old Mrs. Jarvis

Old Mrs. Jarvis, she sits on a cart,
Her pony is quicker to stop than to start,
But always she ambles on fine easy rambles
From village to village, to fair and to mart.

The pony is fat and a-glitter with brass,
The cart it is green as the greenest of grass,
And rabbit skins dangle and old bottles jangle,
And she sits in the midst, and she bows as you pass.

Her eyes are like blackberries shining with dew,
She wears a red kerchief and a jacket of blue;
And a hat with a feather, a-nodding together,
A-nodding, a-nodding, a-nodding at you!

How splendid to sit up so lofty and lone,
To go any whither, a leaf that is blown;
To wander and wander up here and down yonder,
With a pony and trap and a trade all your own!

Elizabeth Fleming

Time, You Old Gipsy Man

Time, you old gipsy man,
    Will you not stay,
Put up your caravan,
    Just for one day?

All things I'll give you
    Will you be my guest;
Bells for your jennet
    Of silver the best.
Goldsmiths shall beat you
    A great golden ring,
Peacocks shall bow to you,
    Little boys sing,
Oh, and sweet girls will
    Festoon you with may;
Time, you old gipsy,
    Why hasten away?

Last week in Babylon,
   Last night in Rome,
Morning, and in the crush
   Under Paul's dome;
Under Paul's dial
   You tighten your rein—
Only a moment,
   And off once again;
Off to some city
   Now blind in the womb,
Off to another
   Ere that's in the tomb.

Time, you old gipsy man,
   Will you not stay,
Put up your caravan,
   Just for one day?

Ralph Hodgson

The Patchwork Quilt

She mixes blue and mauve and green,
   Purple and orange, white and red,
And all the colours in between
   To patch a cover for her bed.

Oblong, triangle, star and square,
   Oval, and round, she makes them fit
Into a wondrous medley there,
   Colour by colour, bit by bit.

Over her knee it swiftly flows,
   And round her feet, a bright cascade,
While at her touch it grows and grows,
   Until at last the quilt is made.

And then across the bed it lies,
   A thing of gorgeous crazy bloom,
As if a rainbow from the skies
   Had shattered in her little room.

Elizabeth Fleming

Open Sesame

Oh, for a book and a shady nook
   Either in-a-door or out,
With the green leaves whispering overhead
   Or the street cry all about,
Where I may read all at my ease,
   Both of the new and old;
For a jolly good book whereon to look
   Is better to me than gold.

The Cobbler

Wandering up and down one day,
  I peeped into a window over the way;
And putting his needle through and through,
There sat a cobbler making a shoe:
For the world he cares never the whisk of a broom—
All he wants is elbow-room.
    Rap-a-tap-tap, tick-a-tack-too,
    That is the way he makes a shoe!

Over laths of wood his bits of leather
He stretches and fits, then sews together;
He puts his wax ends through and through;
And still as he stitches, his body goes too:
For the world he cares never the whisk of a broom—
All he wants is elbow-room.
    Rap-a-tap-tap, tick-a-tack-too,
    This is the way he makes a shoe!

With his little sharp awl he makes a hole
Right through the upper and through the sole;
He puts in one peg, and he puts in two,
And chuckles and laughs as he hammers them through:
For the world he cares never the whisk of a broom—
All he wants is elbow-room.
    Rap-a-tap-tap, tick-a-tack-too,
    This is the way to make a shoe!

Pack, Clouds, Away

Pack, clouds, away! and welcome, day!
  With night we banish sorrow:
Sweet air, blow soft! mount, lark, aloft!
  To give my Love good-morrow;
Wings from the wind, to please her mind,
  Notes from the lark I'll borrow.
Bird, prune thy wing! nightingale, sing!
  To give my Love good-morrow.
  To give my Love good-morrow,
  Notes from them I'll borrow.

Wake from thy nest, robin redbreast!
  Sing, birds, in every furrow!
And from each hill let music shrill
  Give my fair Love good-morrow.
Blackbird and thrush, in every bush—
  Stare, linnet, and cock-sparrow,
You pretty-elves—amongst yourselves
  Sing my fair Love good-morrow!
  To give my Love good-morrow,
  Sing, birds, in every furrow.

Thomas Heywood

The Kite

I wonder what my kite can see,
So high above the world and me;
And if the birds are friends to him,
As I am friends with Jack and Jim,
And are the clouds just really rain,
That melts and pours all down again?
O! he must know a thousand things,
As much as schoolmasters, and kings;
But will he breathe a word to me?
No, he's as quiet as quiet can be.

Pearl Forbes MacEwen

433

Ragged Robin

Rags and tatters,
    Tatters and rags,
A split in my coat
    And a patch on my bags—
My vest is torn
    And outside in.
Can anyone lend me
    A safety pin?

Rags and tatters,
    Darns and tears,
I'm all to pieces
    And nobody cares—
My hat blew away
    In yesterday's wind,
My braces are broken,
    No shoe can I find.

Rags and tatters,
    Tatters and rags,
Bootlaces, buttonhooks,
    Tapes, and tags
Might keep me together
    For one more day—
If they can't be found,
    You must throw me away.

Elizabeth Godley

The Unknown Wind

When the day darkens,
When dusk grows light,
When the dew is falling
    When silence dreams.
I hear a wind
Calling, calling
By day and by night.

What is the wind
That I hear calling
By day and by night,
    The crying of wind?
When the day darkens,
When dusk grows light,
When the dew is falling.

Fiona Macleod

The Wind

Why does the wind so want to be
Here in my little room with me?
He's all the world to blow about,
But just because I keep him out
He cannot be a moment still,
But frets upon my window sill,
And sometimes brings a noisy rain
To help him batter at the pane.

Upon my door he comes to knock.
He rattles, rattles at the lock
And lifts the latch and stirs the key—
Then waits a moment breathlessly,
And soon, more fiercely than before,
He shakes my little trembling door,
And though "Come in, come in!" I say,
He neither comes nor goes away.

Barefoot across the chilly floor
I run and open wide the door;
He rushes in, and back again
He goes to batter door and pane,
Pleased to have blown my candle out.
He's all the world to blow about,
Why does he want so much to be
Here in my little room with me?

Elizabeth Rendall

Travelling

I like to ride in a tramcar
  On a fine and sunny day,
And hear it going clang! clang!
  When someone's in the way.

I like to ride in a railway train
  Through tunnels dark and wide,
Over the bridges crossing the river,
  I feel so safe inside.

Motor cars are jolly too,
  They go so very fast,
Whitewashed houses and fields of cows
  And sheep go flying past.

But an aeroplane is best of all,
  It climbs so very high
That people look like tiny dots,
  And clouds go sailing by.

Dorothy Gradon

From the Train

In England from the train you see
  Green fields and peaceful cows and sheep,
And lazy farmsteads racing by
  In smoke-blue valleys quiet with sleep;

And primroses and meadow sweet,
  And daisies white about the way;
And you can trace the paths that wind
  To where the trees are snowed with may.

In India from the stifling train
  You see great rocky hills go by;
Brown miles of parched, unhappy grass,
  And hot blue tracts of cloudless sky.

436

And slow, indifferent bullocks, too,
　　Well laden on the dusty roads—
And then a station where you stop,
　　With brightly-coloured chattering crowds.

And rows and rows of tiny huts,
　　And young green rice, or sugar-cane,
And little dark-skinned boys and girls
　　Who wonder at the rumbling train.

And many scorching miles you go,
　　And sometimes weary days you spend
Gazing across that burning land
　　And dreaming of your journey's end.

Marjorie Wilson

Moonlit Apples

At the top of the house the apples are laid in rows,
And the skylight lets the moonlight in, and those
Apples are deep-sea apples of green. There goes
　　A cloud on the moon in the autumn night

A mouse in the wainscot scratches, and scratches, and then
There is no sound at the top of the house of men
Or mice; and the cloud is blown, and the moon again
　　Dapples the apples with deep-sea light.

They are lying in rows there, under the gloomy beams;
On the sagging floor; they gather the silver streams
Out of the moon, those moonlit apples of dreams,
　　And quiet is the steep stair under.

In the corridors under there is nothing but sleep.
And stiller than ever on orchard boughs they keep
Tryst with the moon, and deep is the silence, deep
　　On moon-washed apples of wonder.

John Drinkwater
437

The Night Will Never Stay

The night will never stay,
　The night will still go by,
Though with a million stars
　You pin it to the sky,
Though you bind it with the blowing wind
　And buckle it with the moon,
The night will slip away
　Like sorrow or a tune.

Eleanor Farjeon

Little Rain-Drops

Oh, where do you come from,
　You little drops of rain,
Pitter, patter, pitter, patter,
　Down the window pane?

They won't let me walk,
　And they won't let me play,
And they won't let me go
　Out of doors at all to-day.

They put away my playthings
　Because I broke them all,
And then they locked up all my bricks,
　And took away my ball.

Tell me, little rain-drops,
　Is that the way you play,
Pitter, patter, pitter, patter,
　All the rainy day?

They say I'm very naughty,
　But I've nothing else to do
But sit here at the window:
　I should like to play with you.

But "Pitter, patter, pat,"
The little rain-drops cannot speak.
But "Pitter, patter, pat,"
Means "We can play on *this* side,
Why can't you play on *that*?"

Good Night and Good Morning

A fair little girl sat under a tree,
Sewing as long as her eyes could see;
Then smoothed her work, and folded it right,
And said, 'Dear work, Good Night! Good Night!"

Such a number of rooks came over her head,
Crying, "Caw! caw!" on their way to bed;
She said, as she watched their curious flight,
"Little black things, Good Night! Good Night!"

The horses neighed, and the oxen lowed;
The sheep's "Bleat! bleat!" came over the road;
All seeming to say with a quiet delight,
"Good little girl, Good Night! Good Night!"

She did not say to the sun, "Good Night!"
Though she saw him there like a ball of light;
For she knew he had God's time to keep
All over the world, and never could sleep.

The tall pink fox-glove bowed his head—
The violets curtsied and went to bed;
And good little Lucy tied up her hair,
And said, on her knees, her favourite prayer.

And while on her pillow she softly lay
She knew nothing more till again it was day:
And all things said to the beautiful sun,
"Good Morning! Good Morning! our work is begun!"

439

From A Blessing for the Blessed

When the sun has left the hill-top,
   And the daisy-fringe is furled,
When the birds from wood and meadow
   In their hidden nests are curled,
Then I think of all the babies
   That are sleeping in the world.

There are babies in the high lands
   And babies in the low,
There are pale ones wrapped in furry-skins
   On the margin of the snow,
And brown ones naked in the isles
   Where all the spices grow.

L. Alma Tadema

A Sea Song from the Shore

Hail! Ho!
   Sail! Ho!
Ahoy! Ahoy! Ahoy
   Who calls to me
   So far at sea?
Only a little boy.

Sail! Ho!
   Hail! Ho!
The sailor he sails the sea:
   I wish he would capture
   A little sea-horse
And send him home to me.

I wish as he sails
Through the tropical gales,
He would catch me a sea bird, too,
   With its silver wings
   And the song it sings,
And its breast of down and dew!

I wish he would catch me
  A little mermaid,
Some island where he lands,
  With her dripping curls,
  And her crown of pearls,
And the looking-glass in her hands!

Hail! Ho!
  Sail! Ho!
Sail far o'er the fabulous main!
  And if I were a sailor
  I'd sail with you,
Though I never sailed back again.

James Whitcomb Riley

Four and Eight

The Foxglove by the cottage door
Looks down on Joe, and Joe is four.

The Foxglove by the garden gate
Looks down on Joan, and Joan is eight.

"I'm glad we're small," said Joan, "I love
To see inside the fox's glove,
Where taller people cannot see,
And all is ready for the bee;
The door is wide, the feast is spread,
The walls are dotted rosy red."
"And only little people know
How nice it looks in there," said Joe.
Said Joan, "The upper rooms are locked;
A bee went buzzing up—he knocked,
But no one let him in, so then
He bumbled gaily down again."
"Oh dear!" sighed Joe, "if only we
Could grow as little as that bee,
We too might room by room explore
The Foxglove by the cottage door."

The Foxglove by the garden gate
Looked down and smiled on Four and Eight.

ffrida Wolfe

The Witch

I saw her plucking cowslips,
    And marked her where she stood:
She never knew I watched her
    While hiding in the wood.

Her skirt was brightest crimson,
    And black her steeple hat,
Her broomstick lay beside her—
    I'm positive of that.

Her chin was sharp and pointed,
    Her eyes were—I don't know—
For, when she turned towards me—
    I thought it best—to go!

Percy H. Ilott

A Wish

Mine be a cot beside a hill;
A beehive's hum shall soothe my ear;
A willowy brook that turns a mill
With many a fall, shall linger near.

The swallow oft, beneath my thatch,
Shall twitter from her clay-built nest;
Oft shall the pilgrim lift the latch,
And share my meal, a welcome guest.

Around my ivied porch shall spring,
Each fragrant flower that drinks the dew;
And Lucy, at her wheel, shall sing
In russet gown and apron blue.

The village-church among the trees,
Where first our marriage vows were given,
With merry peals shall swell the breeze
And point with taper spire to Heaven.

Samuel Rogers

If I Had But Two Little Wings

If I had but two little wings
And were a little feathery bird,
    To you I'd fly, my dear!
But thoughts like these are idle things
    And I stay here.

But in my sleep to you I fly:
I'm always with you in my sleep!
    The world is all one's own.
But then one wakes, and where am I?
    All, all alone.

Sleep stays not, though a monarch bids:
So I love to wake ere break of day:
    For though my sleep be gone,
Yet while 'tis dark, one shuts one's lids,
    And still dreams on.

Samuel Taylor Coleridge

When all the World is Young

When all the world is young, lad,
    And all the trees are green;
And every goose a swan, lad,
    And every lass a queen;
Then hey for boot and horse, lad,
    And round the world away;
Young blood must have its course, lad,
    And every dog his day.

When all the world is old, lad,
    And all the trees are brown;
And all the sport is stale, lad,
    And all the wheels run down:
Creep home, and take your place there,
    The spent and maimed among:
God grant you find one face there
    You loved when all was young.

Charles Kingsley

443

The Piper

Piping down the valleys wild,
    Piping songs of pleasant glee,
On a cloud I saw a child,
    And he laughing said to me:

"Pipe a song about a Lamb!"
    So I piped with merry cheer.
"Piper, pipe that song again";
    So I piped: he wept to hear.

"Drop thy pipe, thy happy pipe;
    Sing thy songs of happy cheer":
So I sang the same again,
    While he wept with joy to hear.

"Piper, sit thee down and write
    In a book, that all may read."
So he vanish'd from my sight,
    And I pluck'd a hollow reed.

And I made a rural pen,
    And I stain'd the water clear,
And I wrote my happy songs
    Every child may joy to hear.

William Blake

A Feather for my Cap

Seagull flying from the sea,
Drop a feather here for me!
Drop it down into my lap—
I need a feather for my cap!

My satin gown's as white as milk,
My stockings are the finest silk,
My shoes are made of Spanish leather,
But oh! my cap! it lacks a feather!

My girdle is of precious gold,
A bouquet in my hands I hold
Of wild rose buds and lucky heather—
But oh! my cap! it lacks a feather!

What use a gown of satin fine?
What use a grand bouquet—like mine?
What use are shoes of Spanish leather
If caps, or hats, do lack a feather?

Ivy O. Eastwick

The Growing River

At first the river's very small,
And can't float anything at all;
But later, as it journeys on,
It's large enough to float a swan.

It grows till it can safely float
A slim canoe and then a boat;
And later still, as like as not,
It manages to float a yacht.

And presently, when really large,
It takes a steamer, then a barge.
And last it passes busy quays
And floats great ships to foreign seas.

Rodney Bennett

Happy Thought

The world is so full of a number of things,
I'm sure we should all be as happy as kings.

Robert Louis Stevenson

445

Water

Water has no taste at all,
  Water has no smell;
Water's in the waterfall,
  In pump, and tap, and well.

Water's everywhere about;
  Water's in the rain,
In the bath, the pond, and out
  At sea it's there again.

Water comes into my eyes
  And down my cheek in tears,
When mother cries, "Go back and try
  To wash behind those ears."

John R. Crossland

Goldenhair

Lean out of the window,
  Goldenhair,
I heard you singing
  A merry air.

My book is closed;
  I read no more,
Watching the fire dance
  On the floor.

I have left my book;
  I have left my room,
For I heard you singing
  Through the gloom.

Singing and singing
  A merry air,
Lean out of the window,
  Goldenhair.

James Joyce

A Farewell, To C.E.G.

My fairest child, I have no song to sing thee;
No lark could pipe in skies so dull and grey;
Yet, if thou wilt, one lesson I will give thee
For every day.

Be good, sweet maid, and let who will be clever;
Do noble things, not dream them, all day long;
And so make Life, Death, and that vast For Ever
One grand, sweet song.

Charles Kingsley

Song

For Mercy, Courage, Kindness, Mirth
There is no measure upon earth.
Nay, they wither, root and stem,
If an end be set to them.

Overbrim and overflow
If your own heart you would know;
For the spirit born to bless
Lives but in its own excess.

Laurence Binyon

Fables and Stories—
Grave and Gay

Such wondrous tales as childhood loves to hear

The New Duckling

"I want to be new," said the duckling.
    "O, ho!" said the wise old owl,
While the guinea-pig cluttered off chuckling
    To tell all the rest of the fowl.

"I should like a more elegant figure,"
    That child of a duck went on.
"I should like to grow bigger and bigger,
    Until I could swallow a swan.

"I won't be the bond-slave of habit,
    I won't have those webs on my toes,
I want to run round as a rabbit,
    A rabbit as red as a rose.

"I don't want to waddle like mother,
    Or quack like my silly old dad.
I want to be utterly other,
    And frightfully modern and mad."

"Do you know," said the turkey, "you're quacking!
    There's a fox creeping up thro' the rye:
And, if you're not utterly lacking,
    You'll make for that duck-pond. Good-bye!"

But the duckling was perky as perky.
    "Take care of your stuffing!" he called.
(This was horribly rude to a turkey!)
    "But you aren't a real turkey," he bawled.

"You're an early Victorian sparrow!
    A fox is more fun than a sheep!
I shall show that my mind is not narrow
    And give him my feathers—to keep."

Now the curious end of this fable,
    So far as the rest ascertained,
Though they searched from the barn to the stable,
    Was that only his feathers remained.

So he wasn't the bond-slave of habit,
    And he didn't have webs on his toes;
And perhaps he runs round like a rabbit,
    A rabbit as red as a rose.

                                    Alfred Noyes

The Pilgrim Fathers

The breaking waves dashed high
    On a stern and rock-bound coast,
And the woods against a stormy sky
    Their giant branches tossed;

And the heavy night hung dark
    The hills and waters o'er,
When a band of exiles moored their bark
    On the wild New England shore.

Not as the conqueror comes,
    They, the true-hearted, came;
Not with the roll of stirring drums,
    And the trumpet that sings of fame;

Not as the flying come,
    In silence and in fear;
They shook the depths of the desert gloom
    With their hymns of lofty cheer.

Amidst the storm they sang,
    And the stars heard and the sea;
And the sounding aisles of the dim woods rang
    To the anthem of the free!

The ocean eagle soared
    From his nest by the white wave's foam;
And the rocking pines of the forest roared—
    This was their welcome home!

There were men with hoary hair
    Amidst that pilgrim band;
Why had they come to wither there,
    Away from their childhood's land?

There was woman's fearless eye,
    Lit by her deep love's truth;
There was manhood's brow serenely high,
    And the fiery heart of youth.

What sought they thus afar?
    Bright jewels of the mine?
The wealth of seas, the spoils of war?
    They sought a faith's pure shrine!

Ay, call it holy ground,
    The soil where first they trod.
They have left unstained what there they found—
    Freedom to worship God.

Felicia Hemans

The Frog and the Bird

By a quiet little stream on an old mossy log,
Looking very forlorn, sat a little green frog;
He'd a sleek speckled back, and two bright yellow eyes,
And when dining, selected the choicest of flies.

The sun was so hot he scarce opened his eyes,
Far too lazy to stir, let alone watch for flies,
He was nodding, and nodding, and almost asleep,
When a voice in the branches chirped: "Froggie, cheep,
    cheep!"

"You'd better take care," piped the bird to the frog,
"In the water you'll be if you fall off that log.
Can't you see that the streamlet is up to the brim?"
Croaked the froggie: "What odds! You forget I can·swim!"

Then the froggie looked up at the bird perched so high
On a bough that to him seemed to reach to the sky;
So he croaked to the bird: "If you fall, you will die!"
Chirped the birdie: "What odds! You forget I can fly!"

Vera Hessey

Lord Ullin's Daughter

A Chieftain to the Highlands bound
   Cries "Boatman, do not tarry!
And I'll give thee a silver pound
   To row us o'er the ferry!

"Now who would be ye, would cross Lochgyle
   This dark and stormy water?"
"O I'm the chief of Ulva's isle,
   And this, Lord Ullin's daughter.

"And fast before her father's men
   Three days we've fled together,
For should he find us in the glen,
   My blood would stain the heather.

"His horsemen hard behind us ride—
   Should they our steps discover,
Then who would cheer my bonny bride
   When they have slain her lover?"

Out spake the hardy Highland wight,
   "I'll go, my chief, I'm ready:
It is not for your silver bright,
   But for your winsome lady:—

"And by my word! the bonny bird
   In danger shall not tarry;
So though the waves are raging white
   I'll row you o'er the ferry."

By this the storm grew loud apace,
   The water-wraith was shrieking;
And in the scowl of heaven each face
   Grew dark as they were speaking.

But still as wilder blew the wind
   And as the night grew drearer,
Adown the glen rode armèd men,
   Their trampling sounded nearer.

"O haste thee, haste!" the lady cries,
  "Though tempests round us gather;
I'll meet the raging of the skies,
  But not an angry father."

The boat has left a stormy land,
  A stormy sea before her,—
When, oh! too strong for human hand
  The tempest gather'd o'er her.

And still they row'd amidst the roar
  Of waters still prevailing:
Lord Ullin reached that fatal shore,—
  His wrath was changed to wailing.

For, sore dismay'd, through storm and shade
  His child he did discover:—
One lovely hand she stretch'd for aid,
  And one was round her lover.

"Come back! come back!" he cried in grief,
  "Across this stormy water:
And I'll forgive your Highland chief,
  My daughter!—O my daughter!"

'Twas vain: the loud waves lash'd the shore,
  Return or aid preventing:
The waters wild went o'er his child,
  And he was left lamenting.

Thomas Campbell

Sir Nicketty Nox

Sir Nicketty Nox was an ancient knight,
So old was he that he'd lost his sight.
Blind as a mole, and slim as a fox,
And dry as a stick was Sir Nicketty Nox.

His sword and buckler were old and cracked,
So was his charger and that's a fact.
Thin as a rake from head to hocks,
Was this rickety nag of Sir Nicketty Nox.

A wife he had and daughters three,
And all were as old, as old could be.
They mended the shirts and darned the socks
Of that old Antiquity, Nicketty Nox.

Sir Nicketty Nox would fly in a rage
If anyone tried to guess his age.
He'd mouth and mutter and tear his locks,
This very pernickety Nicketty Nox.

Hugh Chesterman

A Tragic Story

There lived a sage in days of yore,
And he a handsome pigtail wore:
But wondered much and sorrowed more
    Because it hung behind him.

He mused upon this curious case,
And swore he'd change the pigtail's place,
And have it hanging at his face,
    Not dangling there behind him.

Says he, "The mystery I've found—
I'll turn me round"—he turned him round;
    But still it hung behind him.

Then round, and round, and out and in,
All day the puzzled sage did spin;
In vain—it mattered not a pin—
    The pigtail hung behind him.

And right and left, and round about,
And up and down, and in and out,
He turned; but still the pigtail stout
    Hung steadily behind him.

And though his efforts never slack,
And though he twist, and twirl, and tack,
Alas! still faithful to his back,
    The pigtail hangs behind him.

W. M. Thackeray

455

From The Piped Piper of Hamelin

Into the street the Piper stept,
  Smiling first a little smile,
As if he knew what magic slept
  In his quiet pipe the while;
Then, like a musical adept,
To blow the pipe his lips he wrinkled,
And green and blue his sharp-eyes twinkled,
Lik a candle-flame where salt is sprinkled;
And ere three shrill notes the pipe uttered,
You heard as if an army muttered;
And the muttering grew to a grumbling;
And the grumbling grew to a mighty rumbling;
And out of the houses the rats came tumbling;
Great rats, small rats, lean rats, brawny rats,
Brown rats, black rats, grey rats, tawny rats,
Grave old plodders, gay young friskers,
  Fathers, mothers, uncles, cousins,
Cocking tails, and pricking whiskers,
  Families by tens and dozens;
Brothers, sisters, husbands, wives—
Followed the piper for their lives.
From street to street he piped, advancing,
And step for step they followed dancing.

Robert Browning

Lochinvar

O, young Lochinvar is come out of the west,
Through all the wide Border his steed was the best;
And save his good broadsword he weapons had none,
He rode all unarm'd, and he rode all alone.
So faithful in love, and so dauntless in war,
There never was knight like the young Lochinvar.

He staid not for brake, and he stopped not for stone,
He swam the Esk river where ford there was none;
But ere he alighted at Netherby gate,
The bride had consented, the gallant came late:
For a laggard in love, and a dastard in war,
Was to wed the fair Ellen of brave Lochinvar.

So boldly he enter'd the Netherby Hall,
Among bride's-men, and kinsmen and brothers, and all:
Then spoke the bride's father, his hand on his sword,
(For the craven bridegroom said never a word),
"O come ye in peace here, or come ye in war,
Or to dance at our bridal, young Lord Lochinvar?"

"I long woo'd your daughter, my suit you denied;—
Love swells like the Solway, but ebbs like its tide—
And now I am come, with this lost love of mine,
To lead but one measure, drink one cup of wine.
There are maidens in Scotland more lovely by far,
That would gladly be bride to young Lochinvar."

The bride kiss'd the goblet: the knight took it up,
He quaff'd of the wine, and he threw down the cup.
She look'd down to blush, and she look's up to sigh,
With a smile on her lips, and a tear in her eye.
He took the soft hand, ere her mother could bar,
"Now tread we a measure!" said young Lochinvar.

So stately his form, and so lovely her face,
That never a hall such a galliard did grace;
While her mother did fret, and her father did fume,
And the bridegroom stood dangling his bonnet and plume,
And the bride-maidens whisper'd, " 'Twere better by far,
To have match'd our fair cousin with young Lochinvar."

One touch of her hand, and one word in her ear,
When they reached the hall-door and the charger stood near;
So light to the croupe the fair lady he swung,
So light to the saddle before her he sprung!
"She is won! we are gone, over bank, bush and scaur;
They'll have fleet steeds that follow," quoth young
    Lochinvar.

There was mounting 'mong Graemes of the Netherby clan;
Forsters, Fenwicks, and Musgraves, they rode and they ran:
There was racing, and chasing, on Cannobie Lee,
  But the lost bride of Netherby ne'er did they see.
  So daring in love, and so dauntless in war,
  Have ye e'er heard of gallant like young Lochinvar?

Walter Scott

457

Jack O' the Inkpot

I dance on your paper,
   I hide in your pen,
I make in your ink-stand
   My little black den;
And when you're not looking
   I hop on your nose,
And leave on your forehead
   The marks of my toes.

When you're trying to finish
   Your "i" with a dot,
I slip down your finger
   And make it a blot;
And when you're so busy
   To cross a bit "t,"
I make on the paper
   A little Black Sea.

I drink blotting-paper,
   Eat penwiper pie,
You never can catch me,
   You never need try!
I leap any distance,
   I use any ink,
I'm on to your fingers
   Before you can wink.

Algernon Blackwood

Stalky Jack

I knew a boy who took long walks,
Who lived on beans and ate the stalks;
To the Giant's Country he lost his way;
They kept him there for a year and a day,
But he has not been the same boy since;
An alteration he did evince;
For you may suppose that he underwent
A change in his notions of extent!

He looks with contempt on a nice high door,
And tries to walk in at the second floor;
He stares with surprise at a basin of soup,
He fancies a bowl as big as a hoop;
He calls the people minniken mites;
He calls a sirloin a couple of bites!
Things having come to these pretty passes,
They bought him some magnifying glasses.

He put on the goggles, and said, "My eyes!
The world has come to its proper size!"
But all the boys cry, "Stalky John!
There you go with your goggles on."
What girl would marry him—and *quite* right—
To be taken for three times her proper height?
So this comes of taking extravagant walks,
And living on beans and eating the stalks.

W. B. Rands

The Wonderful Derby Ram

As I was going to Derby, all on a market day,
I met the finest ram, sir, that ever was fed upon hay,
    Upon hay, upon hay, upon hay;
I met the finest ram, sir, that ever was fed upon hay.

This ram was fat behind, sir, this ram was fat before,
This ram was ten yards round, sir, indeed he was no more,
    No more, no more, no more;
This ram was ten yards round, sir, indeed he was no more.

The horns that grew on his head, sir, they were so wondrous
    high,
As I've been plainly told, sir, they reached up to the sky,
    The sky, the sky, the sky;
As I've been plainly told, sir, they reached up to the sky.

The tail that grew from his back, sir, was six yards and an ell,
And it was sent to Derby to toll the market bell,
    The bell, the bell, the bell,
And it was sent to Derby to toll the market bell.

459

From A Song About Myself

There was a naughty boy,
  A naughty boy was he,
He would not stop at home,
  He could not quiet be—
      He took
      In his knapsack
      A Book
      Full of vowels,
      And a shirt
      With some towels—
      A slight cap
      For night cap—
      A hair brush,
      Comb ditto,
      New stockings,
      For old ones
      Would split O!
      This knapsack
      Tight at 'a back
      He riveted close
And followed his nose
  To the North,
  To the North,
And followed his nose
  To the North.

There was a naughty boy,
  And a naughty boy was he,
For nothing would he do
  But scribble poetry—
      He took
      An inkstand
      In his hand
      And a Pen
      Big as ten
      In the other,
      And away
      In a pother
      He ran
      To the mountains
      And fountains

And ghostes
And witches
And ditches
And wrote
In his coat
When the weather
Was cool
Fearing gout,
And without
When the weather
Was warm—
O the charm
When we choose
To follow one's nose
To the North,
To the North,
To follow one's nose
To the North!

These delightful nonsense verses were written by John Keats to amuse his little sister. Playing with words is a game which amuses many children and some may like to write their own nonsense verses after hearing these.

Just Like a Man

He sat at the dinner table
  With a discontented frown,
The potatoes and steak were underdone
  And the bread was baked too brown;
The pie was too sour and the pudding too sweet,
  And the roast was much too fat;
The soup so greasy, too, and salt,
  'Twas hardly fit for the cat.

"I wish you could eat the bread and pie
  I've seen my mother make,
They are something like, and 'twould do you good
  Just to look at a loaf of her cake."
Said the smiling wife, "I'll improve with age—
  Just now I'm but a beginner;
But your mother has come to visit us,
  And to-day she cooked the dinner."

461

Yussouf

A stranger came one night to Yussouf's tent,
Saying—"Behold one outcast and in dread,
Against whose life the bow of Power is bent,
Who flies, and hath not where to lay his head.
I come to thee for shelter and for food:
To Yussouf, call'd through all our tribes the Good."

"This tent is mine," said Yussouf—"but no more
Than it is God's: come in and be at peace;
Freely shalt thou partake of all my store,
As I of His who buildeth over these
Our tents his glorious roof of night and day,
And at whose door none ever yet heard Nay."

So Yussouf entertain'd his guest that night;
And waking him ere day, said—"Here is gold;
My swiftest horse is saddled for thy flight,—
Depart before the prying day grow bold!"
As one lamp lights another, nor grows less,
So nobleness enkindleth nobleness.

That inward light the stranger's face made grand
Which shines from all self-conquest; kneeling low,
He bow'd his forehead upon Yussouf's hand,
Sobbing—"O Sheikh! I cannot leave thee so.—
I will repay thee,—all this thou has done
Unto that Ibrahim who slew thy son!"

"Take thrice the gold!" said Yussouf,—"for with thee
Into the desert, never to return,
My one black thought shall ride away from me.
First-born, for whom by day and night I yearn,
Balanced and just are all of God's decrees;
Thou art avenged, my First-born! sleep in peace!"

J. R. Lowell

The Owl and the Pussy-Cat

The Owl and the Pussy-Cat went to sea
    In a beautiful pea-green boat.
They took some honey, and plenty of money,
    Wrapped up in a five-pound note.

The Owl looked up to the stars above,
　　And sang to a small guitar,
"O lovely Pussy! O Pussy, my love,
　　What a beautiful Pussy you are,
　　　　You are!
　　What a beautiful Pussy you are!"

Pussy said to the Owl, "You elegant fowl!
　　How charmingly sweet you sing!
O let us be married! too long we have tarried:
　　But what shall we do for a ring?"
They sailed away for a year and a day,
　　To the land where the Bong-tree grows,
And there in a wood a Piggy-wig stood,
　　With a ring at the end of his nose,
　　　　His nose,
　　With a ring at the end of his nose.

"Dear Pig, are you willing to sell for one shilling
　　Your ring?" Said the Piggy, "I will."
So they took it away, and were married next day
　　By the Turkey who lives on the hill.
They dined on mince, and slices of quince,
　　Which they ate with a runcible spoon;
And hand in hand, on the edge of the sand,
　　They danced by the light of the moon.

Edward Lear

The Lobster Quadrille

"Will you walk a little faster?" said a whiting to a snail,
"There's a porpoise close behind us, and he's treading on my
　　tail.
See how eagerly the lobsters and the turtles all advance!
They are waiting on the shingle—will you come and join the
　　dance?
　　Will you, won't you, will you, won't you, will you join the
　　　dance?
　　Will you, won't you, will you, won't you, won't you join
　　　the dance?

"You can really have no notion how delightful it will be,
When they take us up and throw us, with the lobsters, out to
  sea!"
But the snail replied, "Too far, too far!" and gave a look
  askance,
Said he thanked the whiting kindly, but he would not join the
  dance,
Would not, could not, would not, could not, would not
  join the dance,
  Would not, could not, would not, could not, could not
  join the dance.

"What matters it how far we go?" his scaly friend replied.
"There is another shore, you know, upon the other side.
The further off from England the nearer is to France—
Then turn not pale, beloved snail, but come and join the
  dance?
Will you, won't you, will you, won't you, will you join the
  dance?
Will you, won't you, will you, won't you, won't you join
  the dance?"

Lewis Carroll

What Became of Them?

He was a rat, and she was a rat,
  And down in one hole they did dwell,
And both were as black as a witch's cat,
  And they loved one another well.

He had a tail, and she had a tail,
  Both long and curling and fine;
And each said, "Yours is the finest tail
  In the world, excepting mine."

He smelt the cheese, and she smelt the cheese,
  And they both pronounced it good;
And both remarked it would greatly add
  To the charms of their daily food.

So he ventured out, and she ventured out,
  And I saw them go with pain;
For what befell them I never can tell,
  For they never came back again.

Godfrey Gordon Gustavus Gore

Godfrey Gordon Gustavus Gore—
No doubt you have heard that name before—
Was a boy who never would shut a door!

The wind might whistle, the wind might roar,
And teeth be aching and throats be sore,
But still he never would shut the door.

His father would beg, his mother implore,
"Godfrey Gordon Gustavus Gore,
We really do wish you would shut the door!"

Their hands they wrung, their hair they tore;
But Godfrey Gordon Gustavus Gore
Was as deaf as the buoy out at the Nore.

When he walked forth the folks would roar,
"Godfrey Gordon Gustavus Gore,
Why don't you think to shut the door?"

They rigged out a shutter with sail and oar,
And threatened to pack off Gustavus Gore
On a voyage of penance to Singapore.

But he begged for mercy, and said, "No more!
Pray do not send me to Singapore
On a shutter, and then I will shut the door!"

The Wraggle Taggle Gipsies

There were three gipsies a-come to my door,
   And down-stairs ran this lady, O!
One sang high, and another sang low,
   And the other sang, Bonny, bonny, Biscay, O!

Then she pulled off her silk finished gown
   And put on hose of leather, O!
The ragged, ragged rags about our door—
   She's gone with the wraggle taggle gipsies, O!

465

It was late last night, when my lord came home,
  Enquiring for his a-lady, O!
The servants said on every hand:
  "She's gone with the wraggle taggle gipsies, O!"

"O saddle to me my milk-white steed,
  Go and fetch me my pony, O!
That I may ride and seek my bride,
  Who is gone with the wraggle taggle gipsies, O!"

O he rode high and he rode low,
  He rode through woods and copses too,
Until he came to an open field,
  And there he espied his a-lady, O!

"What makes you leave your house and land?
  What makes you leave your money, O?
What makes you leave your new-wedded lord;
  To go with the wraggle taggle gipsies, O?"

"What care I for my house and my land?
  What care I for my money, O?
What care I for my new-wedded lord?
  I'm off with the wraggle taggle gipsies, O!"

"Last night you slept on a goose-feather bed,
  With the sheet turned down so bravely, O!
And to-night you'll sleep in a cold open field,
  Along with the wraggle taggle gipsies, O!"

"What care I for a goose-feather bed,
  With the sheet turned down so bravely, O!
For to-night I shall sleep in a cold open field,
  Along with the wraggle taggle gipsies, O!"

The Three Little Pigs

A jolly old sow once lived in a sty,
  And three little piggies had she;
And she waddled about saying, "Umph! umph! umph!"
  While the little ones said, "Wee! wee!"

"My dear little brothers," said one of the brats,
  "My dear little piggies," said he,
"Let us all for the future say, 'Umph! umph! umph!'
  'Tis so childish to say, 'Wee! wee!' "

Then these three little pigs grew skinny and lean,
  And lean they might very well be;
For somehow they couldn't say, "Umph! umph! umph!"
  And they wouldn't say, "Wee! wee! wee!"

So after a time these little pigs died,
  They all died of felo-de-se;
From trying too hard to say, "Umph! umph! umph!"
  When they only could say, "Wee! wee!"

MORAL:

A moral there is to this little song,
  A moral that's easy to see;
Don't try while yet young to say, "Umph! umph! umph!"
  For you only can say, "Wee! wee!"

Sir Alfred A. Scott-Gatty

Betty at the Party

"When I was at the party,"
  Said Betty, aged just four,
"A little girl fell off her chair
  Right down upon the floor;
And all the other little girls
  Began to laugh, but me—
I didn't laugh a single bit,"
  Said Betty seriously.

"Why not?" her mother asked her,
  Full of delight to find
That Betty—bless her little heart!—
  Had been so sweetly kind.
"Why didn't you laugh, my darling?
  Or don't you like to tell?"
"I didn't laugh," said Betty,
  " 'Cause it was me that fell."

Sons of the King

A little Prince of long ago
  The day that he was six
Put away his birthday toys,
  His soldiers, trains and bricks.

And stealing down the golden stair,
  His slippers in his hand,
He from the shady courtyard stepped
  Into a sunlit land.

And sitting there beside the wall
  He buttoned up his shoes
And wondered—looking up and down
  Which highway should he choose.

When by there rode a gipsy boy,
  His pony dark as he,
Who smiled upon the little Prince
  So golden-fair to see.

"Where are you riding, gipsy boy,
  This lovely summer day?"
"Over the hills and through the woods
  To the land of Far-Away."

"Who is your father, gipsy boy?
  For mine, you know, is king,
And I shall be like him one day
  And wear his crown and ring."

"My father," said the gipsy boy,
  "He also is a king.
Although he sits upon no throne
  And wears no crown or ring.

"He's king of all the gipsy-folk
  Twixt here and Far-Away,
And I, who am his eldest son,
  Shall be a king some day."

"May I go with you, gipsy boy,
    To ride your little horse,
To see your tents and caravans
    Between the golden gorse?

"There I could run without my shoes
    And climb your forest trees,
I seem to smell your smoky fires
    Of crackling twigs and leaves."

Within the Palace voices call,
    The gates are opened wide,
The kindly watchmen see the Prince
    And beckon him inside.

The gipsy smiles and shakes his head,
    He jerks the pony's rein;
"When you and I are kings," he says,
    "Then we shall meet again."

Joan Agnew

Mr. Nobody

I know a funny little man,
    As quiet as a mouse,
Who does the mischief that is done
    In everybody's house!
There's no one ever sees his face,
    And yet we all agree
That every plate we break was cracked
    By Mr. Nobody.

'Tis he who always tears our books,
    Who leaves the door ajar,
He pulls the buttons from our shirts,
    And scatters pins afar;
That squeaking door will always squeak,
    For, prithee, don't you see,
We leave the oiling to be done
    By Mr. Nobody.

469

He puts damp wood upon the fire,
 That kettles cannot boil;
His are the feet that bring in the mud,
 And all the carpets soil.
The papers always are mislaid,
 Who had them last but he?
There's not one tosses them about
 But Mr. Nobody.

The finger-marks upon the door
 By none of us are made;
We never leave the blinds unclosed,
 To let the curtains fade;
The ink we never spill; the boots
 That lying round you see
Are not our boots; they all belong
 To Mr. Nobody.

The Pirates' Tea-party

We'd ever so many kinds of cake
 And at least three sorts of jam.
Doughnuts and cucumber sandwiches,
 Some made with chicken and ham,
Scones and parkin and honey had we
The day that the pirates came to tea.

The oldest, he had twinkly eyes,
 A deep sword-slash on his cheek,
A stubbly beard that was nearly red,
 He hadn't washed for a week.
He showed me his cutlass sharp and bright,
He slept with it 'tween his teeth at night.

The second, he was thin and fair,
 He blushed when they yelled at him;
Tho' young he had killed a dozen Turks,
 They called him "Terrible Tim."
He wore a handkerchief round his head,
Purple and yellow with spots of red.

The third of the crew was extra tall,
   He knew many foreign parts,
He knew some wonderful swearing words,
   He understood all the charts,
But he only whispered one—when he found
His toast with the buttery side on the ground.

The fourth was merely a boy from a school,
   And altho' he wore a belt,
A pistol in it and high sea-boots,
   And a frightful hat of felt,
He is just pretending that he is one
With his "Yo, ho, ho," and "Son of a gun!"

If he is a pirate, I'm one too;
   Says he, "Then be one quick;
Remember whatever the weather's like
   A pirate's never sea-sick."
When the pirates came I wished that we
Had not asked that hateful boy to tea.

                 Dorothy Una Ratcliffe

When Polly Buys a Hat

When Father goes to town with me to buy my Sunday hat,
We can't afford to waste much time in doing things like
    that;
We walk into the nearest shop, and Father tells them then,
"Just bring a hat you think will fit a little girl of ten!"

It may be plain, it may be fine with lace and flowers too;
If it just "feels right" on my head we think that it will do;
It may be red or brown or blue, with ribbons light or dark;
We put it on—and take the car that goes to Central Park.

When Mother buys a hat for me, we choose the shape
    with care;
We ask if it's the best they have, and if they're sure 'twill
    wear;
And when the trimming's rather fine, why, Mother shakes
    her head
And says, "Please take the feathers off—we'd like a bow
instead!"

471

But oh, when Sister buys my hats, you really do not know
The hurry and the worry that we have to undergo!
How many times I've heard her say—and shivered where I
    sat—
"I think I'll go to town to-day, and buy that child a hat!"

They bring great hats with curving brims, but I'm too tall
    for those;
And hats that have no brim at all, which do not suit my
    nose;
I walk about, and turn around, and struggle not to frown:
I wish I had long curly hair like Angelina Brown.

Till when at last the daylight goes, and I'm so tired then,
I hope I'll never, never need another hat again,
And when I've quite made up my mind that shopping is
    the worst
Of all my tasks—then Sister buys the hat that we saw first

And so we take it home with us as quickly as we may,
And Sister lifts it from the box and wonders what they'll
    say;
And I—I peep into the glass, and (promise not to tell!)
I smile, because I really think it suits me very well.

Then slip into the library as quiet as can be,
And this is what my Brother says when first he looks at
    me:
"Upon—my—word! I never saw a queerer sight than that!
Don't tell me this outrageous thing is Polly's Sunday hat!"

E. Hill

Tired Tim

        Poor tired Tim! It's sad for him.
        He lags the long bright morning through,
        Ever so tired of nothing to do;
        He moons and mopes the livelong day,
        Nothing to think about, nothing to say
        Up to bed with his candle to creep,
        Too tired to yawn, too tired to sleep;
        Poor tired Tim! It's sad for him.

        Walter de la Mare.

The Jovial Beggar

There was a jovial beggar,
   He had a wooden leg,
Lame from his cradle,
   And forced for to beg.
And a-begging we will go, will go, will go
And a-begging we will go!

A bag for his oatmeal,
   Another for his salt,
And a pair of crutches,
   To show that he can halt.
And a-begging we will go—

A bag for his wheat,
   Another for his rye,
A little bottle by his side,
   To drink when he's a-dry,
And a-begging we will go—

"Seven years I begged
   For my old Master Wild,
He taught me to beg
   When I was but a child,
And a-begging we will go—

"I begged for my master
   And got him store of pelf;
But, now, Jove be praised!
   I'm begging for myself;
And a-begging we will go—

"In a hollow tree
   I live and pay no rent.
Providence provides for me,
   And I am well content;
And a-begging we will go—

"Of all the occupations
    A beggar's life is best,
For whenever he's a-weary
    He'll lay him down and rest;
And a-begging we will go—

"I fear no plots against me,
    I live in open cell;
Then who would be a king,
    When beggars live so well?
Then a-begging we will go, will go, will go,
    And a-begging we will go!"

The Priest and the Mulberry Tree

Did you hear of the curate who mounted his mare,
And merrily trotted along to the fair?
Of creature more tractable none ever heard:
In the height of her speed she would stop at a word;
But again with a word, when the curate said "Hey,"
She put forth her mettle and gallop'd away.

As near to the gates of the city he rode,
While the sun of September all brilliantly glow'd,
The good priest discover'd, with eyes of desire,
A mulberry tree in a hedge of wild brier;
On boughs long and lofty, in many a green shoot,
Hung, large, black, and glossy, the beautiful fruit.

The curate was hungry and thirsty to boot;
He shrank from the thorns, though he longed for the fruit;
With a word he arrested his courser's keen speed,
And he stood up erect on the back of his steed;
On the saddle he stood while the creature stood still,
And he gather'd the fruit till he took his good fill.

"Sure never," he thought, "was a creature so rare,
So docile, so true, as my excellent mare;
Lo, here now I stand," and he gazed all around,
"As safe and as steady as if on the ground;
Yet how had it been, if some traveller this way,
Had, dreaming no mischief, but chanced to cry 'Hey'?"

He stood with his head in the mulberry tree,
And he spoke out aloud in his fond revery;
At the sound of the word the good mare made a push,
And down went the priest in the wild-brier bush.
He remember'd too late, on his thorny green bed,
Much that well may be thought cannot wisely be said.

Thomas Love Peacock

Barbara Frietchie

Up from the meadows rich with corn,
Clear in the cool September morn,

The clustered spires of Frederick stand
Green-walled by the hills of Maryland.

Round about them orchards sweep,
Apple and peach tree fruited deep,

Fair as the garden of the Lord
To the eyes of the famished rebel horde,

On that pleasant morn of the early fall
When Lee marched over the mountain wall;

Over the mountains winding down,
Horse and foot, into Frederick town.

Forty flags with their silver stars,
Forty flags with their crimson bars,

Flapped in the morning wind: the sun
Of noon looked down, and saw not one.

Up rose old Barbara Frietchie then,
Bowed with her fourscore years and ten;

475

Bravest of all in Frederick town,
She took up the flag the men hauled down

In her attic window the staff she set,
To show one heart was loyal yet.

Up the street came the rebel tread,
Stonewall Jackson riding ahead.

Under his slouched hat left and right
He glanced; the old flag met his sight.

"Halt!"—the dust-brown ranks stood fast.
"Fire!"—out blazed the rifle-blast.

It shivered the window, pane and sash;
It rent the banner with seam and gash.

Quick, as it fell, from the broken staff
Dame Barbara snatched the silken scarf.

She leaned far out on the window-sill,
And shook it forth with a royal will.

"Shoot, if you must, this old grey head,
But spare your country's flag," she said.

A shade of sadness, a blush of shame,
Over the face of the leader came;

The nobler nature within him stirred
To life at that woman's deed and word;

"Who touches a hair of yon grey head
Dies like a dog. March on!" he said.

All day long through Frederick street
Sounded the tramp of marching feet:

All day long that free flag tost
Over the heads of the rebel host.

Ever its torn folds rose and fell
On the loyal winds that loved it well;

And through the hill-gaps sunset light
Shone over it with a warm good-night.

Barbara Frietchie's work is o'er,
And the rebel rides on his raids no more.

Honour to her, and let a tear
Fall, for her sake, on Stonewall's bier.

Over Barbara Frietchie's grave,
Flag of Freedom and Union, wave:

Peace and order and beauty draw
Round the symbol of light and law;

And ever the stars above look down
On thy stars below in Frederick town!

John Greenleaf Whittier

Mountain and the Squirrel

The Mountain and the Squirrel
Had a quarrel,
And the former call'd the latter "Little Prig";
Bun replied,
"You are doubtless very big,
But all sorts of things and weather
Must be taken in together
To make up a year
And a sphere.
And I think it no disgrace
To occupy my place.
If I'm not so large as you,
You are not so small as I,
And not half so spry;
I'll not deny you make
A very pretty squirrel-track;
Talents differ; all is well and wisely put;
If I cannot carry forests on my back,
Neither can you crack a nut."

R. W. Emerson

477

King John and the Abbot of Canterbury

An ancient story I'll tell you anon
Of a notable prince that was called King John;
And he ruled England with main and with might,
For he did great wrong, and maintained little right.

And I'll tell you a story, a story so merrie,
Concerning the Abbot of Canterbury;
How for his housekeeping and high renown,
They rode post for him to fair London town.

An hundred men, the king did hear say,
The abbot kept in his house every day;
And fifty gold chains without any doubt,
In velvet coats waited the abbot about.

"How now, father abbot, I hear it of thee,
Thou keepest a far better house than me;
And for thy housekeeping and high renown,
I fear thou work'st treason against my crown."

"My liege," quo' the abbot, "I would it were known
I never spend nothing, but what is my own;
And I trust your grace will do me no deere,
For spending of my own true-gotten gear."

"Yes, yes, father abbot, thy fault is high,
And now for the same thou needst must die;
For except thou canst answer me questions three,
Thy head shall be smitten from thy bodie.

"And first," quo' the king, "when I'm in this stead,
With my crown of gold so fair on my head,
Among all my liege-men so noble of birth,
Thou must tell me to one penny what I am worth.

"Secondlie, tell me, without any doubt,
How soon I may ride the whole world about;
And at the third question thou must not shrink,
But tell me here truly what I do think."

"Oh, these are hard questions for my shallow wit,
Nor I cannot answer your grace as yet:
But if you will give me but three weeks' space,
I'll do my endeavour to answer your grace."

"Now three weeks' space to thee will I give,
And that is the longest time thou hast to live;
For if thou dost not answer my questions three,
Thy lands and thy livings are forfeit to me."

Away rode the abbot all sad at that word,
And he rode to Cambridge and Oxenford,
But never a doctor there so wise,
That could with his learning an answer devise.

Then home rode the abbot of comfort so cold,
And he met his shepherd a-going to fold;
"How now, my lord abbot, you are welcome home;
What news do you bring us from good King John?"

"Sad news, sad news, shepherd, I must give,
That I have but three days more to live;
For if I do not answer him questions three,
My head will be smitten from my bodie.

"The first is to tell him there in that stead
With his crown of gold so fair on his head,
Among all his liege-men so noble of birth,
To within one penny of what he is worth.

"The second to tell him, without any doubt,
How soon he may ride the whole world about:
And at the third question I must not shrink,
But tell him there truly what he does think."

"Now cheer up, sir abbot, did you never hear yet,
That a fool he may learn a wise man wit?
Lend me your horse and serving men, and your apparel,
And I'll ride to London to answer your quarrel.

"Nay, frown not, if it hath been told unto me,
I am like your lordship as ever may be;
And if you will but lend me your gown,
There is none shall know us at fair London town."

"Now horses and serving men thou shalt have,
With sumptuous array most gallant and brave,
With crozier and mitre, and rochet and cope,
Fit to appear 'fore our father the pope."

"Now welcome, sir abbot," the king he did say,
" 'Tis well thou'rt come back to keep thy day;
For and if thou canst answer my questions three,
Thy life and thy living both savèd shall be.

"And first, when thou seest me here in this stead,
With my crown of gold so fair on my head,
Among my liege-men so noble of birth,
Tell me to one penny what I am worth."

"For thirty pence our Saviour was sold
Among the false Jews, as I have been told:
And twenty-nine is the worth of thee,
For I think thou art one penny worser than he!"

The king laughed, and swore by St. Bittel,
"I did not think I had been worth so little!—
Now secondly, tell me, without any doubt,
How soon I may ride this whole world about."

"You must rise with the sun, and ride with the same
Until the next morning he rises again;
And then your grace need not make any doubt
But in twenty-four hours you'll ride it about."

The king he laughed, and swore by St. John,
"I did not think it could be done so soon!
Now from the third question thou must not shrink,
But tell me here truly what I do think."

"Yes, that shall I do, and make your grace merrie;
You think I'm the abbot of Canterbury;
But I'm his poor shepherd, as plain you may see,
That am come to beg pardon for him and for me."

The king he laughed, and swore by the mass,
"I'll make you lord abbot this day in his place!"
"Now nay, my liege, be not in such speed,
For alack, I can neither write nor read."

"Four nobles a week then I will give thee,
For this merrie jest thou has shown to me;
And tell the old abbot when thou comest home,
Thou hast brought him a pardon from good King John."

Try Again

King Bruce of Scotland flung himself down
    In a lonely mood to think;
'Tis true he was monarch, and wore a crown,
    But his heart was beginning to sink.

For he had been trying to do a great deed,
    To make his people glad;
He had tried and tried, but couldn't succeed
    And so he became quite sad.

He flung himself down in low despair,
    As grieved as man could be;
And after a while he pondered there,
    "I'll give it all up," said he.

Now just at that moment a spider dropped,
    With its silken, filmy clue;
And the King, in the midst of his thinking, stopped
    To see what the spider would do.

'Twas a long way up to the ceiling dome,
    And it hung by a rope so fine;
That how it would get to its cobweb home,
    King Bruce could not divine.

It soon began to cling and crawl
          Straight up with strong endeavour;
But down it came with a slippery sprawl,
          As near to the ground as ever.

Up, up it ran, not a second to stay,
          To utter the least complaint;
Till it fell still lower, and there it lay,
          A little dizzy and faint.

Its head grew steady—again it went,
          And travelled a half-yard higher;
'Twas a delicate thread it had to tread,
          And a road where its feet would tire.

Again it fell and swung below,
          But again it quickly mounted;
Till up and down, now fast, now slow,
          Nine brave attempts were counted.

"Sure," cried the King, "that foolish thing
          Will strive no more to climb;
When it toils so hard to reach and cling,
          And tumbles every time."

But up the insect went once more,
          Ah me! 'tis an anxious minute;
He's only a foot from his cobweb door,
          Oh say, will he lose or win it?

Steadily, steadily, inch by inch,
          Higher and higher he got;
And a bold little run at the very last pinch
          Put him into his native cot.

"Bravo, bravo! the King cried out,
          "All honour to those who try;
The spider up there defied despair;
          He conquered, and why shouldn't I?"

And Bruce of Scotland braced his mind,
    And gossips tell the tale,
That he tried once more as he tried before,
    And that time did not fail.

Eliza Cook

From The Forsaken Merman

Children dear, was it yesterday
We heard the sweet bells over the bay?
In the caverns where we lay,
Through the surf and through the swell,
The far-off sound of a silver bell?
Sand-strewn caverns, cool and deep,
Where the winds are all asleep;
Where the spent lights quiver and gleam,
Where the salt weed sways in the stream,
Where the sea-beasts, ranged all round,
Feed in the ooze of their pasture-ground;
Where the sea-snakes coil and twine,
Dry their mail and bask in the brine;
Where great whales come sailing by,
Sail and sail, with unshut eye,
Round the world for ever and aye?
When did music come this way?
Children dear, was it yesterday?

Children dear, was it yesterday
(Call yet once) that she went away?
Once she sate with you and me,
On a red gold throne in the heart of the sea,
And the youngest sate on her knee.

Children dear, was it yesterday?

Matthew Arnold
483

The Blind Men and the Elephant

It was six men of Hindostan,
  To learning much inclined,
Who went to see the elephant,
  (Though all of them were blind)
That each by observation
  Might satisfy his mind.

The *first* approached the Elephant,
  And happening to fall
Against his broad and sturdy side,
  At once began to bawl:
"Bless me, it seems the Elephant
  Is very like a wall."

The *second,* feeling of his tusk,
  Cried, "Ho! what have we here
So very round and smooth and sharp?
  To me 'tis mighty clear
This wonder of an Elephant
  Is very like a spear."

The *third* approached the animal,
  And happening to take
The squirming trunk within his hands,
  Then boldly up and spake:
"I see," quoth he, "the Elephant
  Is very like a snake."

The *fourth* stretched out his eager hand
  And felt about the knee,
"What most this mighty beast is like
  Is mighty plain; quoth he;
"'Tis clear enough the Elephant
  Is very like a tree."

The *fifth* who chanced to touch the ear
    Said, "Even the blindest man
Can tell what this resembles most;
    Deny the fact who can,
This marvel of an Elephant
    Is very like a fan."

The *sixth* no sooner had begun
    About the beast to grope,
Than, seizing on the swinging tail
    That fell within his scope,
"I see," cried he, "the Elephant
    Is very like a rope."

And so these men of Hindostan
    Disputed loud and long,
Each in his own opinion
    Exceeding stiff and strong,
Though *each* was *partly* in the right
    And all were in the wrong.

                              John Godfrey Saxe

The Beggar Maid

Her arms across her breast she laid;
    She was more fair than words can say:
Bare-footed came the beggar maid
    Before the King Cophetua.
In robe and crown the king stept down,
    To meet and greet her on her way;
"It is no wonder," said the lords,
    "She is more beautiful than day."

As shines the moon in clouded skies,
    She in her poor attire was seen:
One praised her ankles, one her eyes,
    One her dark hair and lovesome mien.
So sweet a face, such angel grace,
    In all that land had never been:
Cophetua sware a royal oath:
    "This beggar maid shall be my queen!"

                              Lord Tennyson

The Tale of a Dog and a Bee

Great big dog,
Head upon his toes;
Tiny little bee
Settles on his noes.

Great big dog
Thinks it is a fly.
Never says a word,
Winks very sly.

Tiny little bee,
Tickles dog's nose—
Thinks like as not
'Tis a pretty rose.

Dog smiles a smile,
Winks his other eye,
Chuckles to himself
How he'll catch a fly.

Then he makes a snap,
Very quick and spry,
Does his level best,
But doesn't catch the fly.

Tiny little bee,
Alive and looking well;
Great big dog,
Mostly gone to swell.

MORAL:

Dear friends and brothers all,
Don't be too fast and free,
And when you catch a fly,
Be sure it's not a bee.

From Goblin Market

Morning and evening
Maids heard the goblins cry:
"Come buy our orchard fruits,
Come buy, come buy:
Apples and quinces,
Lemons and oranges,
Plump unpecked cherries,
Melons and raspberries,
Bloom-down-cheeked peaches,
Swart-headed mulberries,
Wild free-born cranberries,
Crab-apples, dewberries,
Pine-apples, blackberries,
Apricots, strawberries;—
All ripe together
In summer weather—
Morns that pass by,
Fair eaves that fly;
Come buy, come buy:
Our grapes fresh from the vine,
Pomegranates full and fine,
Dates and sharp bullaces,
Rare peaches and greengages,
Damsons and bilberries,
Taste them and try:
Currants and gooseberries,
Bright fire-like barberries,
Figs to fill your mouth,
Citrons from the South,
Sweet to tongue and sound to eye;
Come buy, come buy."

Christina Rossetti

National and Love of Country

I vow to thee, my country—all earthly things above—
Entire and whole and perfect, the service of my love

The Gates to England

The great sea-roads to England
   Have many little gates—
You saw some once—those bustling ports,
   And winding ribbon straits;

And little foreign harbours
   Tucked safely in from blasts;
And lighted dockyards, swaying ships,
   And forests of straight masts.

And somewhere ever waiting
   A slim grey Man of War,
To keep the peace for England,
   Is never very far.

Marjorie Wilson

Home Thoughts from Abroad

Oh! to be in England
Now that April's there,
And whoever wakes in England
Sees, some morning, unaware,
That the lowest boughs and the brushwood sheaf
Round the elm-tree bole are in tiny leaf,
While the chaffinch sings on the orchard bough
In England—now!

And after April, when May follows,
And the whitethroat builds, and all the swallows—
Hark! where my blossomed pear-tree in the hedge
Leans to the field and scatters on the clover
Blossoms and dewdrops—at the bent spray's edge—
That's the wise thrush; he sings each song twice over,
Lest you should think he never could recapture
The first fine careless rapture!
And though the fields look rough with hoary dew
All will be gay when noon-tide wakes anew
The buttercups, the little children's dower—
Far brighter than this gaudy melon flower.

Robert Browning

This is England

And this is England! June's undarkened green
Gleams on far woods; and in the vales between
Gray hamlets, older than the trees that shade
Their ripening meadows, are in quiet laid,
Themselves a part of the warm, fruitful ground.
The little hills of England rise around;
The little streams that wander from them shine
And with their names remembered names entwine
Of old renown and honour, fields of blood
High causes fought on, stubborn hardihood
For freedom spent, and songs, our noblest pride
That in the heart of England never died,
And burning still make splendour of our tongue.

Laurence Binyon

O England, Country of my Heart's Desire

O England, country of my heart's desire,
Land of the hedgerow and the village spire,
Land of thatched cottages and murmuring bees,
And wayside inns where one may take one's ease.
Of village green where cricket may be played
And fat old spaniels sleeping in the shade —
O homeland, far away across the main,
How would I love to see your face again! —
Your daisied meadows and your grassy hills,
Your primrose banks, your parks, your tinkling rills,
Your copses where the purple bluebells grow
Your quiet lanes where lovers loiter so,
Your cottage-gardens with their wallflowers' scent,
Your swallows 'neath the eaves, your sweet content!
And 'mid the fleecy clouds that o'er you spread.
Listen, the skylark singing overhead —
   That's the old country, that's the old home!
   You never forget it wherever you roam.

E. V. Lucas

This Native Land

She is a rich and rare land;
O! she's a fresh and fair land;
She is a dear and rare land—
    This native land of mine.

No men than hers are braver,
Her women's hearts ne'er waver;
I'd freely die to save her
    And think my lot divine.

Thomas Davis

Jerusalem

And did those feet in ancient time
Walk upon England's mountains green?
And was the holy Lamb of God
On England's pleasant pastures seen?

And did the countenance divine
Shine forth upon our clouded hills?
And was Jerusalem builded here
Among these dark Satanic mills?

Bring me my bow of burning gold,
Bring me my arrows of desire,
Bring me my spear, O clouds, unfold!
Bring me my chariot of fire!

I will not cease from mental fight,
Nor shall my sword sleep in my hand,
Till we have built Jerusalem
In England's green and pleasant land.

William Blake

This England

This England never did, nor never shall,
Lie at the proud foot of a conqueror,
But when it first did help to wound itself.
Now these her princes are come home again,
Come the three corners of the world in arms,
And we shall shock them: Naught shall make us rue,
If England to itself do rest but true.

Shakespeare

Land of our Birth

Land of our Birth, we pledge to thee
Our love and toil in the years to be:
When we are grown and take our place,
As men and women with our race.

Father in Heaven who lovest all,
O help Thy children when they call;
That they may build from age to age
An undefilèd heritage.

Teach us to rule ourselves alway,
Controlled and cleanly night and day;
That we may bring, if need arise,
No maimed or worthless sacrifice.

Teach us the strength that cannot seek,
By deed or thought, to hurt the weak:
That, under Thee, we may possess
Man's Strength to comfort man's distress.

Teach us delight in simple things,
And Mirth that has no bitter springs;
Forgiveness free of evil done,
And Love to all men 'neath the sun!

Land of our Birth, our faith, our pride,
For whose dear sake our fathers died;
O Motherland, we pledge to thee
Head, heart and hand through the years to be.

Rudyard Kipling

493

The Best of All

I sometimes think I'd like to be
    A little Eskimo,
And drive a team of dogs before
    My sleigh upon the snow.

Or walk the streets of China, where
    Gay lanterns glow at night,
And have a pair of chopsticks and
    A pigtail and a kite.

Or if I lived in India
    A potter I would be,
And make a row of pots with clay
    For everyone to see.

And if I went to Africa
    Wild animals I'd track,
Or ride the desert mile on mile
    Upon the camel's back.

And Susan says, in blossom-time,
    She'd go to far Japan,
And wear a gay-hued kimono
    And always use a fan.

But all the same we're very sure,
    Although our island's small,
To be an English boy or girl
    Is much the best of all.

Margaret G. Rhodes

I Vow to thee, my Country

I vow to thee, my country—all earthly things above—
Entire and whole and perfect, the service of my love,
The love that asks no question: the love that stands the test,
That lays upon the altar the dearest and the best:
The love that never falters, the love that pays the price,
The love that makes undaunted the final sacrifice.

And there's another country, I've heard of long ago—
Most dear to them that love her, most great to them that
    know—
We may not count her armies; we may not see her King—
Her fortress is a faithful heart, her pride is suffering—
And soul by soul and silently her shining bounds increase,
And her ways are ways of gentleness and all her paths are
    Peace.

Sir Cecil Spring Rice

A Princely Ditty in Praise of the English Rose

Amongst the princely paragons,
Bedeckt with dainty diamonds,
Within mine eye, none doth come nigh
The sweet red rose of England.
    The lilies pass in bravery,
    In Flanders, Spain and Italy,
    And yet the famous flower of France
    Doth honour the Rose of England.

As I abroad was walking,
I heard the small birds talking;
And every one did frame her song
In praise of the Rose of England.
    The lilies, etc.

The bravest lute bring hither,
And let us sing together,
While I do ring, on every string,
The praise of the Rose of England.
    The lilies, etc.

Then fair and princely flower,
That over my heart doth tower,
None may be compared to thee,
Which art the fair Rose of England.
    The lilies, etc.

Thomas Deloney

The Toy Band

Dreary lay the long road, dreary lay the town,
   Lights out and never a glint o' moon:
Weary lay the stragglers, half a thousand down,
   Sad sighed the weary big Dragoon.
"Oh! if I'd a drum here to make them take the road again,
   Oh! if I'd a fife to wheedle—come, boys, come!
You that mean to fight it out, wake and take your load again,
   Fall in! Fall in! Follow the fife and drum!

"Hey, but here's a toy shop, here's a drum for me,
   Penny whistles too to play the tune!
Half a thousand dead men soon shall hear and see
   We're a band!" said the weary big Dragoon.
"Rubadub! Rubadub! Wake and take the road again,
   Wheedle-deedle-deedle-dee, come, boys, come!
You that mean to fight it out, wake and take your load again,
   Fall in! Fall in! Follow the fife and drum!"

Cheerly goes the dark road, cheerly goes the night,
   Cheerly goes the blood to keep the beat:
Half a thousand dead men marching on to fight
   With a little penny drum to lift their feet.
"Rubadub! Rubadub! Wake and take the road again,
   Wheedle-deedle-deedle-dee, come, boys, come!
You that mean to fight it out, wake and take your load again,
   Fall in! Fall in! Follow the fife and drum!"

As long as there's an Englishman to ask a tale of me,
   As long as I can tell the tale aright,
We'll not forget the penny whistle's wheedle-deedle-dee
   And the big Dragoon a-beating down the night,
"Rubadub! Rubadub! Wake and take the road again,
   Wheedle-deedle-deedle-dee, come, boys, come!
You that mean to fight it out, wake and take your load again,
   Fall in! Fall in! Follow the fife and drum!"

Henry Newbolt

The Union Jack

This little flag to us so dear,
    The Union Jack of Fame,
Come, sit by me, and you shall hear
    The way it got its name.

We first must look at other three,
    Please hold them up quite tight,
They all have crosses, you can see,
    Two red ones and one white.

St. Patrick's Cross, to Ireland dear,
    Like letter X it lies;
St. George's Cross, so bright and clear,
    Led England's battle cries.

St. Andrew's Cross is white, you see,
    Upon a bed of blue,
The Scottish flag it used to be,
    To it the folks were true.

In Course of time, the three combin'd,
    It was a famous tack:
We'll do the same, and you will find,
    Great Britain's Union Jack.

Jeannie Kirby

The Thames

The Thames will take us to London town,
"Of wonderful beauty and great renown."
The dew goes up and the rain comes down,
To carry us safely to London town.

We'll meet the ships from every sea,
With cocoa and cotton, with sugar and tea,
From fair lands and fertile, wherever they be,
All faring, all wearing, for you and for me.

M. M. Hutchinson

497

A Ship Sails up to Bideford

A ship sails up to Bideford;
  Upon a western breeze,
Mast by mast, sail over sail,
  She rises from the seas,
And sights the hills of Devon
  And the misty English trees.

She comes from Eastern islands
  The sun is on her hold;
She bears the fruit of Jaffa,
  Dates, oranges and gold.

She brings the silk of China,
  And bales of Persian dyes,
And birds with sparkling feathers,
  And snakes with diamond eyes.

She's gliding in the starlight
  As white as any gull;
The East is gliding with her
  In the shadows of her hull.

A ship sails up to Bideford;
  Upon a western breeze,
With fruits of Eastern summers
  She rises from the seas,
And sights the hills of Devon
  And the misty English trees.

Herbert Asquith

Sea Song

A wet sheet and a flowing sea,
  A wind that follows fast,
And fills the white and rustling sail
  And bends the gallant mast—
And bends the gallant mast, my boys,
  While, like the eagle free,
Away the good ship flies, and leaves
  Old England on the lee.

"Oh for a soft and gentle wind,"
  I heard a fair one cry;
But give to me the snoring breeze,
  And white waves heaving high—
And white waves heaving high, my boys,
  The good ship tight and free;
The world of waters is our home,
  And merry men are we.

There's tempest in yon horned moon,
  And lightning in yon cloud;
But hark the music, mariners!
  The wind is piping loud—
The wind is piping loud, my boys,
  The lightning flashing free,—
While the hollow oak our palace is,
  Our heritage the sea.

A. Cunningham

Prayers, Graces and Thanksgivings, Lullabies and Cradle Songs

He prayeth well, who loveth well
Both man and bird and beast

Evening Song

Soft falls the night,
The day grows dim,
To Thee I lift my evening hymn,
O Lord of dark and light.

My hands I raise,
A little spire,
And send my voice up high and higher
To Thee in happy praise.

For home and friend,
For books and toys,
For all the countless loves and joys
That Thou dost daily send.

Close Thou mine eyes,
That when the day
Returns once more from far away,
I may rejoicing rise.

Edith King

Grace and Thanksgiving

We thank Thee, Lord, for quiet upland lawns,
For misty loveliness of autumn dawns,
For gold and russet of the ripened fruit,
For yet another year's fulfilment, Lord,
  We thank Thee now.

For joy of glowing colour, flash of wings,
We thank Thee, Lord; for all the little things
That make the love and laughter of our days,
For home and happiness and friends, we praise
  And thank Thee now.

Elizabeth Gould

A Child's Prayer

Father, we thank Thee for the night
And for the pleasant morning light,
For rest and food and loving care,
And all that makes the world so fair.
Help us to do the thing we should.
To be to others kind and good,
In all we do, in all we say,
To grow more loving every day.

Prayers

God who created me
Nimble and light of limb,
In three elements free,
To run, to ride, to swim,
Not when the sense is dim,
But now from the heart of joy,
I would remember Him:
Take the thanks of a boy.

Jesu, King and Lord,
Whose army goes to fight,
Gird me with Thy sword,
Swift and sharp and bright.
Thee would I serve if I might
And conquer if I can,
From day-dawn till night,
Take the strength of a man.

Spirit of Love and Truth,
Breathing in grosser clay,
The light and flame of youth,
Delight of men in the fray,
Wisdom in strength's decay;
From pain, strife, wrong to be free,
This best gift I pray,
Take my spirit to Thee.

Henry Charles Beeching

Lovely Things

Bread is a lovely thing to eat—
God bless the barley and the wheat!

A lovely thing to breathe is air—
God bless the sunshine everywhere!

The earth's a lovely place to know—
God bless the folks that come and go!

Alive's a lovely thing to be—
Giver of life—we say—bless Thee!

H. M. Sarson

Morning Thanksgiving

Thank God for sleep in the long quiet night,
　For the clear day calling through the little leaded panes,
For the shining well-water and the warm golden light,
　And the paths washed white by singing rains.

For the treasure of the garden, the gilly-flowers of gold,
　The prouder petalled tulips, the primrose full of spring,
For the crowded orchard boughs, and the swelling buds that
　　hold
　A yet unwoven wonder, to Thee our praise we bring.

Thank God for good bread, for the honey in the comb,
　For the brown-shelled eggs, for the clustered blossom set
Beyond the open window in a pink and cloudy foam,
　For the laughing loves among the branches set.

For earth's little secret and innumerable ways,
　For the carol and the colour, Lord, we bring
What things may be of thanks, and that Thou hast lent
　　our days
　Eyes to see and ears to hear and lips to sing.

John Drinkwater

The Knight's Prayer

God be in my head
  And in my understanding;

God be in mine eyes
  And in my looking;

God be in my mouth
  And in my speaking;

God be in my heart,
  And in my thinking;

God be at my end,
  And at my departing.

The Robin's Song

God bless the field and bless the furrow,
Stream and branch and rabbit burrow,
Hill and stone and flower and tree,
From Bristol town to Wetherby—
Bless the sun and bless the sleet,
Bless the lane and bless the street,
Bless the night and bless the day,
From Somerset and all the way
To the meadows of Cathay;
Bless the minnow, bless the whale,
Bless the rainbow and the hail,
Bless the nest and bless the leaf,
Bless the righteous and the thief,
Bless the wing and bless the fin,
Bless the air I travel in,
Bless the mill and bless the mouse,
Bless the miller's bricken house,
Bless the earth and bless the sea,
God bless you and God bless me!

Old English Rhyme

A Child's Prayer

Thro' the night Thy angels kept
Watch above me while I slept,
Now the dark has passed away,
Thank Thee, Lord, for this new day.

North and south and east and west
May Thy holy name be blest;
Everywhere beneath the sun,
As in Heaven, Thy will be done.

Give me food that I may live;
Every naughtiness forgive;
Keep all evil things away
From Thy little child this day.

William Canton

The Elixir

Teach me, my God and King,
    In all things Thee to see,
And what I do in anything,
    To do it as for Thee.

A man that looks on glass
    On it may stay his eye:
Or, if he pleaseth, through it pass
    And then the heaven espy.

A servant with this clause
    Makes drudgery divine:
Who sweeps a room, as for Thy laws,
    Makes that and th' action fine.

This is the famous stone
    That turneth all to gold:
For that which God doth touch and own
    Cannot for less be told.

George Herbert

He Prayeth Well

From *The Rime of the Ancient Mariner*

He prayeth well, who loveth well
 Both man and bird and beast,
He prayeth best, who loveth best
 All things both great and small;
For the dear God who loveth us,
 He made and loveth all.

Samuel Taylor Coleridge

Praise

Praise the Lord for all the seasons,
 Praise Him for the gentle spring,
Praise the Lord for glorious summer,
 Birds and beasts and everything.
Praise the Lord Who sends the harvest,
 Praise Him for the winter snows;
Praise the Lord, all ye who love Him,
 Praise Him, for all things He knows.

Mary Anderson

The Willow-boughs

Lads and lasses gathering,
Willow-boughs and tapers bring,
 That they homeward bear.

Warmly do the flamelets glow,
Wayfarers cross them as they go;
 Spring-tide scents the air.

Little breeze from far away,
Rain, O rain, with tiny spray,
 Quench ye not the flame.

For Palm Sunday earliest,
I to-morrow stir from rest,
 Holy-day to acclaim.

Alexander Block

507

Good Night

Good night! Good night!
Far flies the light;
But still God's love
Shall shine above,
Making all bright,
Good night! Good night!

Victor Hugo

The Pilgrim

Who would true valour see,
    Let him come hither!
One here will constant be,
    Come wind, come weather;
There's no discouragement
Shall make him once relent
His first-avow'd intent
    To be a Pilgrim.

Whoso beset him round
    With dismal stories,
Do but themselves confound
    His strength the more is.
No lion can him fright;
He'll with a giant fight;
But he will have a right
    To be a Pilgrim.

Nor enemy, nor friend,
    Can daunt his spirit;
He knows he at the end
    Shall Life inherit:—
Then, fancies, fly away;
He'll fear not what men say;
He'll labour, night and day,
    To be a Pilgrim.

John Bunyan

A Child's Grace

Here a little child I stand
Heaving up my either hand;
Cold as paddocks though they be,
Here I lift them up to Thee,
For a benison to fall
On our meat and on us all.   Amen.

R. Herrick

A Child's Morning Prayer

Look down on me, a little one,
Whose life on earth is but begun:
  Dear Saviour, smile on me.

Watch over me from day to day,
And when I work, or when I play,
  Dear Saviour, smile on me.

Help me to do Thy holy will,
With lovely thoughts my mind to fill:
  Dear Saviour, smile on me.

J. Kirby

A Child's Prayer

For Morn, my dome of blue,
For Meadows green and gay,
And Buds who love the twilight of the leaves,
Let Jesus keep me joyful when I pray.

For the big Bees that hum
And hide in bells of flowers;
For the winding roads that come
To Evening's holy door
May Jesus bring me grateful to His arms,
And guard my innocence for evermore.

Siegfried Sassoon

509

Thanks to Spring

We thank Thee, Heavenly Father,
For all the lovely spring,
For primroses and bluebells,
And little birds that sing.

For woods and fields to play in,
For bright blue sky and sea,
For everything we thank Thee.
All beauty comes from Thee.

Mary Anderson

School Creed

This is our school,
Let peace dwell here,
Let the room be full of contentment.
Let love abide here.
Love of one another,
Love of mankind,
Love of life itself,
And love of God.
Let us remember
That as many hands build a house,
So many hearts make a school.

From "The School Creed" of a School in Canada

Go, Pretty Child

Go, pretty Child, and bear this flower
Unto thy little Saviour:
And tell Him, by that bud now blown,
He is the Rose of Sharon known.
When thou hast said so, stick it there
Upon His bib or stomacher.
And tell Him, for good handsel too,
That thou hast brought a whistle new,
Made of a clean straight oaten reed,
To charm His cries at time of need.
Tell Him for coral, thou hast none,
But if thou hadst, He should have one;
And poor thou art, and known to be
Even as moneyless as He.

Robert Herrick

510

The Shepherd Boy's Song

He that is down needs fear no fall,
   He that is low, no pride;
He that is humble ever shall
   Have God to be his guide.

I am content with what I have,
   Little be it or much:
And, Lord, contentment still I crave,
   Because Thou savest such.

Fullness to such a burden is
   That go on pilgrimage:
Here little, and hereafter bliss,
   Is best from age to age.

J. Bunyan

The Divine Image

To Mercy, Pity, Peace and Love
   All pray in their distress:
And to these virtues of delight
   Return their thankfulness.

For Mercy, Pity, Peace and Love
   Is God, our Father dear,
And Mercy, Pity, Peace and Love
   Is man, His child and care.

For Mercy has a human heart,
   Pity a human face,
And Love, the human form divine,
   And Peace, the human dress.

Then every man of every clime,
   That prays in his distress,
Prays to the human form divine,
   Love, Mercy, Pity, Peace.

William Blake

A Thank You for Friends

There are all kinds of men
   Who have done me good turns,
That I still never think about,
   Not for a minute;
Yet if I were making up
   That sort of grace,
They would all of them have
   To be in it.

One man made up stories,
   Another wrote verses
I found, and I liked,
   And I read till I knew them.
Another one saw
   All the things they had written,
Then, being an artist,
   He drew them.

Another took wood
   And a saw and some glue,
And put each of them just
   In the place that would need it—
So that is the chair
   Where I sit with my book
And am so much at ease
   As I read it.

I'm forgetting the one
   Who read tale after tale
When I was too young
   To know letter from letter,
And the other who taught me them,
   Till in the end
I could read for myself—
   Which was better.

Rodney Bennett

The Country Faith

Here in the country's heart,
  Where the grass is green,
Life is the same sweet life
  As it e'er hath been.

Trust in a God still lives,
  And the bell at morn
Flouts with a thought of God
  O'er the rising corn.

God comes down in the rain,
  And the crop grows tall—
This is the country faith,
  And the best of all!

Norman Gale

Ex Ore Infantium

Little Jesus wast Thou shy
Once, and just as small as I?
And what did it feel like to be
Out of Heaven and just like me?
Didst Thou sometimes think of there,
And ask where all the angels were?
I should think that I would cry
For my house all made of sky;
I would look about the air,
And wonder where my angels were;
And at waking 'twould distress me—
Not an angel there to dress me
Hadst Thou ever any toys,
Like us little girls and boys?
And didst Thou play in Heaven with all
The angels that were not too tall,
With stars for marbles? Did the things
Play "can you see me?" through their wings?
And did Thy mother let Thee spoil
Thy robes with playing on our soil?
How nice to have them always new
In Heaven, because 'twas quite clean blue!

513

Didst Thou kneel at night to pray,
And didst Thou join Thy hands this way?
And did they tire sometimes, being young,
And make the prayers seem very long?
And dost Thou like it best that we
Should join our hands to pray to Thee?
I used to think before I knew,
The prayer not said unless we do.
And did Thy mother at the night
Kiss Thee and fold the clothes in right?
And didst Thou feel quite good in bed,
Kissed, and sweet, and Thy prayers said?

Thou canst not have forgotten all
That it feels like to be small:
And Thou knowest I cannot pray
To Thee in my father's way—
When Thou wast so little, say,
Couldst Thou talk Thy Father's way?
So, a little child, come down
And hear a child's tongue like Thy own;
Take me by the hand and walk,
And listen to my baby talk;
To Thy Father show my prayer
(He will look, Thou art so fair)
And say: O Father, I, Thy Son,
Bring the prayer of a little one;
And He will smile, the children's tongue
Hast not changed since Thou wast young.

Francis Thompson

The Vision Clear

Child's eyes to see,
    Child's ears to hear—
God grant to me
    That vision clear.

Grant me the sight
  Of heaven and earth—
Quiet rest at night,
  Day's glorious mirth.
Help me to hear
  Those little things,
Faint, far and clear,
  Rememberings.
So I may learn
  Fully to praise
Thee for my life
  Of happy days.

                                        J. M. Westrup

A Prayer

Teach me, Father, how to go
Softly as the grasses grow;
Hush my soul to meet the shock
Of the wild world as a rock;
But my spirit, prompt with power,
Make as simple as a flower.
Let the dry heart fill its cup,
Like a poppy looking up;
Let life lightly wear her crown,
Like a poppy looking down,
When its heart is filled with dew
And its life begins anew.

Teach me, Father, how to be
Kind and patient as a tree.
Joyfully the crickets croon
Under shady oak at noon;
Beetle, on his mission bent,
Tarries in that cooling tent.
Let me, also, cheer a spot,
Hidden field or garden grot,
Place where passing souls can rest
On the way and be their best.

                                        Edwin Markham

Lines from Invocation of Peace

Deep peace, pure white of the moon to you;
Deep peace, pure green of the grass to you;
Deep peace, pure brown of the earth to you;
Deep peace, pure grey of the dew to you,
Deep peace, pure blue of the sky to you!
Deep peace of the running wave to you,
Deep peace of the flowing air to you,
Deep peace of the quiet earth to you.

"Fiona Macleod"

Hindu Cradle Song

From groves of spice,
O'er fields of rice,
Athwart the lotus-stream,
  I bring for you,
  Aglint with dew,
A little lovely dream.

Sweet, shut your eyes,
The wild fireflies
Dance through the fairy neem,*
  From the poppy bole
  For you I stole
A little lovely dream.

A Danish Cradle Song

Lullaby, sweet baby mine!
Mother spins the thread so fine;
Father o'er the long bridge is gone,
Shoes he'll buy for little John.
Pretty shoes with buckles bright.
Sleep, baby mine, now sleep all night!

*Neem is a lilac tree (Hindustani).

Sweet and Low

Sweet and low, sweet and low,
  Wind of the western sea,
Low, low, breathe and blow,
  Wind of the western sea!
Over the rolling waters go,
Come from the dying moon, and blow,
    Blow him again to me;
While my little one, while my pretty one, sleeps.
  Sleep and rest, sleep and rest,
    Father will come to thee soon;
Rest, rest, on mother's breast,
    Father will come to thee soon;
Father will come to his babe in the nest,
Silver sails all out of the west
     Under the silver moon:
Sleep, my little one, sleep, my pretty one, sleep.

Lord Tennyson

The Dustman

When the shades of night are falling, and the sun goes down,
O! the Dustman comes a-creeping in from Shut-eye Town.
And he throws dust in the eyes of all the babies that he meets,
No matter where he finds them, in the house or in the streets.
Then the babies' eyes grow heavy and the lids drop down,
When the Dustman comes a-creeping in from Shut-eye Town.

When mother lights the lamp and draws the curtains down,
O! the Dustman comes a-creeping in from Shut-eye Town,
And the babies think the Dustman is as mean as he can be,
For he shuts their eyes at nightfall, just when they want to see.
But their little limbs are weary, for all they fret and frown,
When the Dustman comes a-creeping in from Shut-eye Town.

Nod

Softly along the road of evening,
  In a twilight dim with rose,
Wrinkled with age, and drenched with dew,
  Old Nod, the shepherd, goes.

His drowsy flocks stream on before him,
  Their fleeces charged with gold,
To where the sun's last beam leans low
  On Nod the shepherd's fold.

The hedge is quick and green with briar,
  From their sand the conies creep;
And all the birds that fly in heaven
  Flock singing home to sleep.

His lambs outnumber a noon's roses,
  Yet, when night's shadows fall,
His blind old sheep-dog, Slumber-soon,
  Misses not one of all.

His are the quiet steeps of dreamland,
  The waters of no-more-pain,
His ram's bell rings 'neath an arch of stars,
  "Rest, rest, and rest again."

Walter de la Mare

Cradle Hymn

Away in a manger, no crib for a bed,
The little Lord Jesus laid down His sweet head.
The stars in the bright sky looked down where He lay—
The little Lord Jesus asleep in the hay.

The cattle are lowing, the Baby awakes,
But little Lord Jesus, no crying He makes.
I love Thee, Lord Jesus! look down from the sky,
And stay by my cradle till morning is nigh.

Martin Luther

Evening

Hush, hush, little baby,
   The sun's in the west;
The lamb in the meadow
   Has laid down to rest.

The bough rocks the bird now,
   The flower rocks the bee,
The wave rocks the lily,
   The wind rocks the tree;

And I rock the baby
   So softly to sleep—
It must not awaken
   Till daisy-buds peep.

Bed-time

The evening is coming,
   The sun sinks to rest;
The rooks are all flying
   Straight home to the nest.
"Caw!" says the rook, as he flies overhead;
"It's time little people were going to bed!"

The flowers are closing;
   The daisy's asleep;
The primrose is buried
   In slumber so deep.
Shut up for the night is the pimpernel red;
It's time little people were going to bed!

The butterfly, drowsy,
   Has folded its wing;
The bees are returning,
   No more the birds sing.
Their labour is over, their nestlings are fed;
It's time little people were going to bed!

Here comes the pony,
    His work all done;
Down through the meadow
    He takes a good run;
Up goes his heels and down goes his head;
It's time little people were going to bed!

Good night, little people,
    Good night and good night;
Sweet dreams to your eyelids
    Till dawning of light;
The evening has come, there's no more to be said,
It's time little people were going to bed!

Thomas Hood

Norse Lullaby

The sky is dark, and the hills are white,
The Storm King speeds from the North to-night,
And this is the song the Storm King sings,
As over the earth his cloak he flings—
    "Sleep, sleep, little one, sleep!"
He rustles his wings, and gruffly sings,
    "Sleep, little one, sleep!"

On yonder mountain side, a vine
Clings at the foot of a mother pine.
The tree bends over the trembling thing,
And only the vine can hear her sing—
    "Sleep, sleep, little one, sleep!
What can you fear when I am near?
    Sleep, little one, sleep!"

The King may sing in his bitter flight,
The tree may croon to the vine to-night,
But the little snowflake at my breast
Liketh the song I sing the best—
    "Sleep, sleep, little one, sleep!
Weary thou art, a-next my heart,
    Sleep, little one, sleep!"

Eugene Field

Cradle Song

What does little birdie say
In her nest at peep of day?
Let me fly, says little birdie,
Mother, let me fly away.

Birdie, rest a little longer,
Till the little wings are stronger,
So she rests a little longer,
Then she flies away.

What does little baby say,
In her bed at peep of day?
Baby says, like little birdie,
Let me rise and fly away.

Baby, sleep a little longer,
Till the little limbs are stronger,
If she sleeps a little longer,
Baby too shall fly away.

Lord Tennyson

A Summer Lullaby

The sun has gone from the shining skies,
    Bye, baby, bye.
The dandelions have closed their eyes,
    Bye, baby, bye,
And the stars are lighting their lamps to see
If the babies and squirrels and birds, all three,
Are sound asleep as they ought to be—
    Bye, baby, bye.

The squirrel is dressed in a coat of grey,
    Bye, baby, bye.
He wears it by night as well as by day,
    Bye, baby, bye.
The robin sleeps in his feathers of down
With a warm red breast and wings of brown,
But the baby wears a little white gown,
    Bye, baby, bye.

The squirrel's nest is a hole in a tree,
  Bye, baby, bye.
And there he sleeps as snug as can be,
  Bye, baby, bye.
The robin's nest is high overhead
Where the leafy boughs of the maple spread,
But the baby's nest is a little white bed,
  Bye, baby, bye.

Eudora S. Bumstead

A Cradle Song

  Sleep, baby, sleep!
Thy father watches the sheep,
Thy mother is shaking the dreamland tree,
And softly a little dream falls on thee!
  Sleep, baby, sleep!

  Sleep, baby, sleep!
The large stars are the sheep,
The little stars are the lambs, I guess,
The fair moon is the shepherdess;
  Sleep, baby, sleep!

  Sleep, baby, sleep!
I'll buy for thee a sheep,
With a golden bell so fine to see,
And it shall frisk and play with thee;
  Sleep, baby, sleep!

  Sleep, baby, sleep!
Thy father watches the sheep,
The wind is blowing fierce and wild,
It must not wake my little child;
  Sleep, baby, sleep!

  Sleep, baby, sleep!
Our Saviour loves His sheep:
He is the Lamb of God on high,
Who for our sakes came down to die.
  Sleep, baby, sleep!

Lullaby

Lullaby, Lullaby,
Shadows creep across the sky.
See, the sun has gone to rest,
    Lullaby.

Lullaby, Lullaby,
Little one to Dreamland fly,
Till the morning sun awakes,
    Lullaby.

Phyllis Garlick

At Sunset

In the evening
    The sun goes down,
And the lamps are lit
    In the little town.

The bats fly low
    Round the grey church dome,
The thrush and the blackbird
    Are safely home—

Are safely home
    In their quiet nest—
The thrush and the blackbird
    Are both at rest!

Ivy O. Eastwick

Good Night

No more work and no more play,
Every toy is put away,
Ended is the lovely day,
    Then—good night!

Drink the milk all white and creamy,
Have your bath all warm and steamy
Close your eyes all tired and dreamy,
    Then—good night!

Through the window stars are peeping,
From their holes the mice are creeping,
Your white bed is soft for sleeping,
    Then—good night!

Ruth Ainsworth

At Night in the Wood

When night comes down on the children's eyes
    And all in the house is still,
For busy folk it is time to rise
    In the Wood Land over the hill.
There are those who wake when the moon is high;
    They have slept for the whole long day.
With a silent shake or a call or cry,
    They are off on the trail away.
The Owl, who hides from the sunlight's beam,
    Hark!—there is his "Too-hoo-hoo!"
The Vole who lives by the gurgling stream
    Steals out in the darkness too.

The Stoat, the Rat,
And the squeaking Bat
All open their keen little eyes
And rise.
And the Hedgehog peeps from his cosy nest
And hurries out with the rest.
And the bark of the Fox shows he's astir,
And the Rabbit shivers within his fur,
And the sleepy old Dormouse wakes at last—
There's none in the wood can move so fast.
Each one on his trail is off away
And never comes back till the dawn of day.
Oh, when in the night the moon is high
And the stars look down from the dusky sky,
If we crept out—if we only could!—
What wonderful things we should see in the wood!

Nancy M. Hayes

Wynken, Blynken, and Nod

Wynken, Blynken, and Nod one night
   Sailed off in a wooden shoe—
Sailed on a river of crystal light,
   Into a sea of dew.
"Where are you going and what do you wish?"
   The old moon asked the three.
"We have come to fish for the herring-fish
   That live in this beautiful sea;
Nets of silver and gold have we,"
   Said Wynken, Blynken, and Nod.

The old moon laughed and sang a song,
   As they rocked in the wooden shoe,
And the wind that sped them all night long
   Ruffled the waves of dew.
The little stars were the herring-fish
   That lived in that beautiful sea—
"Now cast your nets wherever you wish—
   But never afeared are we";
So cried the stars to the fishermen three:
   Wynken, Blynken, and Nod.

All night long their nets they threw
   To the stars in the twinkling foam—
Then down from the skies came the wooden shoe,
   Bringing the fishermen home;
'Twas all so pretty a sail, it seemed
   As if it could not be,
And some folks thought 'twas a dream they'd dreamed
   Of sailing that beautiful sea—
But I shall name you the fishermen three:
   Wynken, Blynken, and Nod.

Wynken and Blynken are two little eyes,
   And Nod is a little head,
And the wooden shoe that sailed the skies
   Is a wee one's trundle-bed.

So shut your eyes while mother sings
　　Of wonderful sights that be,
And you shall see the beautiful things
　　As you rock on the misty sea,
Where the old shoe rocked the fishermen three:
　　Wynken, Blynken, and Nod.

Eugene Field

The Unwritten Song

Now where's a song for our small dear,
With her quaint voice and her quick ear,
To sing—for gnats and bats to hear—
　　At twilight in her bed?
A song of tiny elfin things
With shiny, silky, silvery wings,
Footing it in fairy rings,
　　And kissing overhead.

A song of starry glow-worms' lights
In the long grass of shadowy nights,
And flitting showers of firefly flights,
　　Where summer woods hang deep;
Of hovering, noiseless owls that find
Their way at dark; and of a kind
And drowsy, drowsy ocean wind
　　That puts the sea to sleep.

But where's the song for our small dear,
With her quaint voice and her quick ear,
To sing—for dreamland things to hear—
　　And hush herself to sleep?

Ford Madox Ford

Lullaby

The wind whistled loud at the window-pane—
   Go away, wind, and let me sleep!
Ruffle the green grass billowy plain,
   Ruffle the billowy deep!
"Hush-a-bye, hush! the wind is fled,
The wind cannot ruffle the soft, smooth bed,—
   Hush thee, darling, sleep!"

The ivy tapped at the window-pane,—
   Silence, ivy! and let me sleep!
Why do you patter like drops of rain,
   And then play creepity-creep?
"Hush-a-bye, hush! the leaves shall lie still,
The moon is walking over the hill,—
   Hush thee, darling, sleep!"

A dream-show rode in on a moonbeam white,—
   Go away, dreams, and let me sleep!
The show may be gay and golden bright,
   But I do not care to peep.
"Hush-a-bye, hush! the dream is fled,
A shining angel guards thy bed,
   Hush thee, darling, sleep!"

W. B. Rands

Christmas and Easter Poems

Why do the bells of Christmas ring?
Why do little children sing?

I Will Keep Christmas

I will keep Christmas in the cold hedgerow,
With red, shining holly and winter snow.
I will keep Christmas far from any town
On the frosted side of the windswept down.

Stars will be candles of sweet silver fire,
Swinging at midnight over tree and spire,
Waves will be booming bells and break the air,
With glory and greeting and wingèd prayer.

I will keep Christmas alone and away,
Praising the Lord of all on Christmas Day.

P. A. Ropes

The Oxen

Christmas Eve, and twelve of the clock.
   "Now they are all on their knees,"
An elder said as we sat in a flock
   By the embers in fireside ease.

We pictured the meek mild creatures where
   They dwelt in their strawy pen,
Nor did it occur to one of us there
   To doubt they were kneeling then.

So fair a fancy few would weave
   In these years! Yet, I feel,
If someone said on Christmas Eve,
   "Come; see the oxen kneel

"In the lonely barton by yonder coomb
   Our childhood used to know,"
I should go with him in the gloom,
   Hoping it might be so.

Thomas Hardy

Silver Bells

Across the snow the silver bells
    Come near and yet more near;
Each day and night, each night and day
    They tinkle soft and clear.

'Tis Father Christmas on his way
    Across the winter snows;
While on his sleigh the silver bells
    Keep chiming as he goes.

I listen for them in the night,
    I listen all the day;
I think these merry silver bells
    Are long, long on the way!

Hamish Hendry

The Carol Singers

Last night the carol-singers came
    When I had gone to bed,
Upon the crisp white path outside
    I heard them softly tread.

I sat upright to listen, for
    I knew they came to tell,
Of all the things that happened on
    The very first Noel.

Upon my ceiling flickering
    I saw their lantern glow,
And then they sang their carols sweet
    Of Christmas long ago.

And when at last they went away,
    Their carol-singing done,
There was a little boy who wished
    They'd only just begun.

Margaret G. Rhodes

Christmas

An azure sky,
All star bestrewn.
A lowly crib,
A hushèd room.
An open door,
A hill afar,
Where little lambs
And shepherds are.
To such a world,
On such a night,
Came Jesus—
Little Lord of Light.

Mary I.

A Christmas Carol

The Christ-child lay on Mary's lap,
His hair was like a light.
(O weary, weary was the world,
But here is all aright.)

The Christ-Child lay on Mary's breast,
His hair was like a star.
(O stern and cunning are the kings,
But here the true hearts are.)

The Christ-child lay on Mary's heart,
His hair was like a fire.
(O weary, weary is the world,
But here the world's desire.)

The Christ-child stood at Mary's knee.
His hair was like a crown,
And all the flowers looked up at Him,
And all the stars looked down.

G. K. C

A Child's Christmas Carol

There was a little Baby once
   Born upon Christmas Day;
The oxen lowed His lullabye
   As in His crib He lay:
His tree, it was a lonely tree
   That stood upon a hill,
Its candles were the mighty stars
   That shine upon us still;
His toys were flocks of little lambs,
   He loved to see them play:
It is for Him we are so glad,
   Now upon Christmas Day.

Christine Chaundler

Cradle Song at Bethlehem

Oh! hush Thee, oh! hush Thee, my Baby so small,
The ass hath her crib and the ox hath his stall,
They shelter Thee, Baby, from Heaven above,
Oh! hush Thee, oh! hush Thee, my Baby, my love.

Oh! hush Thee, oh! hush Thee, my Baby so small,
Dim is the light from the lamp on the wall,
Bright in the night sky shineth a star,
Leading the Kings who come from afar.

Oh! hush Thee, oh! hush Thee, my Baby so small,
Joseph is spreading the straw in the stall,
Soon wilt Thou sleep in the nook of my arm
Safe from all trouble and danger and harm.

E. J. Falconer

533

Christmas Eve

On Christmas Eve my mother read
    The story once again,
Of how the little Child was born,
    And of the Three Wise Men.

And how by following the Star
    They found Him where He lay,
And brought Him gifts; and that is why
    We keep our Christmas Day.

And when she read it all, I went
    And looked across the snow,
And thought of Jesus coming
    As He did so long ago.

I looked into the East, and saw
    A great star blazing bright;
There were three men upon the road
    All black against the light.

I thought I heard the angels sing,
    Away upon the hill . . .
I held my breath . . . it seemed as if
    The whole great world were still.

It seemed to me the little Child
    Was being born again . . .
And very near . . . and Then somehow
    Was Now . . . or Now was Then!
                    Edna Kingsley Walla

Bethlehem

When the herd were watching
    In the midnight chill,
Came a spotless lambkin
    From the heavenly hill.

Snow was on the mountains,
    And the wind was cold,
When from God's own garden
    Dropped a rose of gold.

When 'twas bitter winter,
   Houseless and forlorn,
In a star-lit stable
   Christ the Babe was born.

Welcome, heavenly lambkin;
   Welcome, golden rose;
Alleluia, Baby,
   In the swaddling clothes.

William Canton

As Joseph Was A-Walking

As Joseph was a-walking
   He heard an angel sing:
"This night shall be born
   Our heavenly king.

"He neither shall be born
   In housen nor in hall,
Nor in the place of Paradise,
   But in an ox's stall.

"He neither shall be clothèd
   In purple nor in pall,
But all in fair linen,
   As were babies all.

"He neither shall be rockèd
   In silver nor in gold,
But in a wooden cradle
   That rocks on the mould.

"He neither shall be christened
   In white wine or red,
But with fair spring water,
   With which we were christenèd."

535

The Christmas Party

We're going to have a party
   And a lovely Christmas tea,
And flags and lighted candles
   Upon the Christmas Tree!

And silver balls and lanterns,
   Tied on with golden string,
Will hide among the branches
   By little bells that ring.

And then there will be crackers
   And caps and hats and toys,
A Christmas cake and presents
   For all the girls and boys.

With dancing, games and laughter,
   With music, songs and fun,
We'll make our Christmas Party
   A joy for everyone!

Adeline White

Santa Claus

He comes in the night! He comes in the night!
   He softly, silently comes;
While the little brown heads on the pillows so white
   Are dreaming of bugles and drums.
He cuts through the snow like a ship through the foam,
   While the white flakes around him whirl;
Who tells him I know not, but he findeth the home
   Of each good little boy and girl.

His sleigh it is long, and deep, and wide;
   It will carry a host of things
While dozens of drums hang over the side,
   With the sticks sticking under the strings.
And yet not the sound of a drum is heard,
   Not a bugle blast is blown,
As he mounts to the chimney-top like a bird,
   And drops to the hearth like a stone.

The little red stockings he silently fills,
    Till the stockings will hold no more;
The bright little sleds for the great snow hills
    Are quickly set down on the floor.
Then Santa Claus mounts to the roof like a bird,
    And glides to his seat in the sleigh;
Not the sound of a bugle or drum is heard
    As he noiselessly gallops away.

He rides to the East, and he rides to the West,
    Of his goodies he touches not one;
He eateth the crumbs of the Christmas feast
    When the dear little folks are done.
Old Santa Claus doeth all that he can;
    This beautiful mission is his;
Then, children, be good to the little old man,
    When you find who the little man is.

The Waits

Frost in the air and music in the air,
And the singing is sweet in the street.
She wakes from a dream to a dream—O hark!
    The singing so faint in the dark.

The musicians come and stand at the door,
A fiddler and singers three,
And one with a bright lamp thrusts at the dark,
    And the music comes sudden—O hark!

She hears the singing as sweet as a dream
And the fiddle that climbs to the sky,
With head 'neath the curtain she stares out—O hark!
    The music so strange in the dark.

She listens and looks and sees but the sky,
While the fiddle is sweet in the porch,
And she sings back into the singing dark
    Hark, herald angels, hark!

John Freeman

Carol

He came all so still
   There His mother was,
As dew in April
   That falleth on the grass.

He came all so still
   To His mother's bower,
As dew in April
   That falleth on the flower.

He came all so still
   There His mother lay,
As dew in April
   That falleth on the spray.

Mother and maiden
   Was never done but she!
Well may such a lady
   Goddès mother be.

Christmas Carols

I hear along our street
Pass the minstrel throngs;
Hark! they play so sweet,
On their hautboys, Christmas songs!
   Let us by the fire
   Ever higher
Sing them till the night expire!

In December ring
Every day the chimes;
Loud the gleemen sing
In the street their merry rhymes.
   Let us by the fire
   Ever higher
Sing them till the night expire.

Shepherds at the grange,
Where the Babe was born,
Sang, with many a change,
Christmas carols until morn.
Let us by the fire
Ever higher
Sing them till the night expire!

H. W. Longfellow

The Little Fir Tree

1. At Christmas time so long ago,
The winds were blowing high and low;
A little green fir tree grew by the Inn,
A little fir tree straight and slim.

    "Noel, Noel!" the angels sang,
    "Noel, Noel! Goodwill to man,"
    A little green fir tree grew by the Inn,
    A little green fir tree straight and slim.

2. And, looking up, across the night
The fir tree saw the Star so bright.
The little fir tree wondered why
The star was moving in the sky.

    "Noel, Noel!" etc.

3. The star shone over Bethlehem
Over the stable inn, and then
The little green fir tree shone with light,
Lit by the star that wintry night.

    "Noel, Noel!" etc.

4. The fir tree shone so long ago;
And still in winter's frost and snow,
The little green fir tree comes each year
To bring us joy and Christmas cheer.

    "Noel, Noel!" etc.

Margaret Rose
539

A Christmas Song

Winds through the Olive trees softly did blow
Round little Bethlehem long, long ago.
Sheep on the hill-sides lay white as the snow;
Shepherds were watching them long, long ago.
Shepherds were watching them long, long ago.

Then from the happy skies Angels bent low,
Singing their songs of joy, long, long ago.
For, in His manger bed, cradled, we know,
Christ came to Bethlehem long, long ago,
Christ came to Bethlehem long, long ago.

A Christmas-Tree Song

The Chestnut's a fine tree
    In sunshine of May,
With blossoms like candles
    In shining array;
But they're not half so pretty
    Or so welcome to me
As the little wax candles,
Red-and-white candles,
Lighted four-a-penny candles
    On a little Christmas tree.

The Apple's a gay tree
    With fruit shining red
Like glossy round lanterns
    Alight overhead;
But they're not half so pretty
    Or so welcome to me
As the gay paper lanterns,
Small crinkled lanterns,
Pretty red-and-white lanterns
    On a little Christmas Tree.

The Peach is a rare tree,
  The Plum tree is, too,
With fruit from green turning
  To golden and blue;
But they're not half so pretty
  Or so welcome to me
As the shining round peaches,
Pretty glass peaches,
Mellow plums and golden peaches
  On a little Christmas Tree.

All trees in their season
  Bear fruits that are good,
In hedgerow or garden,
  In orchard or wood;
But they cannot show anything
  So delightful to see
As the brown-paper parcels,
Plump paper parcels,
Jolly ribbon-tied parcels
  On a little Christmas Tree.

Rodney Bennett

Song

Why do the bells of Christmas ring?
Why do little children sing?

Once a lovely shining star,
Seen by shepherds from afar,
Gently moved until its light
Made a manger's cradle bright.

There a darling baby lay,
Pillowed soft upon the hay.
And its Mother sung and smiled:
"This is Christ, the holy Child!"

Therefore bells for Christmas ring,
Therefore little children sing.

Eugene Field
541

A Christmas Wish

To every hearth a little fire,
To every board a little feast,
To every heart a joy,
To every child a toy,
Shelter for bird and beast.

Rose Fyleman

A Child's Song of Christmas

My counterpane is soft as silk,
My blankets white as creamy milk.
  The hay was soft to Him, I know,
  Our little Lord of long ago.

Above the roof the pigeons fly
In silver wheels across the sky.
  The stable doves they cooed to them,
  Mary and Christ in Bethlehem.

Bright shines the sun across the drifts,
And bright upon my Christmas gifts.
  They brought Him incense, myrrh, and gold,
  Our little Lord who lived of old.

O, soft and clear our mother sings
Of Christmas joys and Christmas things.
  God's holy angels sang to them,
  Mary and Christ in Bethlehem.

Our hearts they hold all Christmas dear,
And earth seems sweet and heaven seems near.
  O, heaven was in His sight, I know,
  That little Child of long ago.

Marjorie L. C. Pickthall

The Christmas Tree

With spangles gay and candle light
And many toys, our tree is bright.
And gold and silver birds are there:
While over all there hangs a star.

The toys are given first of all.
For me a doll, for Hugh a ball.
The spangle stuff is pulled about.
The candles are then all put out.

The tree now strip't is dark and bare,
But still the star is shining there
As shone the star the shepherds saw,
Who heard the angels' song of yore.

The star that was a guiding light,
To kings and shepherds, through the night,
Where patient oxen calm and mild,
Shared their bed with Mary's child.

Christmas night is our Saviour's birth.
Joy in heaven, and peace on earth.
This was the story Mummy told me,
As she hung the star in our Christmas tree.

Isabel de Savitzsky

Pudding Charms

Our Christmas pudding was made in November,
All they put in it, I quite well remember:
Currants and raisins, and sugar and spice,
Orange peel, lemon peel—everything nice
Mixed up together, and put in a pan.
"When you've stirred it," said Mother, "as much as you
    can,
We'll cover it over, that nothing may spoil it,
And then, in the copper, to-morrow we'll boil it."
That night, when we children were all fast asleep,
A real fairy godmother came crip-a-creep!

She wore a red cloak, and a tall steeple hat
(Though nobody saw her but Tinker, the cat!)
And out of her pocket a thimble she drew,
A button of silver, a silver horse-shoe,
And, whisp'ring a charm, in the pudding pan popped
    them,
Then flew up the chimney directly she dropped them;
And even old Tinker pretended he slept
(With Tinker a secret is sure to be kept!),
So nobody knew, until Christmas came round,
And there, in the pudding, these treasures we found.

Charlotte Druitt Cole

A Christmas Verse

He had no royal palace,
    Only a stable bare.
He had no watchful servants,
    An ox and ass stood there.
But light shone forth from where He lay;
The King of Love upon the hay!

"Kay"

Christmas Night

Softly, softly, through the darkness
    Snow is falling.
Sharply, sharply, in the meadows
    Lambs are calling.
Coldly, coldly, all around me
    Winds are blowing.
Brightly, brightly, up above me
    Stars are glowing.

B. E. Milner

Christmas Carol

God bless the master of this house,
  Likewise the mistress too:
And all the little children
  That round the table go.
Love and joy come to you,
  And to your wassail too,
And God bless you and send you
  A happy New Year.

Christmas Eve

On Christmas Eve the little stars
  Sparkle and glisten with delight,
Like strings of glitt'ring diamonds,
  Across the darkness of the night.

On Christmas Eve the little stars
  Dance in their places in the sky;
Ah! I would go and trip with them
  If I could only climb as high.

On Christmas Eve the little stars
  Sing merry carols all night long;
But O! I am so far away
  I cannot even hear their song.

On Christmas Eve the little stars
  Sparkle and dance, and sing till dawn;
And I am singing too, because
  To-morrow will be Christmas Morn.

Charlotte Druitt Cole

Ten Little Christmas Trees

Ten little Christmas Trees a-growing in a line.
    The first went to Bedfordshire,
    And that left only nine.

Nine little Christmas Trees all found it long to wait,
    The second went to Monmouthshire,
    And that left only eight.

Eight little Christmas Trees said, "Christmas will be
      heaven."
    The third went to London Town,
    And that left only seven.

Seven little Christmas Trees, and all as straight as sticks!
    The fourth went to Oxfordshire,
    And that left only six.

Six little Christmas Trees, all growing and alive!
    The fifth went to Lancashire,
    And that left only five.

Five little Christmas Trees said, "Will they want some
      more?"
    The sixth went to Devonshire,
    And that left only four.

Four little Christmas Trees, as sturdy as could be!
    The seventh went to Scilly Isles,
    And that left only three.

Three little Christmas Trees all grew and grew and grew,
    The eighth went to Middlesex,
    And that left only two.

Two little Christmas Trees, December almost done!
    The ninth went to Timbuctoo,
    And that left only one.

One little Christmas Tree, feeling very small!
    She came to our school,
    And that was best of all.

Ten little Christmas Trees, with Christmas drawing near,
    Wish you love and gladness
    And a Happy New Year.

Rodney Bennett

All in Red

Red for Santa's fur-lined cloak
    And his scarlet hood.
Red for the holly berries
    Gleaming in the wood.
Red for the breast
Of the bravest little bird,
R-E-D for the brightest Christmas word.

Red for the glow of the yule-log light
And the little crimson slippers
That Santa left last night.
Red for the paper lanterns
    Hanging from the wall.
Of the many Christmas colours
    Red's the best of all.

Eileen Mathias

"How Far is it to Bethlehem?"

How far is it to Bethlehem?
    Not very far.
Shall we find the stable-room
    Lit by a star?

Can we see the little Child?
    Is He within?
If we lift the wooden latch,
    May we go in?

May we stroke the creatures there —
    Ox, ass, or sheep?
May we peep like them and see
    Jesus asleep?

If we touch His tiny hand,
    Will He awake?
Will He know we've come so far
    Just for His sake?

Great kings have precious gifts,
    And we have naught;
Little smiles and little tears
    Are all we brought.

For all weary children
    Mary must weep;
Here, on His bed of straw,
    Sleep, children, sleep.

God, in His mother's arms,
    Babes in the byre,
Sleep, as they sleep who find
    Their heart's desire.

F. Chesterton

The New Year

I am the little New Year, ho, ho!
Here I come tripping it over the snow.
Shaking my bells with a merry din—
So open your doors and let me in!

Presents I bring for each and all—
Big folks, little folks, short and tall;
Each one from me a treasure may win—
So open your doors and let me in!

Some shall have silver and some shall have gold,
Some shall have new clothes and some shall have old;
Some shall have brass and some shall have tin—
So open your doors and let me in!

Some shall have water and some shall have milk,
Some shall have satin and some shall have silk!
But each from me a present may win—
So open your doors and let me in!

A New Year Carol

Here we bring new water
   from the well so clear,
For to worship God with,
   this happy New Year.
Sing, levy dew, sing levy dew,
   the water and the wine;
The seven bright gold wires
   and the bugles that do shine.

Sing reign of Fair Maid,
   with gold upon her toe—
Open you the West Door,
   and turn the Old Year go.

Sing reign of Fair Maid
   with gold upon her chin—
Open you the East Door,
   and let the New Year in.
Sing levy dew, sing levy dew,
   the water and the wine;
The seven bright gold wires
   and the bugles that do shine.

The New Year

Oh! I'm the New Year,
    Come, look at my wares;
I've wishes all good
    And just a few cares.

Oh! what will you have?
    Come, buy, cheap or dear,
Oh! what will you have,
    A hope or a fear?

Oh! what will you have?
    Come, buy, young and old;
I've work and I've play,
    I've days warm and cold.

Oh! what will you have?
    There's no time to lose,
Bright days or dull weather,
    I know which you'll choose.

And for little children
    I've seasons so gay,
And each has a portion
    Of work and of play.

So come, young and old,
    And buy from my pack,
And be sure with each purchase
    Good luck you'll ne'er lack.

Easter Praise

Welcome, happy Easter day!
Winter now is far away.
Through the wide-world children sing
Praises to their Lord and King.

Through the woodlands, buds now doff
Their brown coats, and, throwing off
Winter slumber, bush and tree
Wear an April livery.

Now the wind more softly breathes,
Flowerets cast their sober sheaths,
And, to honour Easter Day,
Strew their petals on His way.

Birds that yesterday were dumb
Find their voices newly come,
And from branches all day long
Pour their joyous Easter Song.

Though but little I can sing,
I my Easter song would bring,
And for joy, as best I may,
In my singing I would pray:

Gentle Jesus, King of kings,
Yet the Lord of little things,
Though but small and young I be,
From Thy glory smile on me.

Keep it ever in my mind
To be kind, as Thou wert kind,
So I may be trusted by
Small things not so strong as I.

Then shall birds and flowers bless
My small hands for gentleness,
And in one thing I shall be
In my living liker Thee.

Help me every hour to make
Something happier for Thy sake,
So through all the year I may
Make each day Thy Easter Day.

Rodney Bennett

Easter

I got me flowers to strew Thy way,
  I got me boughs off many a tree;
But Thou wast up by break of day,
  And brought'st Thy sweets along with Thee.

Yet though my flowers be lost, they say
  A heart can never come too late;
Teach it to sing Thy praise this day,
  And then this day my life shall date.

George Herbert

An Easter Chick

"What a lovely world," said the baby chick,
"I've stepped from my egg to see!"

"What a lovely chick!" said the happy world,
"The spring has brought to me."

The children said, "God sent her to us,"
And fed her joyfully.

Thirza Wakley

Song

From *The Husband of Poverty*

There was a Knight of Bethlehem,
Whose wealth was tears and sorrows;
His men-at-arms were little lambs,
His trumpeters were sparrows;
His castle was a wooden cross,
Whereon He hung so high;
His helmet was a crown of thorns
Whose crest did touch the sky.

Henry Neville Maughan

When Mary Thro' the Garden Went

When Mary thro' the garden went,
  There was no sound of any bird,
And yet, because the night was spent,
  The little grasses lightly stirred,
  The flowers awoke, the lilies heard.

When Mary thro' the garden went,
  The dew lay still on flower and grass,
The waving palms above her sent
  Their fragrance out as she did pass,
  No light upon the branches was.

When Mary thro' the garden went,
  Her eyes, for weeping long, were dim,
The grass beneath her footsteps bent,
  The solemn lilies, white and slim,
  These also stood and wept for Him.

When Mary thro' the garden went,
  She sought, within the garden ground,
One for Whom her heart was rent,
  One Who for her sake was bound,
  One Who sought and she was found.

Mary E. Coleridge

Envoi

Earth puts her colours by,
And veils her in one whispering cloak of shadow;
Green goes from the meadow,
Red leaves and flowers and shining pools are shrouded;
A' few stars sail upon a windy sky,
And the moon is clouded.

The delicate music, traced
In and out of the soft lights and the laughter,
Is hushed, round ledge and rafter
The last faint echoes into silence creeping;
The harp is mute, the violins encased,
And the singers sleeping:

So, now my songs are done,
Leave me to-night awhile and the starlight gleaming,
To silence and sweet dreaming,
Here where no music calls, no beauty shakes me;
Till in my heart the birds sing to the sun
And the new dawn wakes me.

P. H. B. Lyon

Complete Index

Index of Titles

Index of Titles

557

Index of Titles

Index of Titles

Index of Titles

Index of Titles

Index of Titles

Index of Titles

Index of Titles

Index of Titles

566

Index of Titles

Index of Titles

Classified Subject Index

Action Rhymes

Animals, Fish, and Insects

Classified Subject Index

Classified Subject Index

Fables and Poems with a Purpose

Fantasy and Fairyland

Flowers

General

Individual

Classified Subject Index

Classified Subject Index

576

Classified Subject Index

Classified Subject Index

Out of Doors

People and Places

579

Classified Subject Index

Poems for the Very Young

Classified Subject Index

Classified Subject Index

Prayers, Graces, and Thanksgivings

Rain

Sea, Seaside, and Ships

Seasons

General

Spring

Classified Subject Index

Classified Subject Index

Index of First Lines

587

Index of First Lines

Index of First Lines

Index of First Lines

Index of First Lines

591

Index of First Lines

Index of First Lines

Index of First Lines

Index of First Lines

Index of First Lines

Index of First Lines

Index of First Lines

Index of First Lines

Index of First Lines

Index of First Lines

Index of First Lines

Index of First Lines

Index of First Lines

INDEX OF AUTHORS

605

Index of Authors

Index of Authors

607

Index of Authors

608

Index of Authors

Index of Authors

Index of Authors

Index of Authors

612

Index of Authors

613

Index of Authors

614

Index of Authors

Index of Authors

616

Index of Authors

617

Index of Authors

618

Index of Authors

Index of Authors

Index of Authors

623

Acknowledgments

For permission to use copyright material we are indebted to the following authors, literary executors and publishers:

The D. Appleton Century Co. for *A Summer Lullaby* by Eudora Bumstead; Mr. Martin Armstrong for *Gold*; Mr. H. W. Allingham for *Wishing* by W. Allingham; Mr. Herbert Asquith for *The Elephant* and *A Ship sails up to Bideford*; Mr. Norman Ault for *The Pig's Tail* and *Ducks* from "Dreamland Shores" (Oxford Univ. Press); Miss Jean Ayer and The Macmillan Co., New York, for *Everyday Things*; Mr. Laurence Binyon for *The Little Dancers, Song* and the extract *This is England*; Miss Enid Blyton for *What Piggy-Wiggy Found* and *Winter* and Messrs. Methuen and Miss Blyton for *The Field Mouse*; Mr. J. K. Bangs Jr. for *The Little Elf Man*; Messrs. Ernest Benn Ltd. for *The Blackbird* by Humbert Wolfe; Mr. Rodney Bennett for *Christmas Tree Song, Easter Praise, Fluttering Leaves. The Growing River, Little Brown Seed, The Little Old Lady, Merry Birds, Mrs. Jenny Wren, My Dog Spot, The Pigeons, Postman's Knock, Robin's Song, Ten Little Christmas Trees, A Thank You for Friends, There —and Back, Three Little Men in a Boat*, and Mr. Bennett and the University of London Press for *Snail*; Messrs. A. & C. Black for *Five Little Brothers* by Ella Wheeler Wilcox. Messrs. Blackie & Sons Ltd. for *The Big Arm Chair* by E. H. R., *The Frog and the Bird* by Vera Hessey, *Mr. Scarecrow* by Sheila Braine, *The Old Brown Horse* by W. K. Holmes, *Promise* by Florence Lacey, *The Shy Little House* by Nancy M. Hayes, *The Silver House* by John Lea, *Skippets the Bad One* by Christine F. Bradley, *Strange Talk* by L. E. Yates, *A Summer Day* and *The Faerie Fair* by Florence Harrison, *Trains* by Hope Shepherd, *When we are Men* by E. Stella Mead, *The Silver Road, The Upside-Down World* and *Silver Bells* by Hamish Hendry and *Three Dogs* by E. C. Brereton. Messrs. Basil Blackwell & Mott Ltd. and the authors for *The Apple Rhyme, The Caravan*, and *The Scissor-Man* by Madeleine Nightingale; *The Duck, Evening Song, Cobwebs, Pebbles, The Rabbit, The Hedgehog* and *To the Bat* by Edith King; *From the Train, Gates to England, The Light-house, The Little Things that Happen, Jungle Trees* and *Through the Porthole* by Marjorie Wilson, *The Blacksmith* by B. K. Pyke,

Acknowledgments

The King of China's Daughter by Edith Sitwell, *Whale* by Geoffrey Dearmer and *The Wind* by Elizabeth Rendall. The Bobs-Merrill Co. for *Sea Song from the Shore* from "Poems Here at Home" by James Whitcomb Riley; Miss Joyce Brisley for *The Two Families*; Messrs. Jonathan Cape for *Evening* and *The Moon* by Emily Dickinson, and *Secret Joy* and *Foxgloves* by Mary Webb from "Poems and the Spring of Joy," *Goldenhair* by James Joyce, and *Leisure, The Rain, Rich Days* and *White Sheep* by W. H. Davies. Messrs. Chappell & Co. Ltd. for *The Fairy Cobbler* by A. Neil Lyons. Miss Christine Chaundler for *The Tree in the Garden*; Messrs. Charles & Son Ltd. for *A Day at the Farm* by L.J.; Mr. Hugh Chesterman for *Outside, A Rhyme Sheet of Other Lands, Sir Nicketty Nox* and *Yesterday*. The Clarendon Press for *The Cliff-top, Gay Robin is Seen No More, I Love all Beauteous Things, Spring Goeth all in White, The Upper Skies* and *First Spring Morning* from "The Shorter Poems of Robert Bridges." Mr. Aidan Clarke for *The Journey* from "Song and Poems of Richmond Hill"; Messrs. Chatto & Windus and Lady Kilbracken for *Ragged Robin* by Elizabeth Godley; Messrs. Chatto & Windus for *The Far-Farers* and *Song of a Traveller* by R. L. Stevenson; Miss C. Druitt Cole for *Christmas Eve, The Clothes Line* and *Green Lady*. Messrs. Wm. Collins Sons & Co. and the authors for *Amy Elizabeth Ermyntrude Annie* by Queenie Scott-Hopper, *Banbury Fair* by Edith G. Millard, *Billy Boy* by Dorothy King, *The Carol Singers* by Margaret Rhodes, *London Trees* by Beryl Netherclift, *Snowdrops* by Ruth M. Arthur, *Three Mice* by C. Druitt Cole, *Water* by John R. Crossland, and the following poems from "Underneath a Mushroom" (Laurel and Gold Series), *The Fiddle* by Neil Munro, *Jenny and Johnny* by Dorothy King, *Little Betty Blue* by Agnes Grozier Herbertson, *The Yellow Fairy* and *Sun and Moon* by C. Druitt Cole, *My Party* by Queenie Scott-Hopper, *The Little Men* by Flora Fearne, *The King's Wood* by C. S. Holder, *Merry Little Men* by Kathleen M. Chaplin, *The Lace Pedlar* by Catherine A. Morin, *June* by Jane G. Stewart, *All in Red* by Eileen Mathias, *Sowing Seeds* by Ursula Cornwall, *The Christmas Tree* by Isabel de Savitzsky, *The Best of All* by Margaret Rhodes and *The Kite* and *My Little Dog* by Pearl

Acknowledgments

Forbes MacEwan. Padraic Colum for *The Old Woman of the Roads*; Messrs. Constable & Co. Ltd. and the authors for *Dawn* by Gordon Bottomly, *The Lamp Flower* from "The Gift" by Margaret Cecilia Furse and *Envoi* by P. H. B. Lyon. Miss Frances Cornford for *Spring Morning*; Messrs. Coward McCann Inc. for *The Mouse* from "Compass Rose" by Elizabeth Coatsworth; Messrs. Curwen & Sons Ltd. for *Pedlar Jim* by Florence Hoare and *Three Little Pigs* by A. Scott-Gatty. Messrs. J. M. Dent & Sons Ltd. and authors for *Song of Summer Days* by J. W. Foley, *The Witch* by Percy Ilott, *A Rune of Riches* (from "A Masque of Sybils") by Florence Converse, *Bethlehem* and *A Child's Prayer* by William Canton and *Christmas Carol* by G. K. Chesterton. Messrs. Doubleday Doran & Co. Inc. and Miss Rachel Field for *The Playhouse Key*; Messrs. Noel Douglas Ltd. for *Jack Tar, Wandering Jack* and *Who's that a-Knocking* from "Nursery Verseries" by Émile Jacot. Messrs. Gerald Duckworth & Co. Ltd. and the author for *The Elephant* and *The Early Morning* by Hilaire Belloc; Messrs. E. A. Dutton & Co. Inc. for *Christmas Eve* from "Feelings and Things" by Edna Kingsley Wallace; Miss F. Ann Elliott for *Pictures* and *The Snow*; Lady Erskine-Crum for *Goodnight, says the Owl*; Miss Eleanor Farjeon for *The Flower Seller, The Night will never stay, There are big waves, The Children's Bells,* and *There isn't time*; Miss Elizabeth Fleming for *The Balloon-Seller, Fires, The Hedgehog and his Coat, The Hurdy-Gurdy Man, If I were a pig, In the Mirror, The Patchwork Quilt, Old Mrs. Jarvis, The Secret, Toadstools, The Window-Cleaner,* and *Who's In*; the executors of the late Ford Madox Ford for *The Unwritten Song*; Mr. Michael A. E. Franklin for *The Scarecrow*; Miss Rose Fyleman for *A Christmas Wish* from "Small Cruse" (Methuen), *Conversation, The Donkey, The Frog, Good Morning, Mice, Primrose Hill* and *The Weathercock* from "Fifty-One New Nursery Rhymes" (Methuen), *Mrs. Brown* from "The Fairy Green" (Methuen), *The Goblin,* from "Widdy-Widdy-Wurkey" (also by permission of Messrs. Basil Blackwell & Mott), *Jock o' Dreams* and *Pretty Lady*; Miss Elizabeth Gould for *Midsummer Night*; Mr. Robert Graves for *I'd Love to be a Fairy's Child*; Miss Marjorie Greenfield for *Things I'd*

Like; Messrs. Harper & Bros. for *Familiar Friends* from "I Spend the Summer" by James S. Tippett. Messrs. Harrap & Co., Ltd. and the authors for *Dicky-Birds* and *The Kind Mousie* by Natalie Joan, *At Night in the Wood* by Nancy M. Hayes, *Autumn, The Bird Bath* and *Who?* by Florence Hoatson, and *What the Thrush Says* by Queenie Scott-Hopper. Messrs. Heinemann & Co. and the author's executors for *Prayer for Gentleness to all Creatures* from "Collected Poems" by John Galsworthy; *A Ship Sails up to Bideford* and *The Elephant* by Herbert Asquith. Miss Pamela Hinkson and Messrs. Macmillan for *Sheep and Lambs, Leaves,* and *Pink Almond* from "Collected Poems of Katharine Tynan" and to Miss Hinkson for *The Nightingale* and *Slow Spring*; Messrs. Hodder & Stoughton Ltd. and Mrs. Adcock for *Travellers* by St. John Adcock; Miss Ruth Holmes for *No Thoroughfare*. The Houghton Mifflin Co. for *Sea Shell* by Amy Lowell and *Christmas Carols* by H. W. Longfellow. Messrs. John Lane, The Bodley Head, for *Child's Song in Spring* by E. Nesbitt, *Gipsy Jane, Stalky Jack, The Pedlar's Caravan, Lullaby* and *The World* by W. B. Rands; *Jack Frost* and *Romance* by Gabriel Setoun, *The Rock-a-by Lady* and *Wynken, Blynken, and Nod* by Eugene Field. The Little Gem Poetry Books, Bk. 1 (G. Bell & Sons Ltd.) for *Winds through the Olive Trees softly did blow* and *Hindu Cradle Song*; Messrs. Longmans, Green & Co. Ltd. for *Pray, where are the little Bluebells gone* by Jean Ingelow, *Day* and *I Vow to Thee, my Country* from "Poems" by Sir Cecil Spring-Rice; Mr. Louis Loveman for *April Rain* by Robert Loveman; the Lutterworth Press for *Haytime* by C. M. Lowe. Messrs. Macmillan & Co. and the author's representatives for poems by Christina Rossetti, the author or executors and Messrs. Macmillan for *Danny Murphy, Day and Night, The Fifteen Acres, The Night, The Rivals, The Shell, The Snare, White Fields* and *The Wood of Flowers* from "Collected Poems" by James Stephens, *A Frolic* from "Collected Poems by A.E.," *Jack o' the Inkpot* from "The Education of Uncle Paul" by Algernon Blackwood, *Michael's Song* from "Collected Poems 1905–1935" by Wilfrid Gibson, *The Oxen* and *Weathers* by Thomas Hardy (by permission of the Hardy Estate), *Time, you old Gipsy Man*

627

Acknowledgments

and *The Bells of Heaven* from "Poems" by Ralph Hodgson, *Street Scene* by W. E. Henley, *Vespers* from "Collected Poems" by T. E. Brown, *Land of Our Birth* by Rudyard Kipling (also by permission of Mrs. Bambridge). The Macmillan Co., New York, and the author for *Gypsies* by Rachel Field. Mr. Walter de la Mare for *Mrs. Macqueen, Nicholas Nye, Nod, Old Shellover, Silver, Someone, Sooeep* and *Tired Tim*. The executors of the late Mr. W. E. Martyn for *The Little Herd Boy's Song* by Robert Buchanan. Mr. John Masefield for *Roadways* and *Tewkesbury Road* from "Collected Poems of John Masefield" (Wm. Heinemann Ltd.); Miss Stella Mead for *The Last Gate*; Messrs. Meiklejohn for *Haymaking* by A. P. Graves; Messrs Methuen and the executors of E. V. Lucas for *Mr. Coggs*, and *O. England, country of my Heart's Desire* by E. V. Lucas and *Snow in Town* by Rickman Mark, the authors concerned and Messrs. Methuen for *Duck's Ditty* by Kenneth Grahame, *Gypsy Man* by Dorothy King, *Johnny's Farm* by H. M. Adams, *Hay-Harvest, The Puk-Wudjies* and *When Mary Goes Walking* by Patrick R. Chalmers, *Michael Met a White Duck* by J. Dupuy, *Muffin Man* by A. Coasdell, *Puppy and I* by A. A. Milne and *A Sussex Legend* by Charles Dalmon. Mr. Wilfred Meynell for *Chimes* by Alice Meynell and *Ex Ore Infantium* by Francis Thompson. Mr. T. Sturge Moore for *Beautiful Meals*. Mrs. Harold Monro for *Bird at Dawn, Milk for the Cat, One Blackbird* and *Overheard on a Saltmarsh* by Harold Monro. Mr. Christopher Morley and Messrs. J. B. Lippincott Co. for *Song for a Little House*. Messrs. John Murray for *Pensioners* and *Spring the Travelling Man* by W. M. Letts; the National Sunday School Union for *Jack Frost* by Cecily E. Pike. Capt. Francis Newbolt for *The Toy Band* from "Poems New and Old" by Sir Henry Newbolt and *The Deserted House, Street Lanterns, Chillingham, The Train, L'Oiseau Bleu* and *When Mary thro' the Garden Went* from "Poems" by Mary E. Coleridge. Mr. Alfred Noyes and Messrs. Blackwood for *The Barrel Organ, The New Duckling* and *Sherwood* from "The Collected Poems of Alfred Noyes"; Mr. Lloyd Osbourne for *The Wind, A Child's Thought, Farewell to the Farm, Foreign Lands, From a Railway Carriage,*

Acknowledgments

Happy Thought, Marching Song, and *Windy Nights* from "A Child's Garden of Verse" by Robert Louis Stevenson. Mr. Seumas O'Sullivan for *A Piper* and *The Trains.* The Oxford University Press for *From a Walking Song* from "Windows of Night" by Charles Williams. Messrs. A. D. Peters for *The Idlers* by Edmund Blunden; Sir Isaac Pitman & Sons Ltd. for *Little Tommy Tidler* from "Songs and Marching Tunes for Children" by Paul Edmonds; "The Poetry Review" for *Apple Blossoms* by Helen Adams Parker and *The Scarecrow* by Michael Franklin; the Proprietors of "Punch" for *Four-Paws* by Helen Eden Parry, *The Aconite* by A. M. Graham, *The Elfin People Fill the Tubes* by W. M. Letts, *Picnics* and *The Watchmaker's Shop* by Elizabeth Fleming, and to the Proprietors of "Punch" and Miss Rose Fyleman for *A Fairy Went a-Marketing* and *The Fairy Flute.* Miss Dorothy Una Ratcliffe and Messrs. John Lane for *February* and *The Pirates' Tea-Party.* Mrs. Roberts for *Old Morgan* by G. D. Roberts; Miss Margaret Rose for *November, The Little Fir Tree, Little Bird's Song, The Magic Whistle* and *The Butterfly;* Mrs. F. Rogers for *Wishes;* Mr. Clive Sansom and Messrs. A. & C. Black Ltd. for *The Dustman, The Milkman* and *The Postman* from "Speech Rhymes"; Mr. Siegfried Sassoon for *A Child's Prayer, South Wind* and *Daybreak in a Garden* from "Selected Poems" (Heinemann); Messrs. J. Saville & Co. Ltd. for *Fairy Music* by Enid Blyton; Messrs. Charles Scribners Sons Ltd. for *Foreign Children* by R. L. Stevenson; Messrs. Martin Secker & Warburg Ltd. for *Afternoon on a Hill* by Edna St. Vincent Millay, and *The Badgers* by Eden Phillpotts; Mr. R. Farquarson Sharp for *The Wasp* by William Sharp, *Bells of Youth, Invocation of Peace* and *The Unknown Wind* by "Fiona Macleod". Messrs. Silver Burdett Co. for *The Five-Fingered Maple, The Little Plant* and *Lady Moon* by Kate L. Brown; The Society for Promoting Christian Knowledge for *Every Day* by Mary Osborn and *Christmas;* Messrs. Sidgwick & Jackson Ltd. for *Child's Song* from "Poems" by Gerald Gould, *Four and Eight* from "The Very Thing" and *The Poppies in the Garden* by ffrida Wolfe, *Moonlit Apples, Morning Thanksgiving* and *A Town Window* by John Drinkwater and extract from *Ducks* by F. W. Harvey.

Acknowledgments

Mrs. Thomas and Messrs. Faber & Faber Ltd. for *Tall Nettles* by Edward Thomas; Miss A. Alma Tadema for *Bed-Time, A Blessing for the Blessed, Playgrounds, The Robin* and *Snowdrops*; Mr. Wilfrid Thorley for *Fan the Filly* and *Song for a Ball Game.* The University of London Press for *The Squirrel, Cradle Song, Here we come a-Piping, Harvest Song* and *Shell Secrets* from "The London Treasury of Nursery Rhymes"; The University Tutorial Press Ltd. for *A Bit of Colour* by Horace Smith; Messrs. A. P. Watt & Sons and the executrix of the late Frances Chesterton for *How Far Is It to Bethlehem?*; Messrs. Frederick Warne & Co., Ltd. for *Five Sisters* and *A Happy Child,* from "Under the Window" by Kate Greenaway, and *The Owl and the Pussy Cat* from "Nonsense Songs" by Edward Lear. The executors of Sir William Watson and Messrs. Harrap & Co. Ltd. for *April*; Messrs. Wells, Gardner & Darton Ltd. for *The Windmill* by E. V. Lucas and T. Werner Laurie Ltd. for *Song* by Eugene Field.

Whilst every effort has been made to trace the owners of copyrights, in a few cases this has proved impossible, and we take this opportunity of tendering our apologies to any owners whose rights may have been unwittingly infringed.